T0215846

Electron:
From Beginner to Pro

Learn to Build Cross Platform Desktop
Applications using Github's Electron

Chris Griffith

Leif Wells

Apress®

Electron: From Beginner to Pro: Learn to Build Cross Platform Desktop Applications using Github's Electron

Chris Griffith
San Diego, California, USA

Leif Wells
Atlanta, Georgia, USA

ISBN-13 (pbk): 978-1-4842-2825-8
https://doi.org/10.1007/978-1-4842-2826-5

ISBN-13 (electronic): 978-1-4842-2826-5

Library of Congress Control Number: 2017959877

Cover image designed by Freepik

Managing Director: Welmoed Spahr
Editorial Director: Todd Green
Acquisitions Editor: Louise Corrigan
Development Editor: James Markham
Technical Reviewer: Lily Madar
Coordinating Editor: Nancy Chen
Copy Editor: Karen Jameson
Compositor: SPi Global
Indexer: SPi Global
Artist: SPi Global

Distributed to the book trade worldwide by Springer Science+Business Media New York, 233 Spring Street, 6th Floor, New York, NY 10013. Phone 1-800-SPRINGER, fax (201) 348-4505, e-mail orders-ny@springer-sbm.com, or visit www.springeronline.com. Apress Media, LLC is a California LLC and the sole member (owner) is Springer Science + Business Media Finance Inc (SSBM Finance Inc). SSBM Finance Inc is a **Delaware** corporation.

For information on translations, please e-mail rights@apress.com, or visit http://www.apress.com/rights-permissions.

Apress titles may be purchased in bulk for academic, corporate, or promotional use. eBook versions and licenses are also available for most titles. For more information, reference our Print and eBook Bulk Sales web page at http://www.apress.com/bulk-sales.

Any source code or other supplementary material referenced by the author in this book is available to readers on GitHub via the book's product page, located at www.apress.com/9781484228258. For more detailed information, please visit http://www.apress.com/source-code.

Printed on acid-free paper

Contents

About the Authors

Chris Griffith is a User Experience Lead at a home automation and security company and is also an instructor at the University of California, San Diego Extension, teaching mobile application development. He is also an Adobe Community Professional specializing in PhoneGap/Cordova and Experience Design. Chris is regularly invited to speak at conferences such as Fluent, Adobe MAX, and ngConf. He has developed several mobile applications, a variety of code-hinters, and ConfiGAP for PhoneGap Build. In addition, he has served as a technical reviewer for several publications and written for uxmag.com. In his spare time, Chris spends time with his family, sea kayaking, hiking, and drinking craft beer with friends. You can follow him on Twitter @chrisgriffith or at chrisgriffith.wordpress.com.

Leif Wells is a Web and Mobile Application Developer working as a contractor from his home in Atlanta, Georgia. He currently enjoys working with Electron, the Ionic and Angular stack, and has recently become obsessed with automated testing.

His experiences working as a team member on large Enterprise-level projects as well as a single developer on small products have matured him into a seasoned professional. Leif has organized and supported technical communities both online and in Atlanta, and often speaks at conferences and user groups.

Leif enjoys good movies, great sushi, and hanging out with his canine companion, Miss Bonnie. He has been known to blog irregularly at https://leifwells.github.io/ and can be found on Twitter as @leifwells.

About the Technical Reviewer

Lily Madar is a Creative Technologist from London, UK, who, for the last decade, has worked with various web technologies and frameworks for a range of digital creative and media agencies. Some of her work includes interactive displays powered by web technologies and can be seen in the British Museum or the Serpentine Gallery (both in London).

Outside of work, she is an active hackathon participant with recent wins at TADHack and GeoHack.

She also writes tutorials exploring the latest web and digital trends and runs hardware workshops for beginners.

When not coding, she is experimenting with Arduino circuits, crochet, and other crafts, making her a full-stack developer in hardware, software, and yarn-ware!

CHAPTER 1

■ ■ ■

Welcome to Electron

GitHub Electron (or simply Electron) allows you to build desktop applications using just HTML, CSS, and JavaScript. Sounds like a pretty ambitious statement to make. But it is indeed true, just as Apache Cordova (also known as PhoneGap) enables you to create mobile applications also with just HTML, CSS, JS, and so does Electron for the desktop.

Originally released in July 2013 by Cheng Zhao, an engineer at Github, it was part of their effort to produce a new code editor, Atom. Initially, the project was known as the Atom Shell but was soon rebranded simply as Electron. Although other solutions existed, this project quickly gained traction within the development community. In fact, Adobe AIR, released back in 2008, originally supported building desktop applications with HTML, CSS, and JavaScript, in addition to ActionScript. So the desire to leverage web technologies beyond the browser is certainly not a new one.

In this book, we will take you through the entire Electron ecosystem from its initial setup, through its key features, like creating native menus and windows and more, and how to deploy our app so it can be distributed to our users. Rather bog you down in understanding some abstract sample applications, we are going to be focusing on the core code needing to make Electron work. So, you don't need to know the latest framework to use Electron, but having some basic knowledge with Node.js is useful.

Here is a brief outline of what we are going to be covering:

- Setting up Electron

- Exploring creating the application's window

- Adding native menus

- Implementing native dialogs

- Learning how to interact with the user's system

- Creating installable and auto-updating applications

So, if you are ready to start learning about Electron, let's get started.

What Is Electron?

Electron is a blend of two incredibly popular technologies: Node.js (or simply Node) and Chromium. Thus, any web application you have written can run on Electron. Similarly, any Node application you have written can run on Electron. But the power of Electron is that you can use both solutions together.

This book is about how to use these two technologies together to create rich and engaging desktop applications. For example, we have been developing a simple desktop application that will assist developers generate their manifest.json file for their Progressive Web Apps. For those unfamiliar with Progressive Web Apps (PWAs), they are web apps that use modern web capabilities to deliver native app-like experiences

© Chris Griffith, Leif Wells 2017
C. Griffith, L. Wells, *Electron: From Beginner to Pro*, https://doi.org/10.1007/978-1-4842-2826-5_1

within the browser. We could have simply written a Node script that developers could run from the command line. But instead we leverage Electron to create a more compelling desktop application. It is one that allows you to auto-generate the app icons simply by dragging the image on the application, and it will save out the collection for you.

Breaking Electron down into its two components (thankfully the physics naming stopped and we aren't referring to these subparts as quarks), they each have specific functions.

The Node component handles things like file system access, compiled module support, and CommonJS Module support. The Chromium component handles things like rendering HTML and CSS, its own JavaScript engine, and the full suite of Web APIs.

Electron is a straightforward runtime. It is not a massive framework/library like Angular or React, but rather a collection of APIs that we can leverage with those or other frameworks. The structure of an Electron application is also open to personal taste. Usually, the UI framework will have more to say about the directory structure than Electron's requirements. However, there are general guidelines that would be wise to follow when developing.

What Is Node?

Node.js was initially released in 2009 as an open source project, enabling developers to create server-side applications using JavaScript. What made this project interesting was that it leveraged Google's newly open sourced V8 engine to act as its JavaScript runtime. Atop of that runtime, the project added APIs for accessing the local file system, creating servers, as well as the ability to load modules.

Node has enjoyed a tremendous surge of popularity from across the development community. As such, there is a huge collection of modules that are available for use within your Electron application.

What Is Chromium?

Chromium is the open source version of Google's Chrome web browser. Although it shares much of the same code base and feature set, there are a few differences (albeit minor) and it is released under a different license. What is included with Electron is technically the Chromium Content Module (CCM). Quite the mouthful, hence why most simply refer it is as Chromium. But what is the Chromium Content Module? It is the core code that makes a web browser a web browser. It includes the Blink rendering engine and its own V8 JavaScript engine. The CCM will handle retrieving and rendering HTML, loading and parsing CSS, and executing JavaScript as well.

The CCM only focuses on the core needs to render a web page. Additional features, like supporting Chrome Extensions, or syncing your Chrome bookmarks, are not supported. Just remember that its core purpose is to render web content.

Who Is Using Electron?

So many open source projects come and go. Is Electron worth investing your time and energy into learn? Yes. Although, Electron's original purpose was to act as the shell for GitHub's Atom editor, companies large and small found it to be a good solution for their development needs. Since it was backed by a recognizable company, the risks were a bit lower than trusting your next big thing on an unproven project. If you go to atom. electron.io you can see a massive collection of applications that have been released with Electron as its core.

Obviously Github is actively supporting it, as it is the foundation of their Atom editor. But who else? The very popular team messaging application Slack is built atop Electron, enabling them to develop a common UI across the operating systems. If Atom is not your code editor of choice, then Microsoft's Visual Studio Code might be. This popular editor is also built atop Electron. This is currently our editor of choice at the moment. The team at Microsoft has leveraged common development languages of HTML, CSS, and JavaScript to create a very compelling editor tuned for working with TypeScript and more that works across both macOS and Windows.

A variety of familiar web tools have also been able to transform themselves into the desktop-based applications. If you are familiar with Yeoman, a web project generator, there is now a version with a user interface instead of the standard command-line version you are probably familiar with. The team at Basecamp, a popular project management tool, now supports an out of browser experience. If you have worked with Zeplin.io to inspect your visual designs, then the desktop version was developed with Electron. The Postman API inspection tool is another great example of what is possible as an Electron application.

These are just some of the examples of some first-class web applications that have been able to break free from the browser and create desktop-centric versions of their applications. If you would like to explore some other applications that have been built with Electron, visit `https://electron.atom.io/apps/`.

What Do I Need to Know?

Unlike traditional desktop development, the only skills you need to have to develop with Electron are a good understanding of HTML, CSS, and JavaScript, and a touch of Node. Being comfortable with your command line wouldn't hurt either. The fact that we can leverage our existing skills and take them from the browser on to the desktop is what is exciting about Electron. We will be using Git to seed our starter Electron apps, but nothing more than that is needed. But working with a version control system is always a recommended skill.

This book is going to take a slightly different approach to covering how Electron works. Since it is simply a runtime, it is framework agnostic. So rather than working through an application built in the framework that you don't know, we are going to just stick with vanilla JavaScript. Now, you should have a modest understanding of HTML and CSS. As for your JavaScript skills, if you have a general understanding of modern JavaScript (aka ES6), you will be fine.

Another area that can be helpful to have is some experience with Node. We will be using the module system throughout this book. But we will provide some foundations on these and any advanced topics that we might need to cover in this book.

Why Should I Choose Electron?

We can assume by the fact you have bought this book, that either there is a need to build a desktop application for yourself, a client or your employer, or you are simply curious about it.

If you have done any web application developing, you no doubt understand the challenges of having to support a wide range of browsers, each with different levels of standards support. Don't get us wrong, the browser's standard support has come a long way in recent years. But, there are still workarounds and polyfills needed to properly deploy a web application to the world. For those working with enterprise clients, you may be further handicapped to legacy browsers and operating systems. When you create an Electron application, you embed a copy of the Chromium engine with the application, so you know exactly what features your application and support have and how your content will render. For example, if you want to use Flexbox as part of your layout solution, you safely can do so (Figure 1-1). If using the Service Worker or Fetch API is something needed for your application, you only need to make sure that the build Electron supports it.

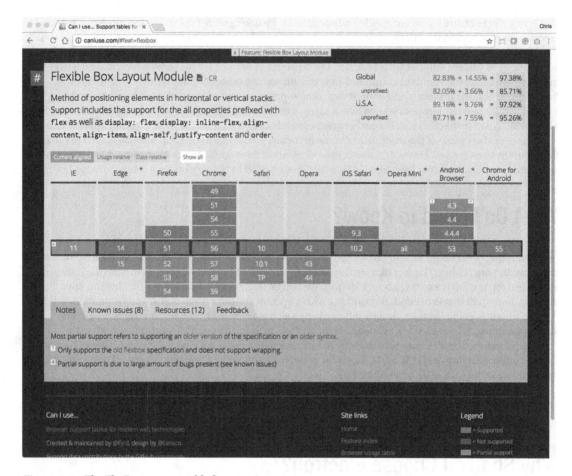

Figure 1-1. *The FlexBox support table from caniuse.com*

No longer will referencing a feature on caniuse.com be disappointing but rather one of possibilities.

As a general rule, Electron updates its Chromium module about two weeks after it is released to the public. The Node component typically takes a bit longer to update. As you begin to embark on larger Electron projects, you will want to also monitor the development process of both of these projects. There might be an issue that you need to be aware or feature added that can greatly make your life easier. But, don't worry – once you can package your application, those runtimes are baked into your application.

Electron's Advantages

Electron applications are just like any other desktop application as they are installed locally on the user's hard drive. They can be launched directly from the Windows taskbar or from the OSX Dock, and there is no need to launch a browser and navigate to some url to run your application. When you need to open or save a file, these dialogs are native in appearance and interaction. Your Electron application can support full drag-and-drop interaction with a local file system, or even associate itself with a file type, so when a user double-clicks the associated file your app will open.

We also have the ability have custom application menus that conform to each platform's user interface guidelines. Contextual menus are available that allow your user to control-click or right-click to display your custom menu. We will show you how to add this functionality in a later chapter.

If you need to trigger a system-wide notification, we can leverage Chromium's Notification API to do so. Electron will go even further that traditional window desktop applications, and create applications that only live in the menubar or system tray.

Electron provides a solid framework that will allow you to develop first-class desktop applications.

Beyond the Sandbox

If you have ever worked with an external API, then you are probably familiar with the restrictions that you have to work. We all have fought with Cross Origin Resource Sharing issues, or establishing proxies in order to allow our web application to work correctly.

Electron operates in a much looser environment with regard to security than your browser. The general assumption is that the user has actively chosen to install and run this application. As such, a degree of trust is then assumed between the user and application.

This allows our Electron application much more freedom, but at the same time we have to use this power with caution.

Offline First Design

With typical web application development, you can usually assume the user is online. Now this is changing with the increase in Progressive Web Apps, but some level of online capability is there for your web app to function. Electron applications have to take the opposite approach. You should not assume that you have an Internet connection. In fact, portions of this chapter were written at 35,000 feet on a plane without WiFi. But I was still able to write in a completely offline mode. Even if your application is dependent on communicating with a back end, you can design your application to function in an offline mode, and sync the data once a connection is reestablished. You will need to take some time to consider how this design pattern will affect the interaction and development of your Electron application.

How Does Electron Work?

Electron-based applications run in two distinct processes: the main process and the render process (Figure 1-2). Each of these two processes has a specific responsibility within your application. While Electron provides a good collection of Node modules for use within your application, many of these modules are only available within a specific process. Knowing these restrictions will help you design the code structure of your application. For example, access to the operating system APIs are restricted to just the main process, and access to the system's clipboard is available to both the main and render process. Knowing this dual-process structure is important, as it will define where some aspects of your application's code need to reside.

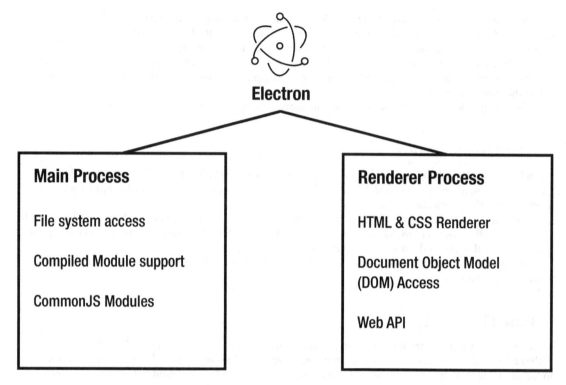

Figure 1-2. *The two processes that power an Electron application*

The Main Process

Within the main process is where your application will handle various system-level activities, like life-cycle events (starting up, preparing to quit, actually quitting, switching between the foreground and background, as just a few examples). This is also the process where application menus are created, as well as any native dialogs, like file open or file save. Our main process is what is used to bootstrap our application. This is the JavaScript file that is referenced within our package.json file, but more on that in the later chapters.

The Render Process

The main process also has another responsibility, which is to spawn any render processes. It is these processes that would display the UI of your application. Each of these render processes will load your content and execute it within its own thread. We can spawn as many windows as we need for our application. Now unlike a standard web app, each of these processes has access to all the installed Node modules, giving you a lot of capabilities.

The render process is isolated from any interaction with any system-level events. Remember, those interactions must be done within the main process. However, Electron does include an interprocess communication system to allow for events and data to be passed back and forth between the main and any renderer process.

One last thing to note, your Electron app actually does not need to have a render process, but it most likely will. This is a perfect option for taking your Node scripts and making them friendlier to use.

Other Solutions

Electron is not the only solution that will enable you to take your web content and enable it to become a desktop application. The most common alternative to using Electron is known as NW.js (originally known as node-webkit). These two projects share some common legacy, remember Cheng Zhao? Well before creating Electron, he was actively involved with the node-webkit project.

Table 1-1 lists some key differences between the projects.

Table 1-1. *Project differences*

	Electron	NW.JS
Chromium Type	Current build of Chromium	A forked version of Chromium
Node Process design	Separate Node processes	Shared Node process
Auto-Updating	Built-in API	Not included
Crash Reporting	Built-in API	Not included
Windows Support	Windows 7 or later	Windows XP or later

Some of the key takeaways from this table are the fact that NW.js uses a forked (or copy of the original code) version of Chromium. This may introduce issues such as standards support or delays in improvements or fixes within the Chromium module. Some use functions like Auto-Updating and Crash Reporting must be handled with your own custom solution, rather than leveraging the built-in APIs. The Node process design is also worth noting. Since Electron uses separate processes, it should be more performant than an NW.js application that must share the Node process. One of NW.js' advantages is the fact it supports a much older version of Windows. If your target audience might include that legacy operating system, then NW.js would be your only option between the two.

Summary

This chapter has given you a general overview of Electron. We have touched on its two core technologies: Node and Chromium, as well as introduced its dual-process design. You should have an initial sense of what an Electron-based application is capable of.

In the coming chapters, we will begin exploring these capabilities in much more detail, as well as some we did not even mention yet.

CHAPTER 2

Installing Electron

Getting your work environment configured to use Electron is fairly straightforward, but there are a couple of items required to get you started. If you are an experienced developer, you probably already have Node and Git installed. If so, feel free to skip to the Install Electron section of this chapter. If not, let's get started by installing Node.

Before Installing

These days, people install new programs on their computers and devices every day without thinking about it. While all of the programs you need to install to work with Electron are safe, any time you wish to install programs on your computer, you should always ensure that you have completed a backup of your computer. Better safe than sorry.

Installing Node

Node is the biggest thing to happen to JavaScript this century. Node is a runtime built with JavaScript that is being used by everyone from hobbyists to Enterprise developers to program anything from Internet of Things (IoT) devices to servers. JavaScript developers use Node daily to assist in the automation of their daily work. Electron uses Node to create cross platform desktop applications.

To install Node, you need to head over to `http://nodejs.org` and download Node using the easily identifiable download buttons on their site (Figure 2-1).

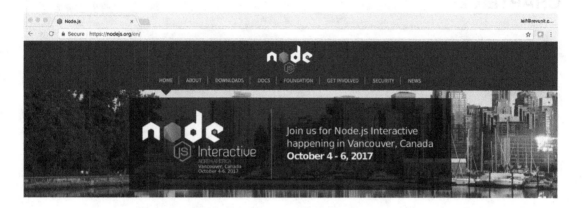

Figure 2-1. *The Node.js Website*

As you can see in this screenshot, there are two buttons available: one for the "LTS" version and another for the "Current" version. "LTS" stands for Long Term Support, meaning that the maintainers of Node decided that version 6 had reached a point of stability that everyone could rely upon; and no more development updates, beyond critical bug fixes and security updates, would be added. They did this so that development on the newer version, the one labeled "Current" could begin in earnest. While the current version can work for you, we are using the LTS version at the time of writing this book. Regardless of that, you need to be aware of your choices in this regard.

Please note: We are also citing version numbers in this chapter at the time of our writing this book. The software you need to install, specifically Node and Electron, are fast-moving projects that are updated regularly. The version numbers cited here may not match the available version numbers at the time of your reading.

Currently, Electron version 1.6.6 ships a version of Node, version 7.4.0, which is slightly behind the currently available version 7.10.0. So what does this mean to you? If there are features of Node 7.4.0 that you would like to use with your Electron app, you should download and install the current version of Node, and be aware that there may be features of 7.10.0 that will not be available in your application when you distribute it.

As mentioned before, for the purposes of this book we will be installing the LTS version of Node.

Installing Node for macOS

Download the LTS version of Node from the Node Website (`http://nodejs.org`), locate the downloaded file, and double-click it. This is a fairly simple installer. Follow the instructions provided and you will install Node (Figure 2-2).

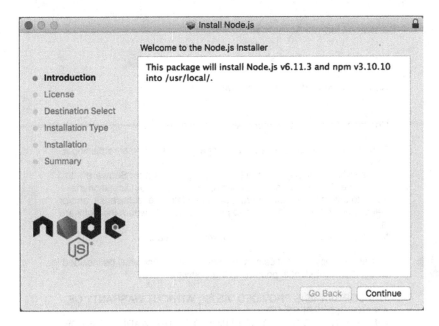

Figure 2-2. *First screen of the Node installer*

Every software that you install these days has to have a Software License Agreement (Figure 2-3). Read it (or not, we won't tell) and hit "Continue," and then click the "Agree" button of the overlaying window that appears.

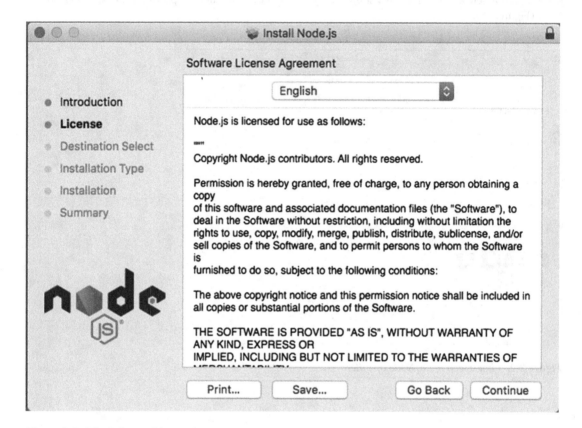

Figure 2-3. *The Software License Agreement*

Select "Install for all users of this computer," and then click "Continue" here (Figure 2-4) as we need to install Node for all users.

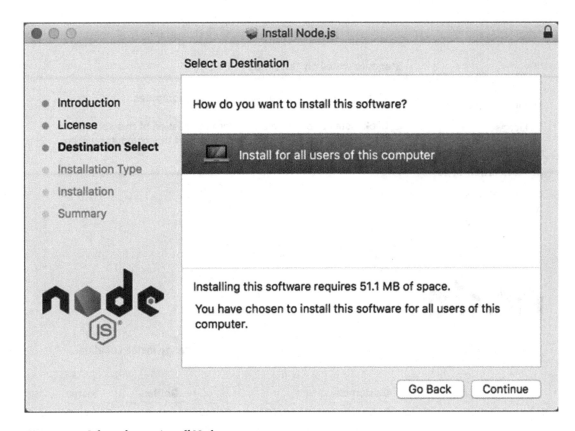

Figure 2-4. *Select where to install Node*

Finally, we are ready to install (Figure 2-5). At this point, when you click "Install" you will be asked for your system's admin password.

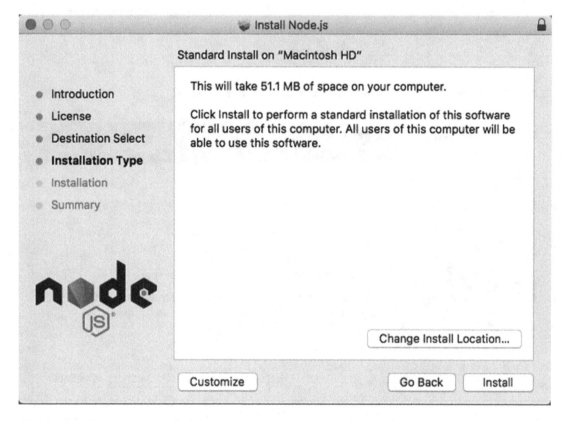

Figure 2-5. *Selecting your installation type*

The installer needs this so that it can install Node into a protected area of your operating system. Once the password is entered, you are off to the races.

Figure 2-6 shows the final screen. You've done it! To test this out, let's open up the terminal application and test the version using the node –version command. You should see the version number you installed.

Figure 2-6. *Installation is complete*

Installing Node on Windows

The installation process for Node on Windows is very similar to the process for macOS.

From the Node Website (http://nodejs.org), download the LTS version of Node for Windows. Once the file is downloaded, find the downloaded file and double-click it to get the install process started (Figure 2-7).

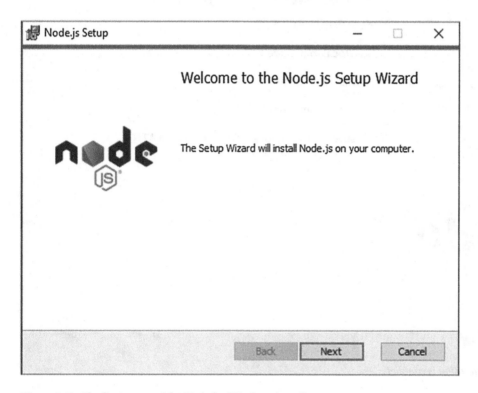

Figure 2-7. *The first screen of the Node for Windows installer*

When you click the Next button, you will see the Software License Agreement (Figure 2-8). Click the check box next to the text "I accept the terms in the License Agreement" and click the Next button to continue.

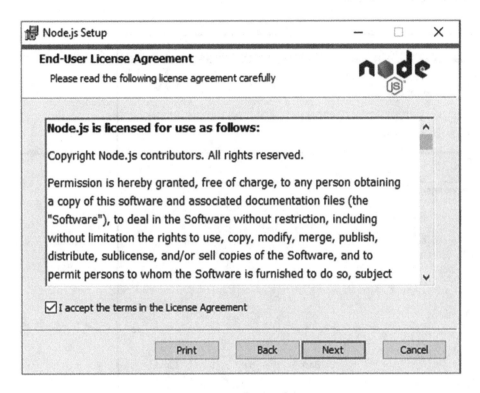

Figure 2-8. *The End-User License Agreement for Windows*

The next screen is the Destination Folder screen (Figure 2-9) where you may choose to customize where Node will be installed. For our purposes, there is no reason to override the default path of "C:\Program Files\nodejs\", but if you wish to change this for your system, this is where you would do that. When you have decided upon a path, click the Next button.

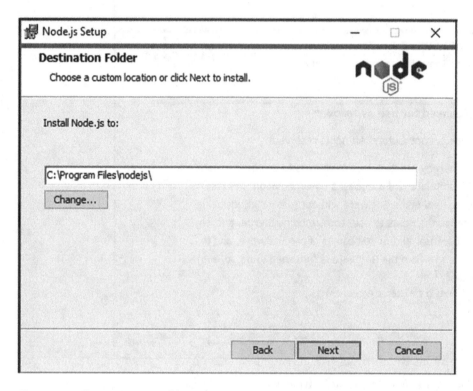

Figure 2-9. *The Destination Folder screen*

The next screen in the Node installer's process is the Custom Setup (Figure 2-10) screen. Again, we recommend accepting the default settings for your Node install.

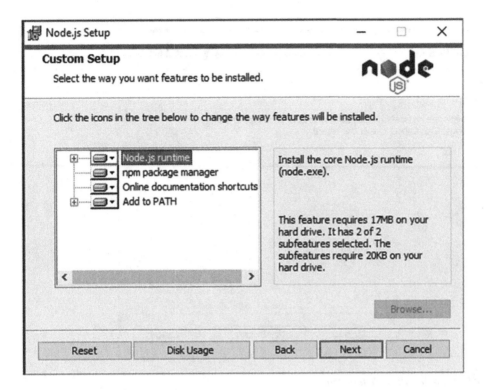

Figure 2-10. *The Custom Setup screen*

The next screen you will be presented is the Ready to install screen (Figure 2-11). Click the Install button.

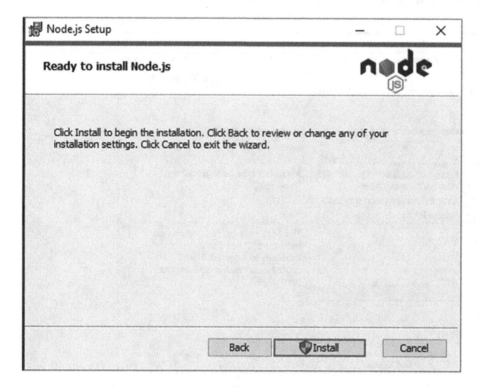

Figure 2-11. *The Ready to install Node.js screen*

After a minute of two, you should be presented with the final screen, the Completed screen (Figure 2-12). Click the Finish button. Open a new Command Prompt window and run the node –version command to assure your installation is working.

Installing Git on macOS

Now that we have Node installed, we need to install a version control system so we can use the starter code and other code repositories that appear in this book. Git, a very popular open source version control system, is what we are using and will install. Git is popular because of its size and ease of use. Older version control systems were often clunky, huge, and inflexible.

To get started, head over to `https://git-scm.com` to find the download link on their site. As you can see in Figure 2-12, you find the link to download the latest version of Git inside the image of the computer.

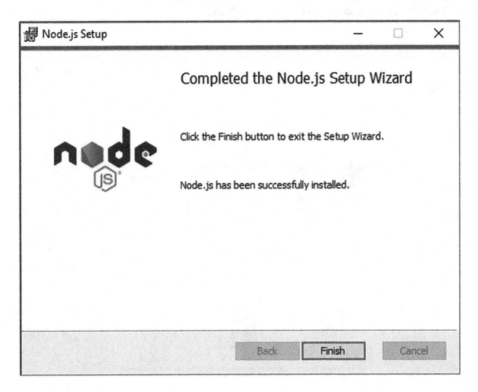

Figure 2-12. *The Git website (`https://git-scm.com/`)*

Installing Node on Windows

The installation process for Node on Windows is very similar to the process for macOS.
Clicking that link will take you to the download page (Figure 2-13).

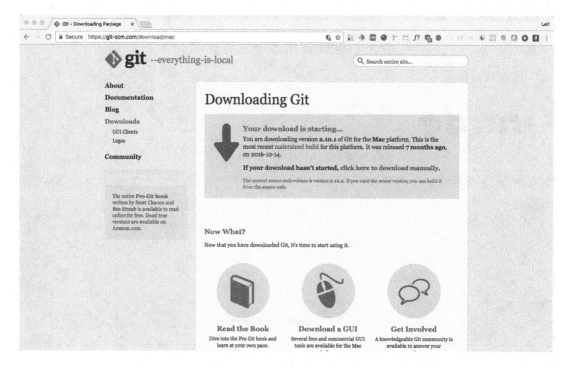

Figure 2-13. *The Git website download page*

Download the file, locate the downloaded file on your system, and double-click the file to mount the installer. You should see a folder like that in Figure 2-14.

Figure 2-14. *The downloaded Git install file opened*

Double-click the installer .pkg file, and you may see a security warning from macOS that will not allow you to install Git.

If you see the screen shown in Figure 2-15, it's ok. This is macOS's way to protect your system from installers from unknown sources. To get around this, you will need to open up System Preferences ➤ Security & Privacy and go to the General tab. There you will find a notification that looks like this.

Figure 2-15. *macOS warning message for Git installer*

Click the "Open Anyway" button (Figure 2-16) to allow the installer to run, and you should see the installer UI load.

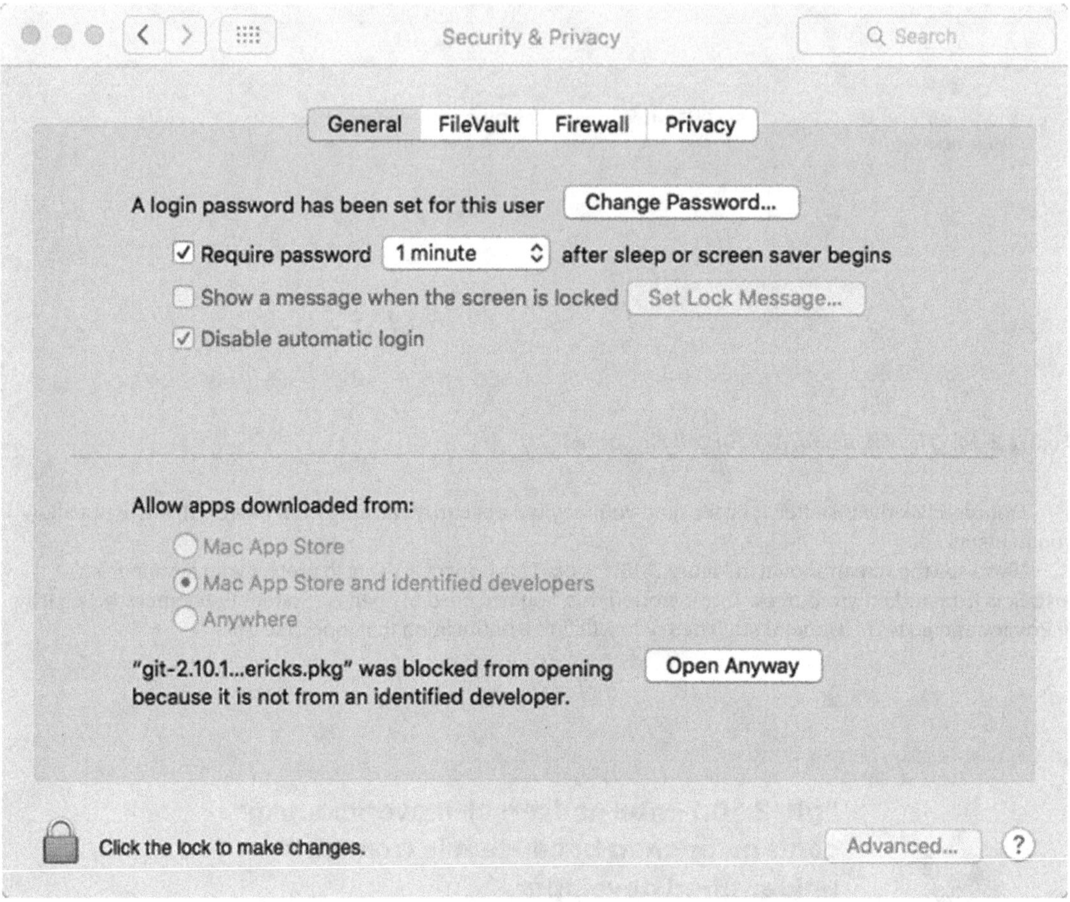

Figure 2-16. *macOS Security & Privacy control panel. Note the "Open Anyway" button*

Continue through the steps of the installer (Figures 2-17 through 2-19) to complete the installation.
Once you have Git installed, let's test the results. Open up a Terminal window and type the following command:

```
git --version
```

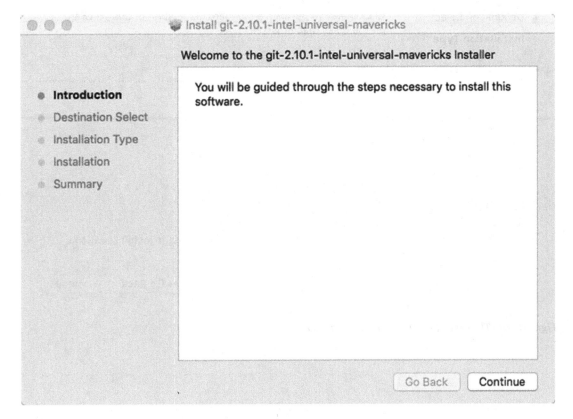

Figure 2-17. *The Git installer's introduction screen*

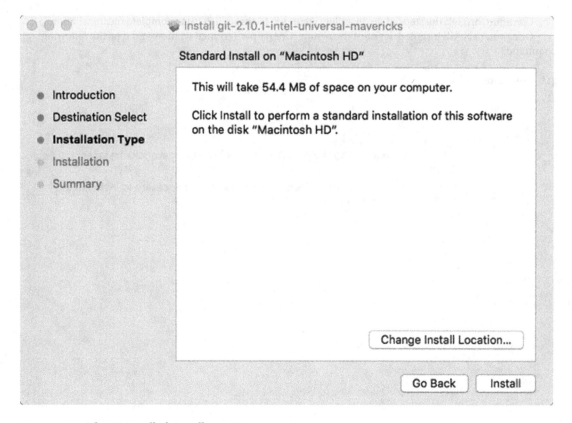

Figure 2-18. *The Git installer's Installation Type screen*

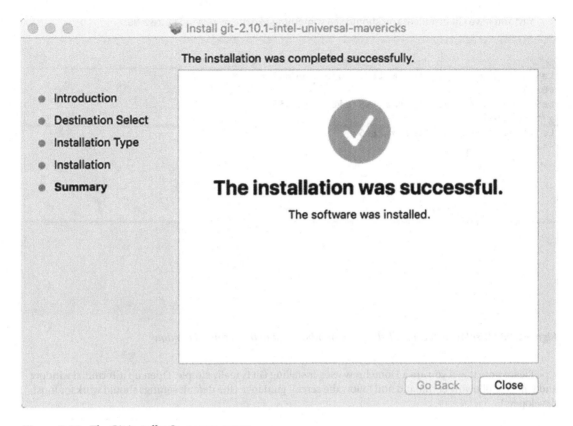

Figure 2-19. *The Git installer Summary screen*

Yay! You have Git installed! You should see something like the results in Figure 2-20.

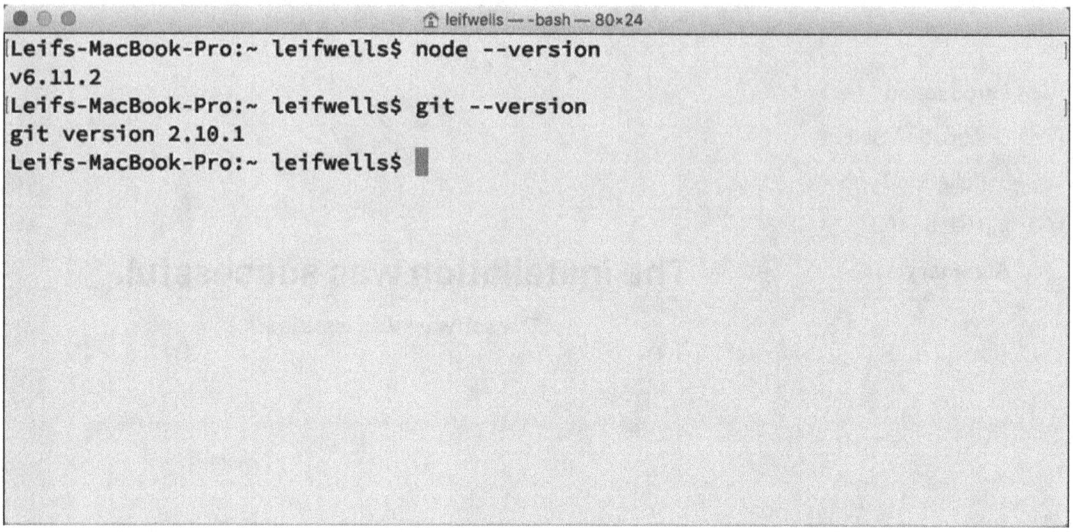

```
● ● ●                         ⌂ leifwells — -bash — 80×24
Leifs-MacBook-Pro:~ leifwells$ node --version
v6.11.2
Leifs-MacBook-Pro:~ leifwells$ git --version
git version 2.10.1
Leifs-MacBook-Pro:~ leifwells$
```

Figure 2-20. *Displaying the installed version number of git in the Terminal window*

Please note that if you are a Homebrew user, installing Git is really simple. Open up a Terminal window and type the following command and follow the screen guidance (the default settings should work for most developers):

```
brew install git
```

Installing Git on Windows

Installing Git on Windows is a very similar process as on macOS. When you arrive at the Git Website (http://git-scm.com) on a Windows system, you are presented with the latest version of Git for Windows (Figure 2-21). In our case, the version 2.14.3, but by the time you read this book that version may have changed.

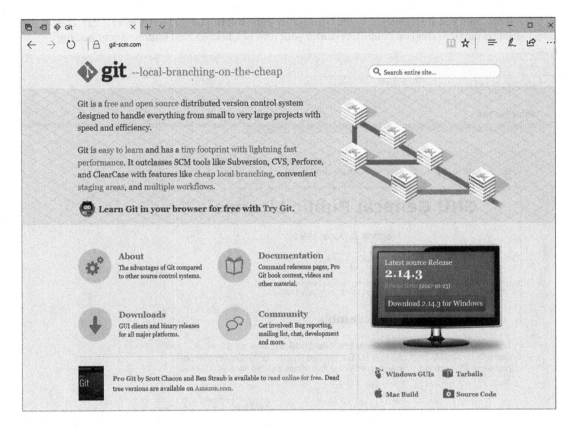

Figure 2-21. *The Git Website as it appears on a Windows system*

Select the link to download Git for Windows to begin the download process. Once the file is downloaded, find and doubleclick the file to get the installation process started.

The first screen you are presented by the Git installer is the Information screen (Figure 2-22). This screen displays the GNU General Public License for your review. Click the Next button to continue the process.

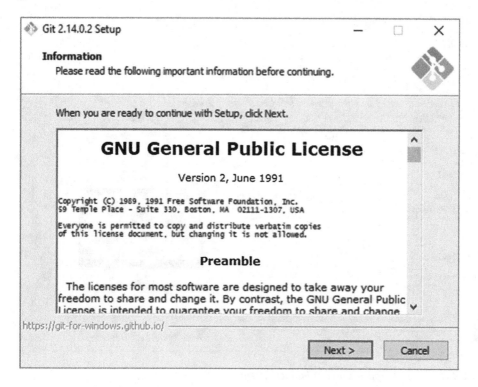

Figure 2-22. *The Information Screen*

The next screen displayed is the Select Components screen (Figure 2-23) where you may choose which of the Git components you wish to install. For our purposes, the default settings are what we suggest you use, so click Next for the next screen.

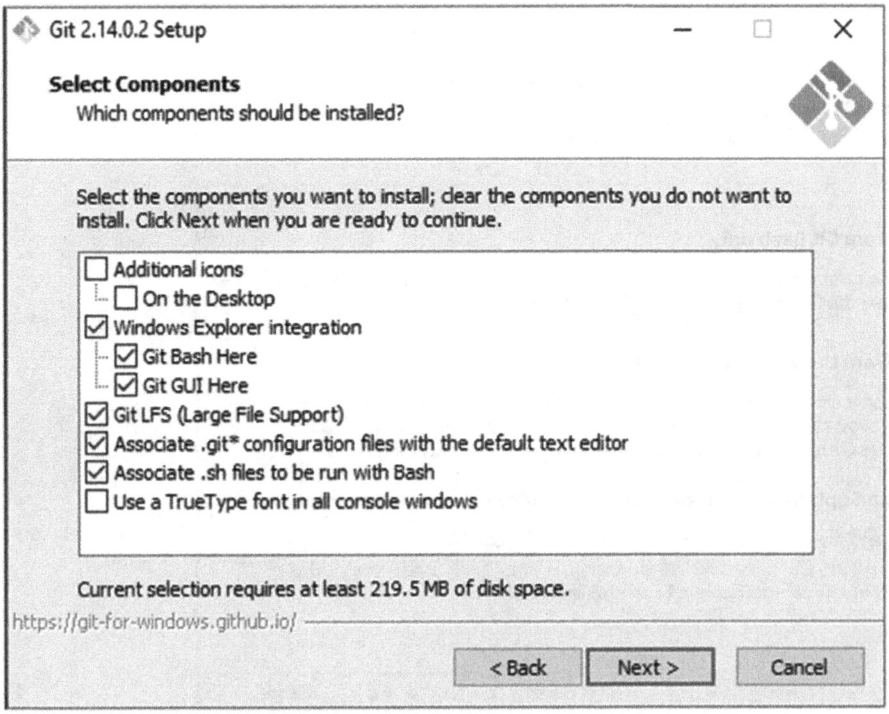

Figure 2-23. The Select Components screen

The next screen is the Adjusting your PATH environment screen (Figure 2-24) where you choose how you want to use Git on the command line, setting the PATH for your application for your system. The second option "Use Git from the Windows Command Prompt" is the choice we made because it gave us the flexibility to use either the Git Bash application or the Windows Command Prompt. Click Next to continue.

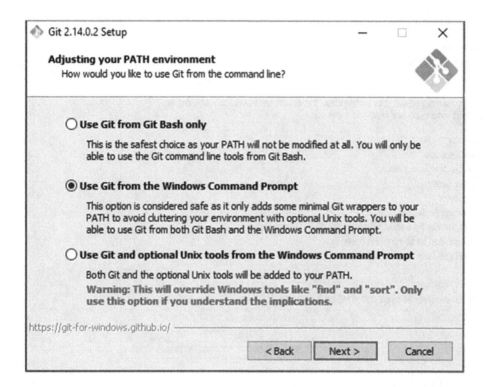

Figure 2-24. *The Adjusting your PATH environment screen*

The next screen presented by the Git installer is the Choosing HTTPS transport backend (Figure 2-25) screen. This screen allows you to choose how to communicate over a secure connection while using Git. Our suggestion is to choose the default "Use the OpenSSL library" option which should work for most developers. If you work on a system in a more strict corporate environment, you may need to select the "Use the native Windows Secure Channel library." Check with your System Administrator if you have any doubts about which option is best for you. Make your choice, then click the Next button.

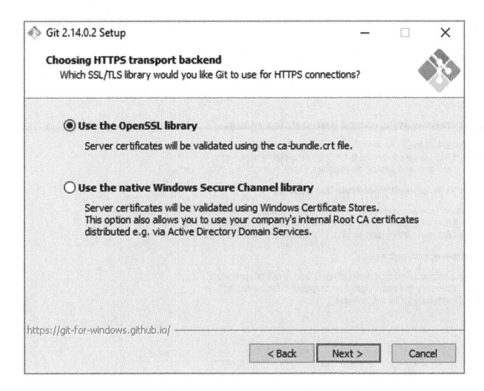

Figure 2-25. *The Choosing HTTPS transport backend screen*

The next screen is the Configuring the line ending conversions screen (Figure 2-26) where you need to decide how Git will handle line endings for files downloaded and uploaded by Git. Windows systems handle line endings differently than Unix systems, and Git accounts for those differences by changing the line endings at download to a Windows-friendly type and changes them to a Unix-friendly type upon committing to the repository. The "Checkout Windows-style, commit Unix-style line endings" is the option we are recommending, but we are making the assumption that you will be working alone. If you plan on using Git in a team environment, you may wish to choose one of the other options, though the default option will most likely be the one your team has chosen. Before making your choice, you should check with a team leader to make sure you conform to team requirements otherwise you may create problems when committing new code to the team repository. Make your selection and click the Next button.

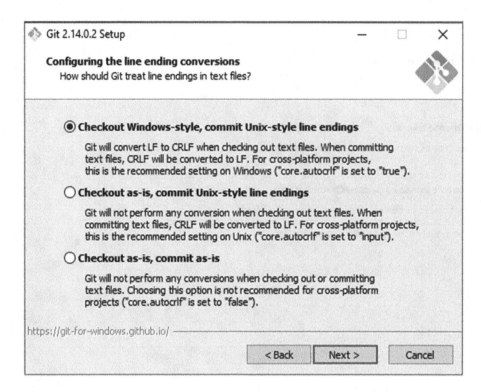

Figure 2-26. *The Configuring the line ending conversions screen*

The Configuring the terminal emulator to use with Git Bash screen (Figure 2-27) is the next screen and, again, we recommend using the default setting which is "Use MinTTY." The "Use Windows' default console window" option can be limiting. This will only effect developers who choose to use the Git Bash application.

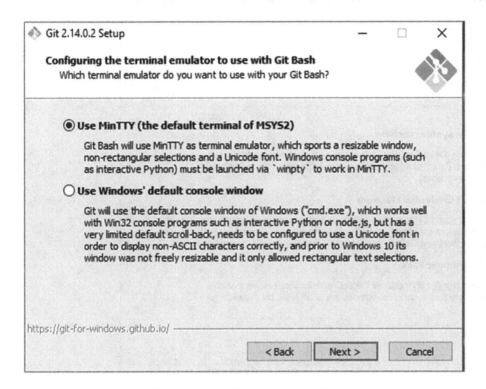

Figure 2-27. *Configuring the terminal emulator to use with Git Bash screen*

The next screen in the Git installation process is the Configuring extra options screen (Figure 2-28). The first item, Enable file system caching, is recommended as the description states it provides significant performance. The second option, Enable Git Credential Manager, also recommended, will assist you with accessing your repositories securely. Finally, we can click the Install button to continue.

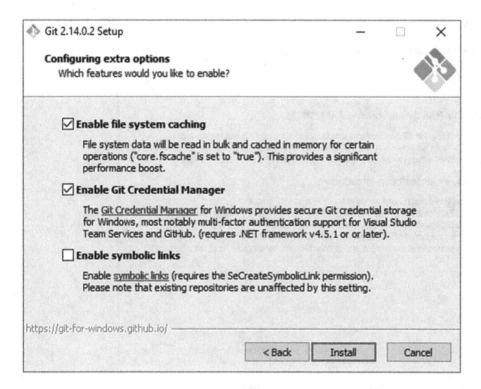

Figure 2-28. *The Configuring extra options screen*

The Git installer will run for a few moments and then present you with the Completing the Git Setup Wizard screen (Figure 2-29). On this screen you see two check boxes. We recommend selecting the Launch Git Bash check box, and deselecting the View Release Notes check box (unless you wish to view the notes). Once you click the Finish button, you will be presented with the Git Bash application. Verify out your installation by entering the git –version command as seen in Figure 2-30.

Figure 2-29. *Completing the Git Setup Wizard screen*

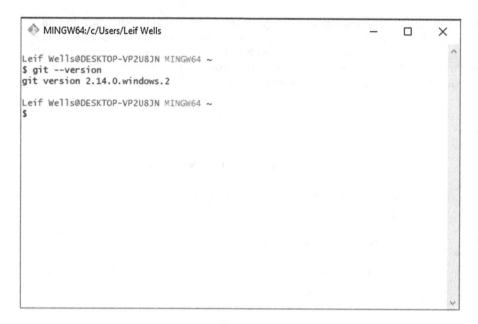

Figure 2-30. *Terminal showing the results of running the git –version command*

Installing Electron

One of the best features of Node is NPM, the Node Package Manager. Node Package Manager is how thousands of code libraries are distributed across the Internet. Need to add a feature or API to your project? Fire up a terminal window and use NPM to install it. With NPM, Node has truly standardized code distribution.

So, of course, we need to use NPM to install Electron. When installing a package like Electron, we have two options: (1) to install Electron locally, on a per project basis; or (2) globally so that any project can use it. Since you will be using Electron with each code sample in this book, we suggest installing Electron globally. Open a Terminal window and enter the following command:

```
npm install -g electron
```

Later, if you need to install Electron in a project, you should use this command:

```
npm install --save-dev electron
```

This is a commonly used command so let's break it down so that you understand how it works. First, npm is the utility we are using to install Electron. Second, install is the command. Third, the –g is shorthand for global, meaning our intention is to install Electron globally, making it accessible from anywhere on our computer. Finally, electron, obviously, is the name of the package we are installing. Note that the name is lowercase.

Once you hit enter, the command kicks in and messages should begin filling your screen. Don't freak out. This is expected. At the end of the process, you should be seeing something like Figure 2-31.

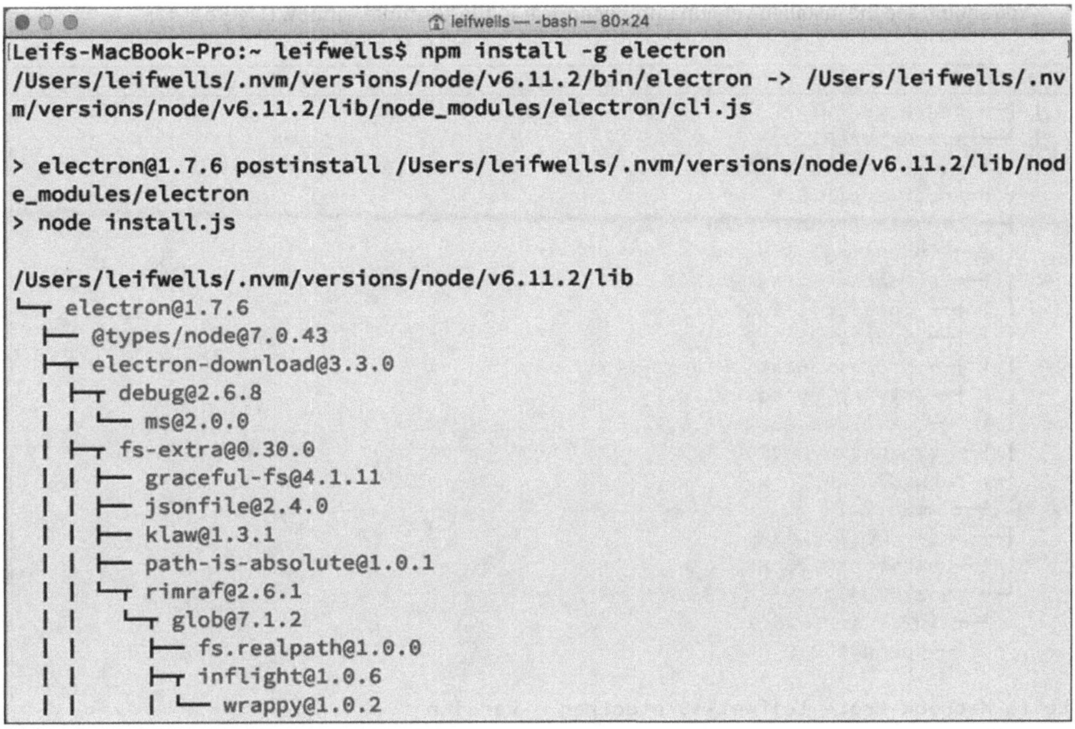

```
● ● ●                        ⬆ leifwells — -bash — 80×24
[Leifs-MacBook-Pro:~ leifwells$ npm install -g electron
/Users/leifwells/.nvm/versions/node/v6.11.2/bin/electron -> /Users/leifwells/.nv
m/versions/node/v6.11.2/lib/node_modules/electron/cli.js

> electron@1.7.6 postinstall /Users/leifwells/.nvm/versions/node/v6.11.2/lib/nod
e_modules/electron
> node install.js

/Users/leifwells/.nvm/versions/node/v6.11.2/lib
└─┬ electron@1.7.6
  ├── @types/node@7.0.43
  ├─┬ electron-download@3.3.0
  │ ├─┬ debug@2.6.8
  │ │ └── ms@2.0.0
  │ ├─┬ fs-extra@0.30.0
  │ │ ├── graceful-fs@4.1.11
  │ │ ├── jsonfile@2.4.0
  │ │ ├── klaw@1.3.1
  │ │ ├── path-is-absolute@1.0.1
  │ │ └─┬ rimraf@2.6.1
  │ │   └─┬ glob@7.1.2
  │ │     ├── fs.realpath@1.0.0
  │ │     ├─┬ inflight@1.0.6
  │ │     │ └── wrappy@1.0.2
```

Figure 2-31. *Installing Electron globally*

To test your install, enter the following command:

electron -version

You should see the installed version number appear in the Terminal window (Figure 2-32).

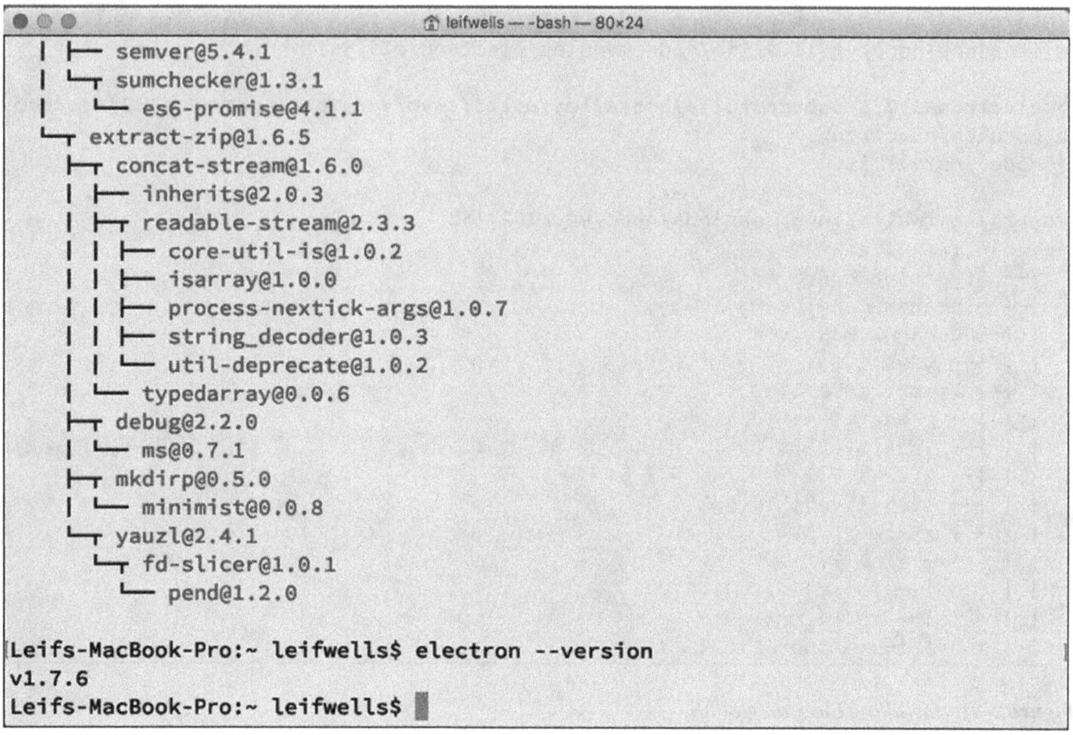

```
● ● ●                    ⌂ leifwells — -bash — 80×24
│  ├── semver@5.4.1
│  └┬ sumchecker@1.3.1
│   └── es6-promise@4.1.1
└┬ extract-zip@1.6.5
 ├┬ concat-stream@1.6.0
 │ ├── inherits@2.0.3
 │ ├┬ readable-stream@2.3.3
 │ │ ├── core-util-is@1.0.2
 │ │ ├── isarray@1.0.0
 │ │ ├── process-nextick-args@1.0.7
 │ │ ├── string_decoder@1.0.3
 │ │ └── util-deprecate@1.0.2
 │ └── typedarray@0.0.6
 ├┬ debug@2.2.0
 │ └── ms@0.7.1
 ├┬ mkdirp@0.5.0
 │ └── minimist@0.0.8
 └┬ yauzl@2.4.1
   └┬ fd-slicer@1.0.1
     └── pend@1.2.0

Leifs-MacBook-Pro:~ leifwells$ electron --version
v1.7.6
Leifs-MacBook-Pro:~ leifwells$ ▌
```

Figure 2-32. *Checking the installed version of Electron*

You can also enter electron to see an Electron application that allows you to drag and drop a Web application into the window to see it run.

Summary

You now have everything you need to work with Electron, as well as being able to participate with the samples used in this book. Good luck and enjoy coding with Electron.

CHAPTER 3

The Electron Quick Start

Getting started with Electron can be confusing. Where do you put files? What do you name files? What code do you need to start with? How should your code be organized?

Luckily for us, folks who work on Electron have created a Github repository to assist you, and us, with getting started with Electron. We will be using the Electron Quick Start as the starting point for our example applications in this book. The Electron Quick Start is located at https://github.com/electron/electron-quick-start on Github. Review the code in this repository. It is very simple, and it contains code to handle the basic needs of an Electron application.

There are many ways to write the code for Electron's Renderer Process. You could use any number of frameworks: Angular, React, Vue... frankly, too many to be named here. We're leaving this decision to you. Our goal with this book is to ensure you understand how to code for Electron, in both the Main and Renderer Processes, and by using a vanilla approach as the Quick Start's code can focus on Electron's features and create a foundation upon which you may build.

Getting the Quick Start Code

You will need to have Git, Node, and npm installed on your computer to build from the Electron Quick Start.

Developers usually have a directory on their system where they keep their code projects. Typically, there can be a HOME/Code/ directory. For the purposes of this book, we are going to assume this is where your code is kept. Please remember to use the path to the code on your system when you see HOME/Code/.

Open your terminal application. On Mac OS X, this application is located in the Applications/Utilities folder. On Windows it is located *in Start | Program Files | Accessories | Command Prompt, although you might prefer using Git Bash, to download examples more easily.*

From your terminal application, change directories to your Code folder. From your Code folder, enter the following command:

```
git clone https://github.com/electron/electron-quick-start quick-start
```

This command creates a copy of the Electron Quick Start repository inside the quick-start folder in the path from which the command was made.

Now, change directories into the quick-start directory:

```
cd quick-start
```

Now clear the repository's history so we can start from scratch from Git's perspective:

```
git init
```

© Chris Griffith, Leif Wells 2017
C. Griffith, L. Wells, *Electron: From Beginner to Pro*, https://doi.org/10.1007/978-1-4842-2826-5_3

You should see a message like the following:

```
Reinitialized existing Git repository in /Users/<username>/Code//quick-start/.git/
```

One of the nice things about Git repositories and npm is that you don't need to carry around external modular code with you all the time. We just need to ask npm to install the node modules associated with this project by using the following command:

```
npm install
```

Now you are ready to open your new project inside your favorite integrated development environment. We are using Microsoft Visual Studio Code, so you will see that UI in many of our screenshots.

Updating the Project to Make It Yours

The first step after setting up your new Electron project is to update the package.json file. If you are starting a completely new project, without example files, the package.json file will be created when running npm init.

Right now, the file should look something like this:

```
{
  "name": "electron-quick-start",
  "version": "1.0.0",
  "description": "A minimal Electron application",
  "main": "main.js",
  "scripts": {
    "start": "electron ."
  },
  "repository": "https://github.com/electron/electron-quick-start",
  "keywords": [
    "Electron",
    "quick",
    "start",
    "tutorial",
    "demo"
  ],
  "author": "GitHub",
  "license": "CC0-1.0",
  "devDependencies": {
    "electron": "^1.4.1"
  }
}
```

Some things to take note of here:

- "name": The name of your application. The expected format is using lowercase letters with dashes between words. In the samples we are building for this book, the name isn't all that important, but for future application, the name may be critical. Make certain to update this to the name you wish to use and keep it up to date.

- "version": This represents the version of your application's code. It should be updated to match the current release of the application.

- "description": This key, oddly enough, is where you place a brief description of your application.

- "main": This key is critical. This is where you tell Electron to locate the code for the Main Process. If you decide to create a directory for this file to keep your project's structure neat, you will need to update this node to reflect that change. Otherwise, Electron will fail to run.

- "scripts": This key tells Node Package Manager (npm) what actions to take for specific commands. Here, entering npm run start results in the command **electron**. being run. This is a convenient way to organize commands.

- "repository": This key points to the repository where your code is stored. Feel free to change this to your repository.

- "keywords": Enter any keywords that may be used to describe your application.

- "author": That's you! Put your name or your organization's name here.

- "license": This is the code representing which license you've decided to release your code under. You'll find over 500 license types at this link: https://gist.github. com/robertkowalski/7620849. Before releasing an application or the code for a repository, you should take the time to examine your licensing options.

- "Dependencies" and "devDependencies": These are a list of names and versions of modules that are required for the project. There is currently no dependencies key for this project. The devDependencies key contains "electron," which is used to create our application. These properties will get updated when you install new modules.

Now that we've examined the package.json file, let's take a look at the application by using this command:

```
npm start
```

You should see something similar to Figure 3-1 on your screen.

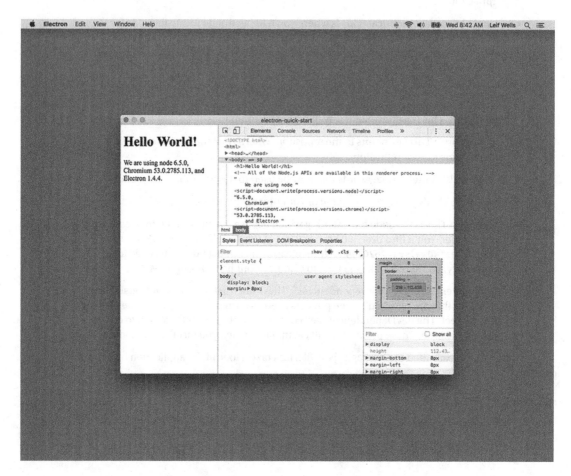

Figure 3-1. *The starter Electron application's main window and development tools*

■ **Note**   You can quit this application using the typical means: command-q, Electron ➤ Quit on Mac OS X or File ➤ Quit on Windows. From the terminal application you may also enter the control-c key combination to quit the application.

Next we'll take a look at the code that makes this starter project work.

The Main Process File

As we mentioned before, Electron has two processes: the Main Process and the Renderer Process. In our starter project, the code for the Main Process resides inside the main.js file.

> ■ **Note** Naming the Main Process file `main.js` is a best practice. And it makes good sense: the `main.js` file represents the starting point for Node to fire up your Main Process. While you may decide to organize the code for your Main Process into a sensible directory and file structure, you should keep a `main.js` file to represent the starting point for your project.

The `main.js` file contains basic code required for any Electron application as well as some helpful comments, as shown in Listing 3-1.

Listing 3-1. `main.js`

```
const electron = require('electron')
// Module to control application life.
const app = electron.app
// Module to create native browser window.
const BrowserWindow = electron.BrowserWindow

const path = require('path')
const url = require('url')

// Keep a global reference of the window object, if you don't, the window will
// be closed automatically when the JavaScript object is garbage collected.
let mainWindow

function createWindow () {
  // Create the browser window.
  mainWindow = new BrowserWindow({width: 800, height: 600})

  // and load the index.html of the app.
  mainWindow.loadURL(url.format({
    pathname: path.join(__dirname, 'index.html'),
    protocol: 'file:',
    slashes: true
  }))

  // Open the DevTools.
  mainWindow.webContents.openDevTools()

  // Emitted when the window is closed.
  mainWindow.on('closed', function () {
    // Dereference the window object, usually you would store windows
    // in an array if your app supports multi windows, this is the time
    // when you should delete the corresponding element.
    mainWindow = null
  })
}

// This method will be called when Electron has finished
// initialization and is ready to create browser windows.
// Some APIs can only be used after this event occurs.
app.on('ready', createWindow)
```

```
// Quit when all windows are closed.
app.on('window-all-closed', function () {
  // On OS X it is common for applications and their menu bar
  // to stay active until the user quits explicitly with Cmd + Q
  if (process.platform !== 'darwin') {
    app.quit()
  }
})

app.on('activate', function () {
  // On OS X it's common to re-create a window in the app when the
  // dock icon is clicked and there are no other windows open.
  if (mainWindow === null) {
    createWindow()
  }
})

// In this file you can include the rest of your app's specific main process
// code. You can also put them in separate files and require them here.
```

The top of the file gives us access to the modules required for this application:

```
const electron = require('electron')
// Module to control application life.
const app = electron.app
// Module to create native browser window.
const BrowserWindow = electron.BrowserWindow

const path = require('path')
const url = require('url')
```

The electron constant is, as you'd expect, the Electron module. It gives you access to all of the Electron APIs as well as any extensions to Node that Electron provides.

The app constant is the part of the Electron API that gives you access to the event life cycle of our application. We'll see examples of how app is used further down in the code.

The BrowserWindow constant represents your Renderer Process. We will use BrowserWindow to create an instance of Chromium, the windows that make up the UIs of our application.

The path and url constants represent Node modules, part of the Node API that is accessible by any Electron application. url is used to help with creating URLs. path helps with dealing with files and directories.

The next piece of code comes with some guidance in the form of a comment:

```
// Keep a global reference of the window object, if you don't, the window will
// be closed automatically when the JavaScript object is garbage collected.
let mainWindow
```

■ **Note** if you start working with a project and you open a window but it disappears, the Main Process may not have a reference to the mainWindow. This will also occur with any other windows you may create.

The next bit of code is the createWindow method that creates your main window:

```
function createWindow () {
  // Create the browser window.
  mainWindow = new BrowserWindow({width: 800, height: 600})

  // and load the index.html of the app.
  mainWindow.loadURL(url.format({
    pathname: path.join(__dirname, 'index.html'),
    protocol: 'file:',
    slashes: true
  }))

  // Open the DevTools.
  mainWindow.webContents.openDevTools()

  // Emitted when the window is closed.
  mainWindow.on('closed', function () {
    // Dereference the window object, usually you would store windows
    // in an array if your app supports multi windows, this is the time
    // when you should delete the corresponding element.
    mainWindow = null
  })
}
```

This method does the following steps:

- Creates an instance of a BrowserWindow, passing along an object used to configure that window to be 800 pixels wide and 600 pixels high.

- Loads that window using the path and url modules to access the index.html file. This file is the starting point for your Renderer Process.

- The line `mainWindow.webContents.openDevTools()` does what you think it does: opens up the Developer Tools that are part of Chromium. These tools are extremely helpful for debugging the Renderer Process.

- Listens for the `closed` event on the new window instance. The guidance here is around how to manage multiple windows, if the app uses them. The function here merely nulls your window instance, but this is where you may wish to add code in the future.

Finally, we get to the part of the code where the app listeners control when the window is created, and when the application quits.

```
// This method will be called when Electron has finished
// initialization and is ready to create browser windows.
// Some APIs can only be used after this event occurs.
app.on('ready', createWindow)

// Quit when all windows are closed.
app.on('window-all-closed', function () {
  // On OS X it is common for applications and their menu bar
  // to stay active until the user quits explicitly with Cmd + Q
```

```
  if (process.platform !== 'darwin') {
    app.quit()
  }
})

app.on('activate', function () {
  // On OS X it's common to re-create a window in the app when the
  // dock icon is clicked and there are no other windows open.
  if (mainWindow === null) {
    createWindow()
  }
})

// In this file you can include the rest of your app's specific main process
// code. You can also put them in separate files and require them here.
```

The app instance is listening to three events here: `ready`, `window-all-closed`, and `activate`.

Upon receiving the `ready` event, the createWindow that we discussed above is called.

As the commented guidance references, the `windows-all-closed` is listened for because on the Mac OS X platform you can close all of an application's windows but not quit the application. That is not true on Windows and Linux, so this code quits the application on those platforms.

Also of note, here is the use of `process`, part of the Node API. For instance, `process.platform` will return `darwin` for Mac OS X, and `win32` for the Windows platform. Even on Windows 64-bit, process. platform will read `win32`, while process.arch (stands for Architecture) will return `x64`.And since you can have an application open without any windows open on the Mac OS X platform, the `active` event is listened for and creates a new window when emitted. This bit of code is not testing to see which platform the application is on because this condition - where the `active` event is emitted and `mainWindow === null` will only occur on the Mac OS X platform.

Finally, at the very bottom of the main.js file we are given more guidance, letting us know that we should add more Main Process code here or require other files if that is how you wish to organize your code.

The Quick Start's Renderer Process

As we mentioned before, the main.js file identifies the html file used to start up Electron's renderer process. The process is started using the mainWindow.loadURL() call in this code block:

```
  // and load the index.html of the app.
  mainWindow.loadURL(url.format({
    pathname: path.join(__dirname, 'index.html'),
    protocol: 'file:',
    slashes: true
  }))
```

Using Node's url.format() method, this code creates a path to the index.html file by joining the file name with the Electron variable __dirname that points us to the file in the root of our project.

Let's review the index.html file:

```html
<!DOCTYPE html>
<html>
  <head>
    <meta charset="UTF-8">
    <title>Hello World!</title>
  </head>
  <body>
    <h1>Hello World!</h1>
    <!-- All of the Node.js APIs are available in this renderer process. -->
    We are using Node.js <script>document.write(process.versions.node)</script>,
    Chromium <script>document.write(process.versions.chrome)</script>,
    and Electron <script>document.write(process.versions.electron)</script>.
  </body>

  <script>
    // You can also require other files to run in this process
    require('./renderer.js')
  </script>
</html>
```

Again, another simple file, this one is a basic HTML file. But there are a few important points to remember about this file to help you understand how Electron works.

First, in the middle of the page there are several script tags that contain calls to Node's process API:

```html
<!-- All of the Node.js APIs are available in this renderer process. -->
    We are using Node.js <script>document.write(process.versions.node)</script>,
    Chromium <script>document.write(process.versions.chrome)</script>,
    and Electron <script>document.write(process.versions.electron)</script>.
```

As you can see from the comment, all of Node's APIs are available to the renderer process, which is why you have access to the process API inside this HTML file. In this instance, the code lets us see which versions of Node, Chromium, and Electron are being used with this application. Figure 3-1 shows how this renders.

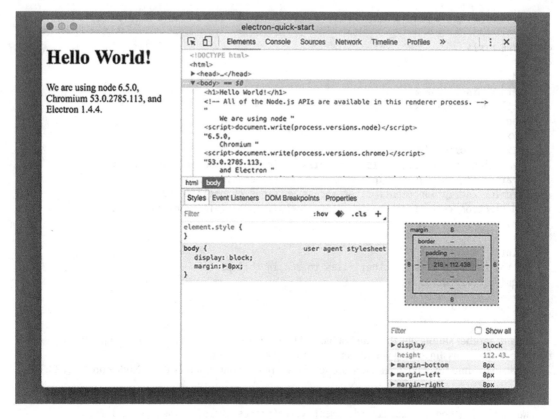

Figure 3-2. *The starter Electron application, the version numbers dynamically added*

This code isn't necessary but it is useful in helping us understand how Electron works. The other important piece to the index.html file is the script tag at the bottom of the file:

```
<script>
    // You can also require other files to run in this process
    require('./renderer.js')
</script>
```

This tag uses require to import the renderer.js file. In most cases, this will be the starting point for the JavaScript for your application. If we take a look at the actual file, we will see it only contains the following comment:

```
// This file is required by the index.html file and will
// be executed in the renderer process for that window.
// All of the Node.js APIs are available in this process.
```

Summary

There are many ways you can build your Electron application. If you go with a vanilla approach - that is, just using plain old JavaScript instead of a framework - this is the file you'll be working in. Since there are so many ways to build an Electron application, far too many to cover in one book, we will be focusing on leveraging Electron's features using simple JavaScript examples. Using the Electron Quick Start as a starting point for our exercises will be helpful in keeping this focus.

CHAPTER 4

BrowserWindow Basics

As explained in earlier chapters, the Renderer Process is where your application appears. The Renderer Process uses Chromium to render your user interface. The Main Process creates Renderer Processes by creating instances of the BrowserWindow object.

In this chapter, we explore the basic options for creating BrowserWindow instances as well as explore the frameless and transparent window types.

Getting Started

Let's take a moment to make this `package.json` match our own by updating some nodes.

1. Change the name node to `"browser-window-sample"`.

2. Change the version number to `"0.0.1"` since we are just starting out. If you are unfamiliar with semantic versioning, version numbers are broken into three elements: MAJOR.MINOR.PATCH. As this is our starting point, we will begin numbering with 0.0.1.

3. In the description let's use something like `"A sample Electron application to demonstrate BrowserWindow creation"`.

4. Remove the repository property. If you decide to put your results in a repository you can change or re-add this property with the correct address.

5. Keywords can be `"Electron,"` `"BrowserWindow,"` `"sample"`.

6. `"author"`: Your name goes here.

7. If you wish to change the licensing type, you can do that with this property. By default, it is set to Creative Commons 1.0 Universal. There are many alternative options available; choose the one that best suits your needs.

Disabling Chrome DevTools

In this chapter, we will be repeatedly starting and stopping our project to see how different settings affect the window our project creates. We also need to make sure that Dev Tools are turned off so they don't interfere with what we see. Open the `main.js` file and find the line in the code that makes the Dev Tools appear and comment it like this (note the highlighted code added):

```
// Open the DevTools.
// mainWindow.webContents.openDevTools()
```

Now that the Dev Tools are out of the way, let's take a look at what the default code without the Dev Tools creates (Figure 4-1). From the terminal application, navigate to the project folder and run the following command:

```
npm start
```

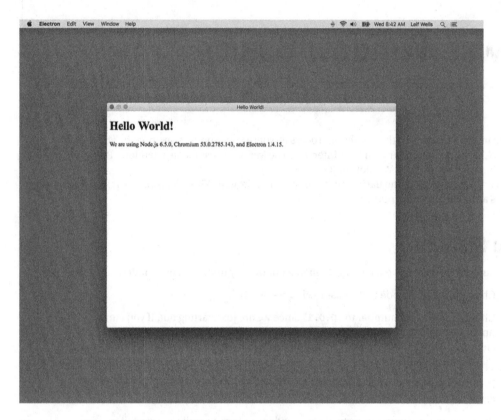

Figure 4-1. *The starter Electron window without the Chrome DevTools*

Remember this command as we will be using it many times in this chapter.

As you can see, this is a simple window. Nothing exciting here. Let's review the code that initializes this window in the createWindow method inside the main.js file:

```
function createWindow () {
  // Create the browser window.
  mainWindow = new BrowserWindow({width: 800, height: 600})

  // and load the index.html of the app.
  mainWindow.loadURL(url.format({
    pathname: path.join(__dirname, 'index.html'),
    protocol: 'file:',
    slashes: true
  }))
```

```
// Open the DevTools.
// mainWindow.webContents.openDevTools()

// Emitted when the window is closed.
mainWindow.on('closed', function () {
  // Dereference the window object, usually you would store windows
  // in an array if your app supports multi windows, this is the time
  // when you should delete the corresponding element.
  mainWindow = null
})
}
```

When createWindow is called, the mainWindow variable is created by calling the new BrowserWindow constructor. There is an argument being passed to the constructor in the form of an object with the properties of width and height.

Lower in that code block we call the loadURL method on the mainWindow. The argument required for the loadURL method is created using Node's url module, a utility module that assists in the creation and formatting of URLs:

```
// and load the index.html of the app.
mainWindow.loadURL(url.format({
        pathname: path.join(__dirname, 'index.html'),
        protocol: 'file:',
        slashes: true
 }))
```

The format method from the url module allows you to create a link to the file that the Renderer Process will use to render. Note the properties used in the argument for the format method. This is the way Node likes to have URLs created:

- pathname: uses Node's path module to create a string by connecting the two pieces of the path, __dirname (a Node global), and the name of the file to be rendered.

- protocol: the loading protocol to use. Typically for Electron, 'file:' is the setting. Please note the use of the colon.

- slashes: Setting this to true adds '//' to the protocol making it 'file:///', in this case making it properly use three slashes.

After we load the file for the window, we need to add a listener to the window so we can capture the 'closed' event and, as is best practice for desktop applications, clear the mainWindow variable:

```
// Emitted when the window is closed.
mainWindow.on('closed', function () {
        // Dereference the window object, usually you would store windows
        // in an array if your app supports multi windows, this is the time
        // when you should delete the corresponding element.
        mainWindow = null
})
```

Update Code to Use the ready-to-show Event

The first change we will make to our code is to establish a best practice of waiting for the BrowserWindow's ready-to-show event before showing the window. This best practice is recommended in Electron's documentation and is often overlooked. When you create a BrowserWindow directly, as our code does currently, the Renderer Process starts and immediately displays. But the content you are displaying may not be fully rendered. To avoid this condition we will listen for the 'ready-to-show' event and call the BrowserWindow's show() method to display the window. Make the following changes to the createWindow method:

```
function createWindow () {
  // Create the browser window.
  mainWindow = new BrowserWindow({
    show: false,
    backgroundColor: '#FFF',
    width: 800,
    height: 600
  })

  // and load the index.html of the app.
  mainWindow.loadURL(url.format({
    pathname: path.join(__dirname, 'index.html'),
    protocol: 'file:',
    slashes: true
  }))

  // Open the DevTools.
  // mainWindow.webContents.openDevTools()

  // Wait for 'ready-to-show' to display our window
  mainWindow.once('ready-to-show', () => {
    mainWindow.show()
  })

  // Emitted when the window is closed.
  mainWindow.on('closed', function () {
    // Dereference the window object, usually you would store windows
    // in an array if your app supports multi windows, this is the time
    // when you should delete the corresponding element.
    mainWindow = null
  })
}
```

At the top of this code block we've added the show property set to false, which prevents the created window from displaying.

The next new property is the backgroundColor. The best practice here is to try to match the background color used in your application so that if the window does display before the content is rendered, there won't be a flash between displaying the window's default background color of '#FFF' (white) and the background color of your application. This setting is effective with the show property set to true but is a good practice to generally follow. This property only accepts hexcodes for its value and not colors defined in rgb() or rgba(). It is worth noting that this parameter only accepts hexadecimal values, and nothing of the form rgb() or rgba().

Later in the code block we've added the listener for the 'ready-to-show' event. In our current code, this event occurs quickly since we are not loading up a lot of code and assets in our sample like you might with a real application. We are also using one of the new ES6 features, the fat arrow function. If you are not familiar with this feature, it provides a shorthand notation to have a callback execute it function.

In ES5, we would have written a simple multiply function like this:

```
var multiply = function (x,y) {
 return x * y;
}
```

But in ES6, using the new arrow function formation, we can write the same function this way:

```
var multiply = (x, y) => { return x * y };
```

The arrow function example allows us to accomplish the same result with fewer lines of code and approximately half the typing.

Now that we have established these best practices, let's explore BrowserWindow's options.

BrowserWindow Options Argument

Let's do an experiment here to give us some insight into how the BrowserWindow's argument works. If you haven't done so already, quit the application and delete the argument object making that line of code look like this:

```
mainWindow = new BrowserWindow()
```

Run the npm start command to see how the window appears (Figure 4-2).

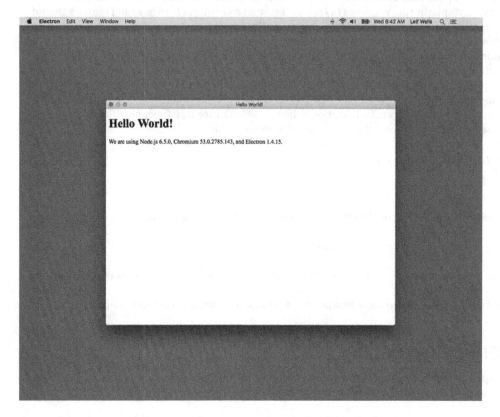

Figure 4-2. *The starter Electron window opening using the 'ready-to-show' event*

If it appears that nothing has changed, you are correct. The window is centered on the screen and is 800 pixels wide, 600 pixels high. If you grab the title bar, the window will move. Grab the any edge of the window and you can resize it to any size you would like.

The points being made here are:

- The BrowserWindow's options argument is not required.

- The BrowserWindow has defaults in place so that, if you do not enter options like the width and height properties in the argument, the window will still appear.

A list of all available options can be found in the Electron documentation <https://electron.atom.io/docs/api/browser-window/#class-browserwindow>

In this case, the default for width is 800(px) and the default is 600(px). The documentation for the BrowserWindow cites over 40 optional properties, all with defaults. Let's continue by looking at some of the other window properties to which we have access.

Basic Window Properties (width, height, minWidth, minHeight, maxWidth, maxHeight)

Let's update the code to add an argument to the BrowserWindow method.

```
// Create the browser window.
mainWindow = new BrowserWindow({
        show: false,                    // DEFAULT: true
        backgroundColor: "#FFF",        // DEFAULT: '#FFF'
        width: 800,                     // DEFAULT: 800
        height: 600,                    // DEFAULT: 600
        minWidth: 800,                  // DEFAULT: 0
        maxWidth: 1024,                 // DEFAULT: UNLIMITED
        minHeight: 600,                 // DEFAULT: 0
        maxHeight: 768,                 // DEFAULT: UNLIMITED
        resizable: true,                // DEFAULT: true
        movable: true                   // DEFAULT: true
})
```

Take a moment to note what we are trying to illustrate with the comments in this code. On the left side are the window properties we wish to affect. On the right side are comments informing us of the default for each of these properties. While these comments aren't required, they will help us moving through this chapter.

Now, run npm start in the terminal and see how these additional properties change our window. No need to give you a screenshot. The initial appearance of the window hasn't changed. While the screen size is 800 x 600 pixels, if you try resizing the window you'll find that you cannot make it smaller than it currently is and no larger than 1024 x 768 pixels.

Please be aware that these sizing constraints are user-oriented constraints. Once the window is created, you may resize it using BrowserWindow methods like setBounds(bounds) and setSize(width, height) to change the size of your window. If you do decide to resize your window, you should take a look at the setMinimumSize(width, height) and setMaximumSize(width, height) to apply new resize constraints.

The center, x and y Properties

You may notice that this code is not passing a center property in the options argument. Best practices suggest that if your application is a single window application, it should initially appear in the center of the screen. Since our example application is loading in the center of the screen, we can assume that the default setting for center is true even though the default is not currently documented.

Also, not appearing in our code are the x and y options, which control where the top left corner of the window will appear. The defaults for these options are to center the window. That is, when you do not pass the x and y options as part of the options argument for BrowserWindow, Electron does the math taking the width and height properties along with screen dimensions and sets the x and y properties so that the window is centered. Setting the x and y options essentially turns the center option to false.

The x and y options are the only options that are optionally required. What does that mean? If you pass the x option you must pass the y option. The same goes when passing the y option; the x option must be passed as well. If you pass either of these options by themselves, the option is ignored.

For the purposes of this exercise, these properties will not be added to our code. The default settings will do.

The `resizable` and `movable` Properties

Let's make another change to the code so we can see how changing the `resizable` and `movable` properties affect the other properties:

```
// Create the browser window.
mainWindow = new BrowserWindow({
        show: false,                  // DEFAULT: true
        backgroundColor: '#FFF'       // DEFAULT: '#FFF'
        width: 800,                   // DEFAULT: 800
        height: 600,                  // DEFAULT: 600
        minWidth: 800,                // DEFAULT: 0
        maxWidth: 1024,               // DEFAULT: UNLIMITED
        minHeight: 600,               // DEFAULT: 0
        maxHeight: 768,               // DEFAULT: UNLIMITED
        resizable: false,             // DEFAULT: true
        movable: false                // DEFAULT: true
})
```

After you quit the application and run npm start again you'll find that changing the `resizable` property to false restricts any resizing of the application. In effect, the `minWidth`, `minHeight`, `maxWidth`, and `maxHeight` properties are basically ignored. That doesn't mean you should ignore these properties if your window is not resizable. You may wish to turn the resizable property on and off. Setting minimum and maximum sizes is a good practice.

Now try moving the window by dragging the title bar. This window will not move. A best practice here would be to always use the default setting of `movable: true` unless there is a compelling reason to make it immovable. Most desktop applications allow a user to decide where they want the application's windows to appear.

The `alwaysOnTop` property is another setting that is important. The default setting for this property is `false`. Setting `alwaysOnTop` to `true` means that while the application is running, this window is above all other windows in the application and on the computer. We can add `alwaysOnTop` to the bottom of our options argument and reset our `resizable` and `movable` properties so our code looks like this:

```
// Create the browser window.
mainWindow = new BrowserWindow({
        show: false,                  // DEFAULT: true
        backgroundColor: '#FFF'       // DEFAULT: '#FFF'
        width: 800,                   // DEFAULT: 800
        height: 600,                  // DEFAULT: 600
        minWidth: 800,                // DEFAULT: 0
        maxWidth: 1024,               // DEFAULT: UNLIMITED
        minHeight: 600,               // DEFAULT: 0
        maxHeight: 768,               // DEFAULT: UNLIMITED
        resizable: true,              // DEFAULT: true
        movable: true,                // DEFAULT: true
        alwaysOnTop: true             // DEFAULT: false
})
```

Quit the application and run npm start to see this in action. As described, the window stays on top of everything, even windows belonging to the operating system. Again, the best practice is to go with the default setting of false with this property unless there is a compelling reason for blocking all other user interfaces and irritating users.

The title Property

You would think that something like the title property would be something simple. Well, it is, but it may not work the way you might think, so pay attention. The title property is used in the title bar of your window. The Electron documentation says that the title property is, like all the other properties, and the default for title is "Electron." But let's look at how it really works.

Without adding any code to our project, run the npm start command and look at the text that appears in the title bar (Figure 4-3):

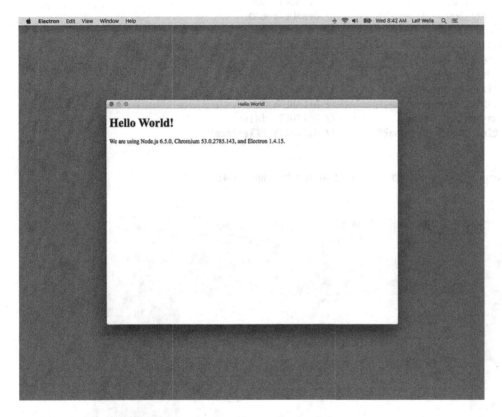

Figure 4-3. *Our application name shown in the window's title bar*

See, there it is: "Hello, World!" Where is that coming from? Let's find out. Quit the application and open the index.html file in the project. This is the file that our BrowserWindow is being told to render. Up in the head element of that file you will see the title element:

```
<head>
        <meta charset="UTF-8">
        <title>Hello World!</title>
</head>
```

So, we've learned that the text in the title element of the head element of our rendered HTML file will be used in the title bar of our application. But let's dig a little deeper. Open the main.js file in the project and add the title option to the BrowserWindow argument object (make sure you reset alwaysOnTop to false):

```
// Create the browser window.
mainWindow = new BrowserWindow({
        show: false,                    // DEFAULT: true
        backgroundColor: '#FFF'         // DEFAULT: '#FFF'
        width: 800,                     // DEFAULT: 800
        height: 600,                    // DEFAULT: 600
        minWidth: 800,                  // DEFAULT: 0
        maxWidth: 1024,                 // DEFAULT: UNLIMITED
        minHeight: 600,                 // DEFAULT: 0
        maxHeight: 768,                 // DEFAULT: UNLIMITED
        resizable: true,                // DEFAULT: true
        movable: true,                  // DEFAULT: true
        alwaysOnTop: false,             // DEFAULT: false
        title: "Goodbye, Moon?"         // DEFAULT: "Electron"
})
```

Run the npm start command and look at our results (Figure 4-4).

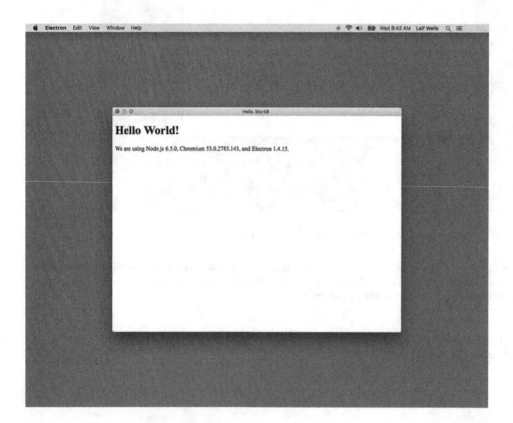

Figure 4-4. *Updating the Electron Window title*

Wait, what? Why aren't we seeing "Goodbye, Moon?" in our title bar? You see, the HTML content that the Renderer Process is rendering overrides the optional title argument. Let's prove this out. Go back to the index.html file and comment out the title element:

```
<head>
        <meta charset="UTF-8">
        <!-- <title>Hello World!</title> -->
</head>
```

Now run npm start and see what displays in the title bar (Figure 4-5).

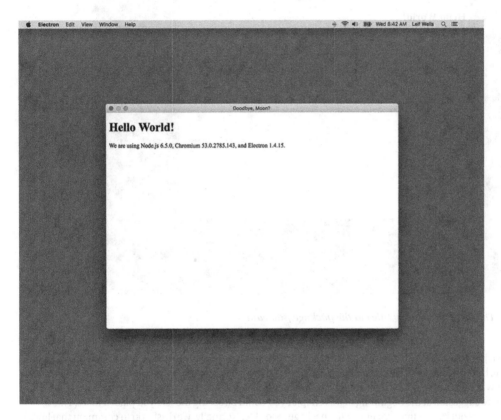

Figure 4-5. *Our Electron window title properly updated*

There's our "Goodbye, Moon?" Nice. Let's take this experiment one step further and comment out the title optional argument.

```
// title: "Goodbye, Moon?" // DEFAULT: "Electron"
```

Now our code has the title argument commented in the main.js file as well as the title element comment in the index.html file commented so we should see the default setting of "Electron" in our title bar, right? Run the npm start command to see (Figure 4-6):

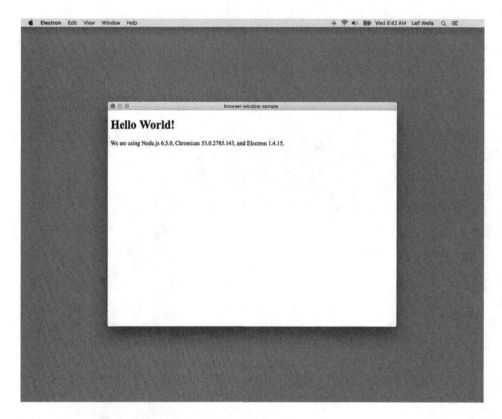

Figure 4-6. *The Electron window title via the package.json value*

OK, what just happened? Are you seeing what we are seeing? We're seeing the text "browser-window-sample" in the title bar, but you may see something else. At the time of this writing, we asked the contributors to the Electron project if this was on purpose but haven't gotten a response. Needless to say, if you changed the package.json property like we suggested at the beginning of this chapter you could be seeing the text you placed there. Weird, right? Let's test this out by deleting that line in the package.json file. Normally, we'd ask you to comment that line, but commenting isn't allowed in JSON. Please remember to re-create that line after this experiment. So, without the name property in our package.json file we can run the npm start command and finally see (Figure 4-7):

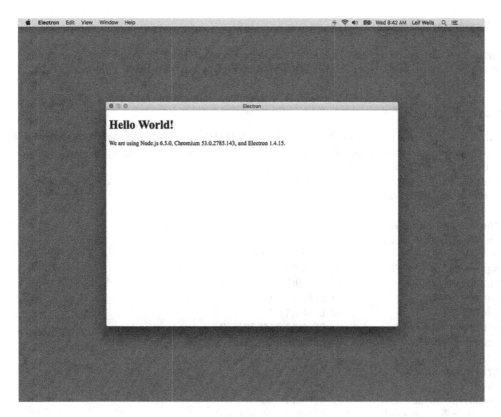

Figure 4-7. *The Electron window title restored*

"Electron"! Hizzah! We were confused at first, too. But we learned something, right? If you do not provide a title argument when you create a BrowserWindow instance, or you do not provide a title in the HTML file you are rendering you will probably get a title that you don't want. (Make sure you re-create the name line in the package.json file.)

Best practices for the title option are to take control of the text that appears in your title bar. You may wish to do this in the Main Process or the Renderer Process. Depending on what kind of application you've created, the text that appears in the title bar could be dynamic. You may need to add a "*" at the end or beginning of the title text to indicate that a file hasn't been saved. The file being loaded by the Renderer Process might be a template that dynamically loads other files, or even navigates to other files. Making sure that the title element is in the HTML file by default may work in many cases, but if not give thought to which of the processes makes sense to manage the text that appears in the title bar.

To change the title dynamically on macOS, you can call mainWindow.setTitle ('Goodbye, Moon'); this will override your window title (even when it is set in the HTML). Windows (the Operating System) is trickier and will retain the default title (either from HTML or package.json until the user interacts with the window (maximize/minimize/resize).

Other Window Types

While the windows we have been creating so far in this chapter are typically the kind of windows applications will use, there are two other window types we should mention: frameless and transparent windows.

Frameless Windows

A frameless window is a window that has no chrome. This means that the window will appear without any borders or toolbars associated with a browser window and only display the HTML content provided. Let's look at how a frameless window is created.

Frameless windows can be created by using the frame option and setting it to false. Add this option at the bottom of our BrowserWindow code like so:

```
// Create the browser window.
mainWindow = new BrowserWindow({
        show: false,               // DEFAULT: true
        backgroundColor: '#FFF'    // DEFAULT: '#FFF'
        width: 800,                // DEFAULT: 800
        height: 600,               // DEFAULT: 600
        minWidth: 800,             // DEFAULT: 0
        maxWidth: 1024,            // DEFAULT: UNLIMITED
        minHeight: 600,            // DEFAULT: 0
        maxHeight: 768,            // DEFAULT: UNLIMITED
        resizable: true,           // DEFAULT: true
        movable: true,             // DEFAULT: true
        alwaysOnTop: false         // DEFAULT: false
        title: 'Goodbye, Moon?',   // DEFAULT: "Electron"
        frame: false               // DEFAULT: true
})
```

Now we can run the npm start command and look at a frameless window (Figure 4-8).

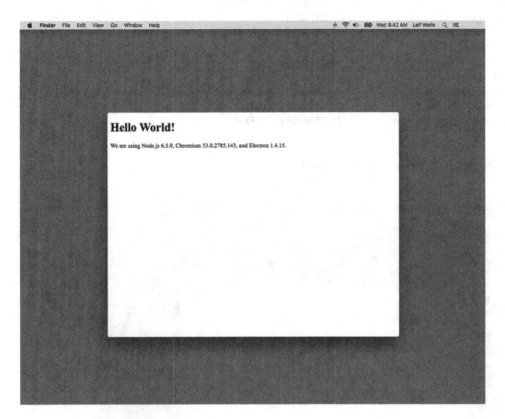

Figure 4-8. *Our Electron application in a frameless window*

There it is, a frameless, naked window. No borders. No title bar. No toolbars. Just the bare window. But we need to review some of the things that we can't see that are missing. If you are running on macOS, the first thing you may notice is the normal windows controls that appear in the upper left corner aren't there. You know, the traffic light on its side with a red, yellow, and green button. With those controls missing, you can't close this window using the mouse. Speaking of the mouse, try moving this window. You can't. There is no title bar for you to grab. In some cases, this behavior may be desirable. But we might want to have the window appear as frameless but still give users typical control over the window, so we need to make sure we can get these features back if we need them.

To get a frameless window on macOS that has the window controls, we must create the frameless window a different way. To get the desired window, we do not use the frame option at all. We need to use the titleBarStyle option. The default option for titleBarStyle is 'default', but we want to use the 'hidden' or 'hidden-inset' options. Comment the line with the frame option and then add the following code:

```
// Create the browser window.
mainWindow = new BrowserWindow({
        show: false,                  // DEFAULT: true
        backgroundColor: '#FFF'       // DEFAULT: '#FFF'
        width: 800,                   // DEFAULT: 800
        height: 600,                  // DEFAULT: 600
```

```
      minWidth: 800,              // DEFAULT: 0
      maxWidth: 1024,             // DEFAULT: UNLIMITED
      minHeight: 600,             // DEFAULT: 0
      maxHeight: 768,             // DEFAULT: UNLIMITED
      resizable: true,            // DEFAULT: true
      movable: true,              // DEFAULT: true
      alwaysOnTop: false,         // DEFAULT: false
      title: 'Goodbye, Moon?',    // DEFAULT: "Electron"
      // frame: false,            // DEFAULT: true
      titleBarStyle: 'hidden'     // DEFAULT: 'default'
})
```

Run the npm start command and look (Figure 4-9).

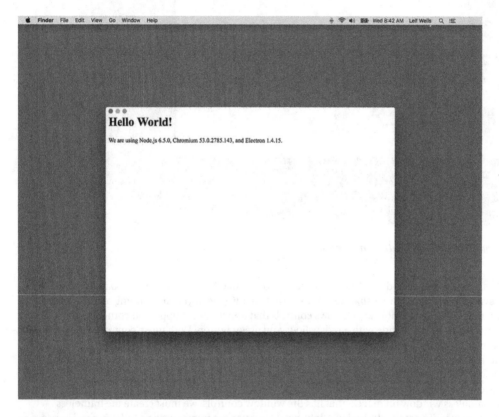

Figure 4-9. *The Electron application in a frameless window with window controls added*

Here we see that the window controls are shown, but, as the option 'hidden' suggests, the title bar is not seen. The other option for titleBarStyle is 'hidden-inset'. We can change that code and take a look at how that window displays. Quit the application if it is still running, make the following change to the code, and run the npm start command:

```
titleBarStyle: 'hidden-inset' // DEFAULT: 'default'
```

The change is subtle (Figure 4-10). As compared to the 'hidden' setting, the controls have slightly inset into the window. Choose which option to suit your purposes. Note: this property has no effect on Windows OS.

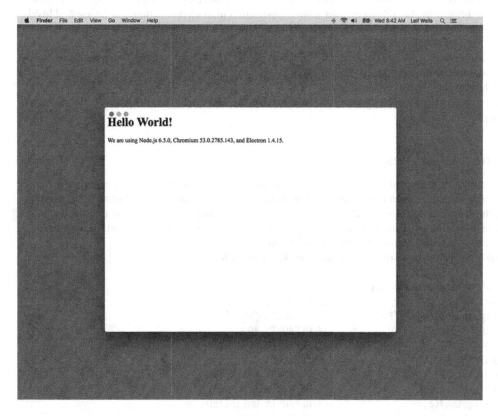

Figure 4-10. *The Electron application in a frameless window with window controls added in the inset mode*

Now, we need to see about getting the ability to move our frameless window back. For this issue we need to rely upon some CSS. If we want to make the whole window movable, we can simple apply a style to the body of the HTML being rendered. Quit the application if it is still running, open the index.html, and make the following change to the body element:

```
<body style="-webkit-app-region: drag">
```

Run the npm start command and test out our application.

No reason to show you a screenshot, but we should discuss the effects this change has made. Use your mouse to click-hold anywhere near the top area of the window and move the window around. Yes! We can move our window. But let's check doing the same on the bottom area of the window. No dice. What is going on here?

Since we are applying the CSS fix to the body element, only that element will trigger dragging, but the body element is restricted to the size of the content. Quit the application so we may make a change to our CSS so we can see what is really happening:

```
<body style="border:1px solid red;-webkit-app-region: drag">
```

When we run the npm start command we see a red box around the content at the top of the window. Now we can see where we can drag the window around and where we cannot. This is because the boundaries of body element are constrained by the content it holds. So, this technique may not be the best way to re-create this feature. Let's also consider what happens to button elements that may be applied inside the body element. The CSS overrides the button behavior so now your buttons don't work. What about selecting text? No, that won't work either.

What have we learned from this experiment? The best practice for moving a frameless window would be to provide an element at the top of the window that can be made draggable. The user expects this behavior and not click-holding anywhere on the window.

Note that if you set the window property movable to false, it will override the CSS property we've set on the body and prevent dragging.

Transparent Windows

Another window type we can explore is a transparent window. This window type is just what you might expect: you can see anything underneath the window. Before we explore making our window transparent, take heed to this warning: you may find that you have lost your application. At 100% transparent, you won't see it. It can be disorienting, so don't panic. If you get confused, go back to your terminal window and use the control-c keyboard combination to stop the application.

Let's make some changes to our main.js file to make a transparent window possible:

```
mainWindow = new BrowserWindow({
        show: false,                        // DEFAULT: true
        backgroundColor: '#FFF'             // DEFAULT: '#FFF'
        width: 800,                         // DEFAULT: 800
        height: 600,                        // DEFAULT: 600
        minWidth: 800,                      // DEFAULT: 0
        maxWidth: 1024,                     // DEFAULT: UNLIMITED
        minHeight: 600,                     // DEFAULT: 0
        maxHeight: 768,                     // DEFAULT: UNLIMITED
        resizable: true,                    // DEFAULT: true
        movable: true,                      // DEFAULT: true
        alwaysOnTop: false                  // DEFAULT: false
        frame: false,                       //  DEFAULT: true
        //  title: 'Goodbye, Moon?',        //  DEFAULT: 'default'
        transparent: true                   //  DEFAULT: false
})
```

Run the npm start command and prepare yourself to be amazed (Figure 4-11).

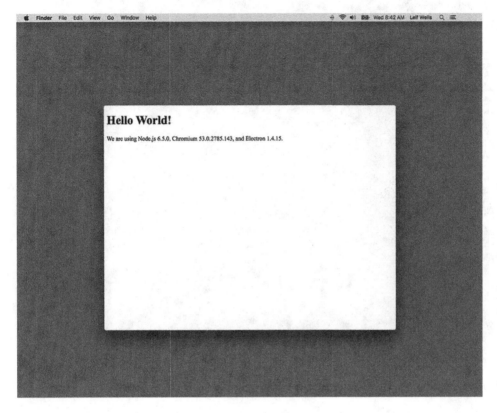

Figure 4-11. *The Electron window with transparency enabled*

Wait a minute. That's not a transparent window. It looks exactly like a frameless window. It seems that just setting the transparent option to true isn't enough. Let's change one more option, the backgroundColor option, and see what we get. Specifically, we will comment out the option:

```
mainWindow = new BrowserWindow({
        show: false,                    // DEFAULT: true
        // backgroundColor: '#FFF'      // DEFAULT: '#FFF'
        width: 800,                     // DEFAULT: 800
        height: 600,                    // DEFAULT: 600
        minWidth: 800,                  // DEFAULT: 0
        maxWidth: 1024,                 // DEFAULT: UNLIMITED
        minHeight: 600,                 // DEFAULT: 0
        maxHeight: 768,                 // DEFAULT: UNLIMITED
        resizable: true,                // DEFAULT: true
        movable: true,                  // DEFAULT: true
        alwaysOnTop: false              // DEFAULT: false
        frame: false                    //  DEFAULT: true
        //  titleBarStyle: 'hidden'     // DEFAULT: 'default'
        transparent: true               // DEFAULT: false
})
```

Figure 4-12. *The Electron window with transparency properly enabled*

Yeah, that is more like it. Depending on what is on your screen, you can barely see the text of the index. html. We've made a transparent window, but we need to know about the restrictions for this window, too. With the frame option set to false, you have all the restrictions as a typical frameless window: no title bar, no toolbars, and the window will not move without modification. Add to these restrictions that you may find it nearly impossible to resize a transparent window. How could you? You can't see the edges of the window. Be aware: setting the reset option to true can make a transparent window stop working. More restrictions and information about creating transparent windows on different platforms can be found in Electron's documentation. Please note that on Windows, this property has for effect to make the whole window and its content disappear, rendering the application unusable.

Please be responsible when you use transparent windows. You do not want the users of your application to think you are playing tricks; but you could set an rgba() background-color on your <html> or <body> tags to obtain a semi-transparent window that gives you a background but lets you see what's underneath.

Summary

In this chapter, we explored the basic options of BrowserWindow creation: show, width, height, minWidth, maxWidth, minHeight, maxHeight, resizable, movable, and alwaysOnTop. We also explored two window types: frameless and transparent. The knowledge we gained here will help us as we move into the next chapters.

CHAPTER 5

Adding Custom Menus

Menus are also something that traditional web app have never had access to. The application menus were always that of the browsers. If the user accessed a contextual menu on the page, the default browser contextual menu would appear. Web apps had no ability to change either one. However, Electron gives you full control over creating both application-level menus, as well as contextual menus.

We will explore creating both the application-level menus and the contextual menus. Electron uses the Menu and the MenuItem modules together to create the custom menus that your application will use.

Getting Started

Let's clone a fresh copy of the Electron Quick Start example.

```
git clone https://github.com/electron/electron-quick-start custom-menu-demo
```

Next, change your active directory to electron-quick-start.

```
cd custom-menu-demo
```

Now, we need to install the dependencies:

```
npm install
```

Finally, reset Git with

```
git init
```

You might have noticed that our previous Electron samples already included a standard application menu. In fact, it is a robust menu system with many of the standard functions already defined (Figure 5-1).

© Chris Griffith, Leif Wells 2017
C. Griffith, L. Wells, *Electron: From Beginner to Pro*, https://doi.org/10.1007/978-1-4842-2826-5_5

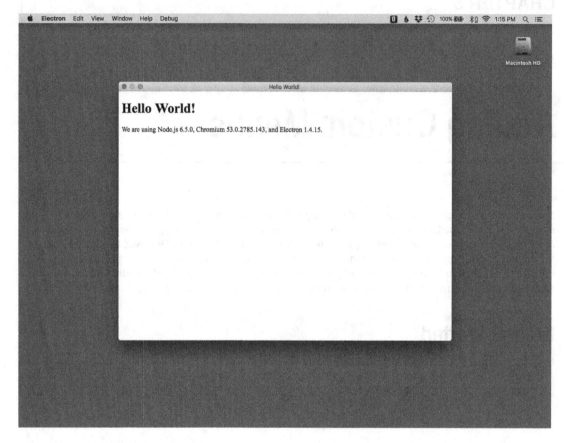

Figure 5-1. *The default Electron menu*

But if we want to have a custom menu in our application, then the creation of the entire menu must be defined by the developer. So, let's get started building our basic application menu. Figure 5-2 shows what our final menu structure will look like on macOS.

Electron	Edit	View	Window	Help
About electron-quick-start	Undo	Reload	Minimize	Search
------	Redo	Toggle Full Screen	Close	Learn More
Services	------	Toggle Developer Tools	------	
------	Cut	------	Reopen Window	
Hide electron-quick-start	Copy	App Menu Demo	------	
Hide Others	Paste		Being All to Front	
Show All	Select All		------	
------	------		Hello World	
Quit	Start Dictation			
	Emoji & Symbols			

Figure 5-2. *Menu hierarchy diagram*

Now the application menu is only available in the main process, so let's open the main.js file in our editor. Within our existing constants, we will define another for our Menu module:

```
const Menu = electron.Menu
```

Then once our application is ready, we can attach our menu. Locate this function in main.js

```
app.on('ready', createWindow)
```

and replace it with this:

```
app.on('ready', function () {
  const menu = Menu.buildFromTemplate(template)
  Menu.setApplicationMenu(menu)
  createWindow()
})
```

One of the methods in the Menu module is the ability to create a menu object from a template. Rather than append each menu item one by one, Electron gives us the ability to create a menu template and have it properly generate our menu object for us. Once we have created our menu object, we can replace the default application menu that the Electron shell provides.

■ **Note**   If you run the application in its current state, you will encounter an error, as we have not defined a template yet.

Menu Templates

Let's start creating our menu template. For any modest application, you will have quite a lengthy template, so we are going to build up our template in steps to ensure that the formatting is correct.

After we define the mainWindow variable, add this code block for a simple menu that will have two top-level menus, and each with a single menu item:

```
let template = [{
  label: 'Menu 1',
  submenu: [{
    label: 'Menu item 1'
  }]
}, {
  label: 'Menu 2',
  submenu: [{
    label: 'Another Menu item'
  }, {
    label: 'One More Menu Item'
  }]
}]
```

The menu template is an array of objects. Each object will define an individual menu that will be shown in the application's menu bar. To define text that will be shown, we assign that value to its label property. In this code sample, we are defining two menus: Menu 1 and Menu 2.

To define the menu items – the elements that are shown when a user selects that menu – we set the submenu property to an array of menu objects. For Menu 1, we only define one menu item with a label of Menu item 1. For the second menu, Menu 2, we will define two menu items: Another Menu Item and One More Menu Item.

Before we test out our menu, we need to make a special adjustment for running on macOS.

macOS's Application Menu

Ignoring the Apple menu, which is systemwide, on macOS, the first menu item of the application menu is the application's name. Currently, this menu is labeled Electron, since that is the root application that we are using. Once we build our application for distribution, this label will reflect our actual application name.

This application menu is where you will find the applications preference's menu, the ability to hide the application or other applications, and the quit menu. If we simply define our menu template without accommodating for this special menu, we will have an issue. Our first menu definition will be incorrectly displayed. The main menu label will not be shown, but the menu items will be inserted under the application menu.

To solve this, we will need to shift our menus one position if we are running on macOS. After the template definition in the main.js file, we can add this code to offset our template if we are running on a macOS system:

```
if (process.platform === 'darwin') {
  const name = electron.app.getName()
  template.unshift({
    label: name,
    submenu: [{
      label: 'Quit',
      accelerator: 'Command+Q',
      click: function () {
        app.quit()
      }
    }]
  })
}
```

This will only adjust our menu structure. The traditional menu items that we typically would see in this menu will not be there. However, we did include the Quit menu item to make working with this sample a bit easier. We will address adding in the rest of the menu items for the macOS application menu later in the chapter. For now, let's explore expanding our menus.

Defining Keyboard Shortcuts and Menu Item Roles

Let's replace our simple menu template with one that is more complex, like a standard Edit menu. Here is the template we will use:

```
let template = [{
  label: 'Edit App',
  submenu: [{
    label: 'Undo',
    accelerator: 'CmdOrCtrl+Z',
    role: 'undo'
  }, {
    label: 'Redo',
    accelerator: 'Shift+CmdOrCtrl+Z',
    role: 'redo'
  }, {
    type: 'separator'
  }, {
```

```
    label: 'Cut',
    accelerator: 'CmdOrCtrl+X',
    role: 'cut'
  }, {
    label: 'Copy',
    accelerator: 'CmdOrCtrl+C',
    role: 'copy'
  }, {
    label: 'Paste',
    accelerator: 'CmdOrCtrl+V',
    role: 'paste'
  }, {
    label: 'Select All',
    accelerator: 'CmdOrCtrl+A',
    role: 'selectall'
  }]
}]
```

We set the top-level menu's name through using the label property. Now, standard convention for the Edit menu is simply to call it Edit; we are changing it to Edit App so you can verify that the menu is your menu and not the predefined Electron Edit menu.

■ **Note**   You should always follow the platform convention for keyboard shortcuts and menu naming. Refer to each platform's user interface guidelines forfurther information.

Next, we will set the submenu with an array of menu items. Let's look at the first submenu:

```
{
  label: 'Undo',
  accelerator: 'CmdOrCtrl+Z',
  role: 'undo'
}
```

Again, we set the menu's name through using the label property. Next, we define the accelerator. This is an optional property, but this is how you define the keyboard shortcut for the menu item. We can listen for the following modifiers:

- Command (or Cmd for short)
- Control (or Ctrl for short)
- CommandOrControl (or CmdOrCtrl for short)
- Alt
- Option
- AltGr
- Shift
- Super

The modifier is then combined with a keycode to define our accelerator. In our snippet, our accelerator is set to be 'CmdOrCtrl+Z'. This means that if the user presses either the Command key or the Control key (based on the platform) and the Z key, the menu item will be triggered.

Since our Electron application will be running on a variety of platforms, we need a solution to properly map our accelerators to the platform's conventions. For example, on Windows and Linux, there Is no Command key. But by using the CommandOrControl modifier, Electron will properly map the modifier to the correct key based on the platform.

Although the Option modifier does exist, it is recommended that you use Alt instead. The Option key only exists on macOS, whereas the Alt key is available on all platforms.

The Super key is mapped to the Windows key on Windows and Linux and Cmd on macOS.

It is also possible to combine modifiers together. Typically, this is just including the Shift modifier as an additional keypress.

The next property that is defined is role. While many of our menu items might trigger custom actions within our application, many of them will simply map to a standard role. Rather than try to implement the behavior of each action in a click function, we can leverage the built-in role behavior.

The role property can have the following values:

- undo

- redo

- cut

- copy

- paste

- pasteandmatchstyle

- selectall

- delete

- minimize - Minimize current window

- close - Close current window

- quit- Quit the application

- reload - Reload the current window

- toggledevtools - Toggle developer tools in the current window

- togglefullscreen- Toggle full screen mode on the current window

- resetzoom - Reset the focused page's zoom level to the original size

- zoomin - Zoom in the focused page by 10%

- zoomout - Zoom out the focused page by 10%

On OSX, the role can also have following additional values:

- about - Map to the orderFrontStandardAboutPanel action

- hide - Map to the hide action

- hideothers - Map to the hideOtherApplications action

- unhide - Map to the unhideAllApplications action

- startspeaking - Map to the startSpeaking action

- stopspeaking - Map to the stopSpeaking action

- front - Map to the arrangeInFront action

- zoom - Map to the performZoom action

- window - The submenu is a "Window" menu

- help - The submenu is a "Help" menu

- services - The submenu is a "Services" menu

If you don't want to use one of the predefined roles, you can set the click property to call a custom function

```
{
  label: 'Generate Icon',
  click: doGenerateIcon
}
```

Now when the user selects the Generate Icon menu item, our custom function doGenerateIcon will be called. Electron will automatically pass in three parameters: menuItem, browserWIndow, and event, into our function. The menuItem parameter can be used to determine which menu item the function was called from. The browserWindow parameter will tell us which window had focus when the function was called. This is important when you have a multi-window application and need to affect something in a specific renderer view. The final parameter, event, will tell have the state of the modifier keys when the function was triggered.

■ **Note**   On macOS, if you specify a menu item's role, you can only affect the label and the accelerator. All other menu item options are ignored.

There are several other menu item properties that you should be aware of. The first is the simple separator. This menu item will insert the horizontal line in the menu (Figure 5-3).

```
{
    type: 'separator'
}
```

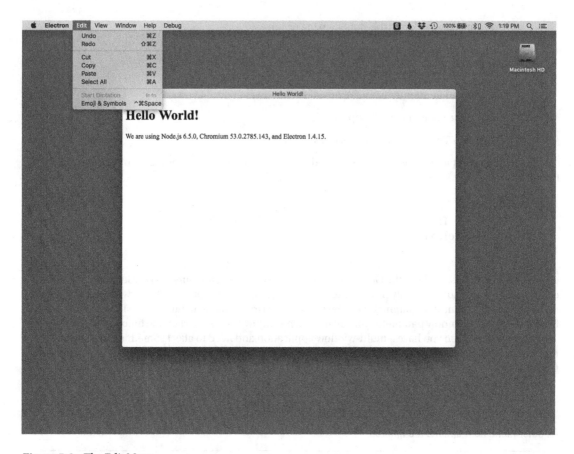

Figure 5-3. *The Edit Menu*

Creating Submenus and Checkmarks

Another menu type that you will use is the submenu. We already used it to define the menus under each menu name. But if you want to create a submenu from a menu item, this is the type you will use. After the Select All definition in our Edit App menu, let's add a demonstration of both the separator and a submenu:

```
{
    label: 'Select All',
    accelerator: 'CmdOrCtrl+A',
    role: 'selectall'
}, {
    type: 'separator'
}, {
    label: 'My Submenu',
    submenu: [
      {
        label: 'Item 1'
      },
```

```
      {
        label: 'Item 2'
      }
    ]
  }
```

Figure 5-4 shows what this looks like.

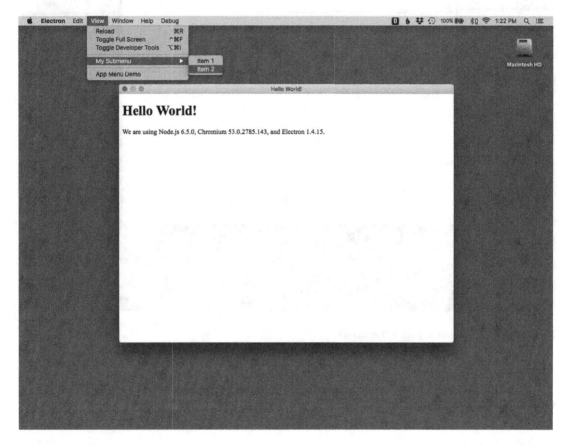

Figure 5-4. *Our custom submenu*

In addition to these menu item types, there are several other properties that can be set on a menu item. These are setting the enable property. If this is set to false, the menu item will be grayed out and unclickable. To hidden a menu completely, set the visible property to false.

Often you might want to indicate that a menu item's function is active. Typically, this is shown through using a checkmark next to the menu name (see Figure 5-5). Electron offers two methods to achieve this. The first is the checkbox type. Set the type of the menu item to 'checkbox'. The status checkbox is set via the checked property.

```
{
  label: 'Item 1',
  type: 'checkbox',
  checked: true
}
```

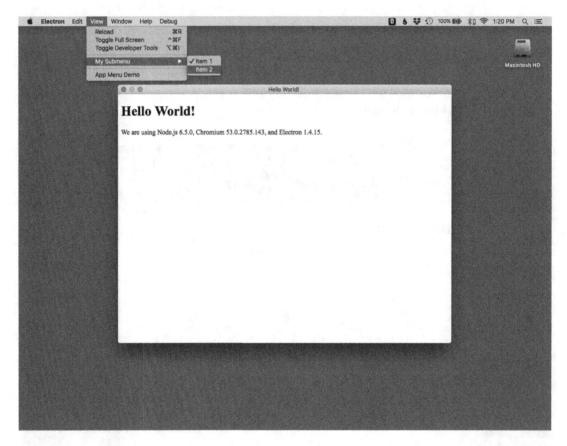

Figure 5-5. *The menuitem with a checkmark*

The toggling of the checkbox will be managed completely by your application.

If your menu item is a part of collection of options, where one item must always be selected, then you can use the menu item type 'radio'.

```
{
  label: 'Item 1',
  type: 'radio',
  checked: false
},
{
  label: 'Item 2',
  type: 'radio'
,
  checked: true
}
```

Electron will handle the switching of the checkmark between the menu items automatically for you, but you will still need to handle the application logic of that selection yourself.

Completing the macOS's Application Menu

Earlier in this chapter, we added a brief bit of code, to adjust our menus on macOS to render correctly. Now, let's return to that code block and replace it with the completed version (see Figure 5-6).

```
if (process.platform === 'darwin') {
  let name = 'App Name'
  template.unshift({
    label: name,
    submenu: [
      {
        label: `About ${name}`,
        role: 'about',
      },
      { type: 'separator' },
      {
        label: 'Preferences',
        accelerator: 'Command+,',
        click: appPrefs
      },
      { type: 'separator' },
      {
        label: 'Services',
        role: 'services',
        submenu: [],
      },
      { type: 'separator' },
      {
        label: `Hide ${name}`,
        accelerator: 'Command+H',
        role: 'hide',
      }, {
        label: 'Hide Others',
        accelerator: 'Command+Alt+H',
        role: 'hideothers',

      }, {
        label: 'Show All',
        role: 'unhide',
      },
      { type: 'separator' },
      {
        label: `Quit ${name}`,
        accelerator: 'Command+Q',
        click: function () {
              app.quit()
            }
      }]
  })
}
```

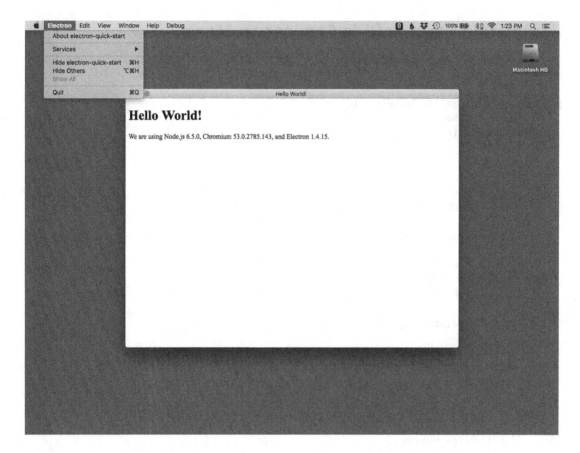

Figure 5-6. *The application menu on macOS*

■ **Note**   The Preferences menu calls a custom function, appPrefs, which is not defined; the rest of the template can rely on the built menu roles. Also, our quit menu item will perform an immediate quit. If your application needs to check if a file needs to be saved, you will need to expand this function to allow for that functionality.

---

macOS's Window Menu Modifications

OSX also has another menu modification that is needed to align with its user interface guidelines. The 'Window' menu has some additional menu items that need to be included, such as 'Bring All to Front'. There is also the ability to close or minimize the current window from this menu as well.

The standard Window menu will look like this:

```
{
  label: 'Window',
  role: 'window',
  submenu: [{
    label: 'Minimize',
    accelerator: 'CmdOrCtrl+M',
    role: 'minimize'
  }, {
    label: 'Close',
    accelerator: 'CmdOrCtrl+W',
    role: 'close'
  }, {
    type: 'separator'
  }, {
    label: 'Reopen Window',
    accelerator: 'CmdOrCtrl+Shift+T',
    enabled: false,
    key: 'reopenMenuItem',
    click: function () {
      app.emit('activate')
    }
  }]
}
```

Add this new menu to our template. Since the menu templates can get very lengthy and have complex nesting, we will assign each menu to its own variable then push it onto the template array. This helps keep the code a bit more manageable.

```
let windowMenu = {
  label: 'Window',
  role: 'window',
  submenu: [{
    label: 'Minimize',
    accelerator: 'CmdOrCtrl+M',
    role: 'minimize'
  }, {
    label: 'Close',
    accelerator: 'CmdOrCtrl+W',
    role: 'close'
  }, {
    type: 'separator'
  }, {
    label: 'Reopen Window',
    accelerator: 'CmdOrCtrl+Shift+T',
    enabled: false,
    key: 'reopenMenuItem',
```

```
    click: function () {
      app.emit('activate')
    }
  }]
}
```

```
template.push(windowMenu)
```

We can then extend this base menu to include a 'Bring All to Front' menu item, and a separator before it. Since the template is just an array of objects, we can just select the correct index, then adjust the submenu. For our sample menu template, our Window menu is at index 2. Remember, we shifted the menus by 1 to accommodate the Application menu on macOS (see Figure 5-7).

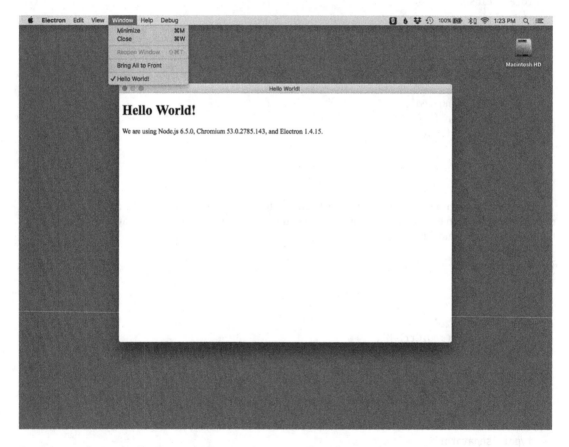

Figure 5-7. *The Bring All to Front menu inserted into the Window Menu*

Then we simply push our two new menu items onto the submenu.

```
if (process.platform === 'darwin') {
  ...

  template[2].submenu.push({
    type: 'separator'
  }, {
      label: 'Bring All to Front',
      role: 'front'
    })
}
```

Here is a complete starter menu system for your Electron application:

```
let template = [{
  label: 'Edit',
  submenu: [{
    label: 'Undo',
    accelerator: 'CmdOrCtrl+Z',
    role: 'undo'
  }, {
    label: 'Redo',
    accelerator: 'Shift+CmdOrCtrl+Z',
    role: 'redo'
  }, {
    type: 'separator'
  }, {
    label: 'Cut',
    accelerator: 'CmdOrCtrl+X',
    role: 'cut'
  }, {
    label: 'Copy',
    accelerator: 'CmdOrCtrl+C',
    role: 'copy'
  }, {
    label: 'Paste',
    accelerator: 'CmdOrCtrl+V',
    role: 'paste'
  }, {
    label: 'Select All',
    accelerator: 'CmdOrCtrl+A',
    role: 'selectall'
  }]
}, {
  label: 'View',
  submenu: [{
    label: 'Reload',
    accelerator: 'CmdOrCtrl+R',
    click: function (item, focusedWindow) {
```

```
      if (focusedWindow) {
        // on reload, start fresh and close any old
        // open secondary windows
        if (focusedWindow.id === 1) {
          BrowserWindow.getAllWindows().forEach(function (win) {
            if (win.id > 1) {
              win.close()
            }
          })
        }
        focusedWindow.reload()
      }
    }
  }, {
    label: 'Toggle Full Screen',
    accelerator: (function () {
      if (process.platform === 'darwin') {
        return 'Ctrl+Command+F'
      } else {
        return 'F11'
      }
    })(),
    click: function (item, focusedWindow) {
      if (focusedWindow) {
        focusedWindow.setFullScreen(!focusedWindow.isFullScreen())
      }
    }
  }, {
    label: 'Toggle Developer Tools',
    accelerator: (function () {
      if (process.platform === 'darwin') {
        return 'Alt+Command+I'
      } else {
        return 'Ctrl+Shift+I'
      }
    })(),
    click: function (item, focusedWindow) {
      if (focusedWindow) {
        focusedWindow.toggleDevTools()
      }
    }
  }]
}, {
  label: 'Window',
  role: 'window',
  submenu: [{
    label: 'Minimize',
    accelerator: 'CmdOrCtrl+M',
    role: 'minimize'
  }, {
```

```
      label: 'Close',
      accelerator: 'CmdOrCtrl+W',
      role: 'close'
    }, {
      type: 'separator'
    }, {
      label: 'Reopen Window',
      accelerator: 'CmdOrCtrl+Shift+T',
      enabled: false,
      key: 'reopenMenuItem',
      click: function () {
        app.emit('activate')
      }
    }]
  }, {
    label: 'Help',
    role: 'help',
    submenu: [{
      label: 'Learn More',
      click: function () {
        electron.shell.openExternal('http://electron.atom.io')
      }
    }]
}]
```

Since we have now included a View menu into our template, we will adjust the index value for the Bring All to Front menuitem by one.

```
template[3].submenu.push({
  type: 'separator'
}, {
    label: 'Bring All to Front',
    role: 'front'
  }
)
```

Contextual Menus

Electron can also create a context, or right-click menu, with the Menu and MenuItem modules as well. Figure 5-8 shows what a contextual menu looks like.

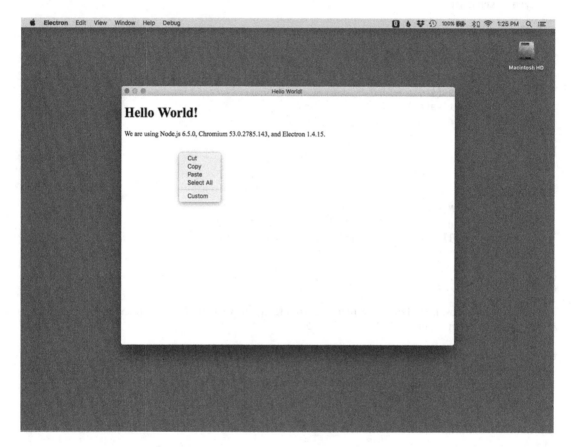

Figure 5-8. *The contextual menu*

Unlike the application menu, where a default one is included, there is no default contextual menu built in. This functionality must be completely written by us. However, since the user action occurs within the window itself, the click event is occurring within the Renderer Process. But, the Menu and MenuItem modules can only be directly used by the Main Process. We can't directly mix using APIs that are allowed in the specific processes. There are two solutions to this problem of using an API in a different process. The first solution is to leverage the Remote module. From the documentation, the remote module provides a simple way to do inter-process communication (IPC) between the renderer process (web page) and the main process.

By importing this module in the renderer.js file, we can in turn access the Menu module within our Render process. Here is a simple contextual menu sample.

```
const { remote } = require('electron')
const { Menu } = remote

const myContextMenu = Menu.buildFromTemplate ([
    { label: 'Cut', role: 'cut' },
```

```
    { label: 'Copy', role: 'copy' },
    { label: 'Paste', role: 'paste' },
    { label: 'Select All', role: 'selectall' },
    { type: 'separator' },
    { label: 'Custom', click() { console.log('Custom Menu') } }
])

window.addEventListener('contextmenu', (event) => {
    event.preventDefault()
    myContextMenu.popup()
} )
```

The other solution is to use the IPC (Inter-Process Communication) module directly. This method might be preferred since interactions with the contextual menu might have an impact on the application's menu. Keeping all the menu-related code in one process might make more organizational sense. Although we will cover the IPC module in detail in a later chapter, let's outline the code to show this solution.

Main Process (in main.js)

```
////
//Contextual Menu Imports
const MenuItem = electron.MenuItem
const ipc = electron.ipcMain


...


//////
//Contextual Menu
//////
const contextMenu = new Menu()
contextMenu.append(new MenuItem({ label: 'Cut', role: 'cut' }))
contextMenu.append(new MenuItem({ label: 'Copy', role: 'copy' }))
contextMenu.append(new MenuItem({ label: 'Paste', role: 'paste' }))
contextMenu.append(new MenuItem({ label: 'Select All', role: 'selectall' }))
contextMenu.append(new MenuItem({ type: 'separator' }))
contextMenu.append(new MenuItem({ label: 'Custom', click() { console.log('Custom Menu') }
}))

ipc.on('show-context-menu', function (event) {
  const win = BrowserWindow.fromWebContents(event.sender)
  contextMenu.popup(win)
})

Renderer Process [in renderer.js]
const { remote, ipcRenderer } = require('electron')
const ipc = ipcRenderer

window.addEventListener('contextmenu', (event) => {
    event.preventDefault()
    ipc.send('show-context-menu')
})
```

In this code sample, we are recreating the same menu from our first contextual menu sample using the direct menu style. Then we create an IPC event listener. This listener will listen for our custom event, 'show-context-menu'. It will then resolve from which window our message came from, then trigger the contextual menu using the popup method.

On the Renderer process, we have the same event listener for the contextmenu event. But instead of directly triggering the menu, we use the IPC send command to broadcast our custom event to the Main process.

Summary

In this chapter, we have explored the various options you have when creating your application's menu system. We covered how to assign key commands, or accelerators, to menu items; how to enable or disable an menuitem; and how to have it trigger either prebuilt actions or custom code.

We also briefly looked at how to have custom context, or right-click, menus with our Electron application, giving it one more layer of a 'native' feel.

CHAPTER 6

■ ■ ■

Understanding the IPC Module

We briefly saw the use of the inter-process communication (IPC) module as one solution for having contextual menus in our application. In this chapter, we are going to explore this module in greater depth. Now, this is not the most glamorous part of API, but it is certainly the workhorse that much of our real-world applications will rely upon.

Getting Started

Since Electron applications are broken into two separate processes (main and render), we need a system to communicate between them. That system is in the IPC module. This module allows you to send and receive synchronous and asynchronous messages between the processes. Each process has a specific module: ipcRenderer and ipcMain (Figure 6-1).

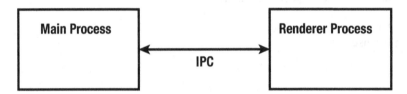

Figure 6-1. *The IPC API provides a communication bridge between the processes.*

Let's clone a fresh copy of Electron.

```
git clone https://github.com/electron/electron-quick-start ipc-example
```

Next, change your active directory to electron-quick-start.

```
cd ipc-example
```

Now, we need to install the dependencies:

```
npm install
```

Finally, reset Git with

```
git init
```

With our fresh copy of Electron, let's begin exploring the various IPC solutions.

© Chris Griffith, Leif Wells 2017
C. Griffith, L. Wells, *Electron: From Beginner to Pro*, https://doi.org/10.1007/978-1-4842-2826-5_6

Synchronous IPC Messaging

Let's begin by defining a few quick styles for our button and response field, the result of this can be seen in Figure 6-2. Open the index.html file and place this style block within our <head> tag:

```
<style>
  p {
    font-family: sans-serif;
    border: 1px solid #ccc;
    border-radius: 4px;
    padding: .5rem;
    background-color: #ddd;
    box-shadow: inset 0 0 2px #aaa;
  }

  button {
    color: rebeccapurple;
    font-family: sans-serif;
    font-weight: bold;
    padding: .5rem;
    background-color: #ccc;
    box-shadow: 2px 2px 2px #ccc;
  }
</style>
```

Next, replace the content within the <body> tag with the following:

```
<button id="sendSyncMsgBtn">Ping Main Process</button>
<p id="syncReply">Awaiting response</p>
```

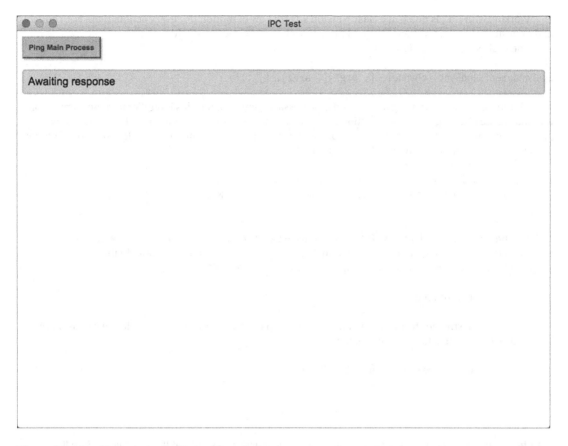

Figure 6-2. *Our Electron application with our button*

Now, let's open the renderer.js to add the code that will be triggered when we click our button, as well as the code needed to accept the response back.

First, we need to import the correct IPC module. Since this code will be executed in the Renderer process, we will use the IPCRenderer module.

```
const ipc = require('electron').ipcRenderer
```

Next, we need to get the reference to our button.

```
const syncMsgBtn = document.getElementById('sendSyncMsgBtn')
```

With our reference, we can attach our event listener to it:

```
syncMsgBtn.addEventListener('click', function () {

})
```

Working with IPC, is much like Isaac Newton's Third Law of motion (for every action, there is an equal and opposite reaction), for every IPC send there must be an IPC receive method.

The basic structure of this call is

```
ipcRenderer.sendSync (channel, [, arg1][, arg2], [,...})
```

The channel value is a string that is used as a message identifier. It is this identifier that the companion method will be listening for. You can optionally send additional values as arguments. These can be any JavaScript primitive (string, number, arrays, objects). In the spirit of communications, let's have our function send the famous words from Alexander Graham Bell:

```
syncMsgBtn.addEventListener('click', function () {
  const reply = ipc.sendSync('synchronous-message', 'Mr. Watson, come here.')
})
```

Whenever, we are working with IPC events, once we write our sending function, we switch to the other process and write the companion stub function. So, let's switch to the main.js file and do this.

The Main process will also need to import the IPC module as well.

```
const ipc = electron.ipcMain
```

Now, we can write our receiver function. The function is straightforward, and we define which channel it should listen on, and a function to execute.

```
ipc.on('synchronous-message', function (event, arg) {

})
```

■ **Note**   Often when coding Electron application, we have multiple files open at the same time. More than once, we have forgotten to save all the files and wonder why our code does not work. You might want to start to learn the key command to perform a Save All to ensure all the files are saved and your code will execute properly.

The callback function has two arguments: the event object and the arguments. While the arguments will contain the data that our sending function passed over, the event object has some special functions. The event object has the built-in ability to respond to the sender. Meaning, there is no need to write another set of listeners and receivers to communicate a response.

For synchronous IPC messages, the method is

```
event.returnValue
```

This value can be a string, a number or an object. For this example, let's just keep it a string.

```
ipc.on('synchronous-message', function (event, arg) {
  event.returnValue = 'I heard you!'
})
```

Switching back to the renderer.js file, we can now add the code to handle this returned value. The value that we sent over from the main process will be stored in the reply.

```
syncMsgBtn.addEventListener('click', function () {
  const reply = ipc.sendSync('synchronous-message', 'Mr. Watson, come here.')
  console.log(reply)
})
```

We will then craft a simple message that we will display. Let's use the new templating feature in ES6 to do this. This is done using the $() syntax, so the message can be written as such:

```
const message = `Synchronous message reply: ${reply}`
```

If you have not used the ${} syntax before, it greatly improves the readability of your concatenated strings. You will also note we are using ` or back ticks instead of ' or ". This is another new habit to try to pick up. The advantage of using ` is you can now have your string extend for more than one line. However, in this case we don't need it.

With our message string constructed, we can update the innerHTML our paragraph:

```
document.getElementById('syncReply').innerHTML = message
```

Here is the complete code:

```
syncMsgBtn.addEventListener('click', function () {
  const reply = ipc.sendSync('synchronous-message', 'Mr. Watson, come here.')
  console.log(reply)
  const message = `Synchronous message reply: ${reply}`
  document.getElementById('syncReply').innerHTML = message
})
```

Save all the files and run the application. Click the button, and our message should appear in the window (Figure 6-3).

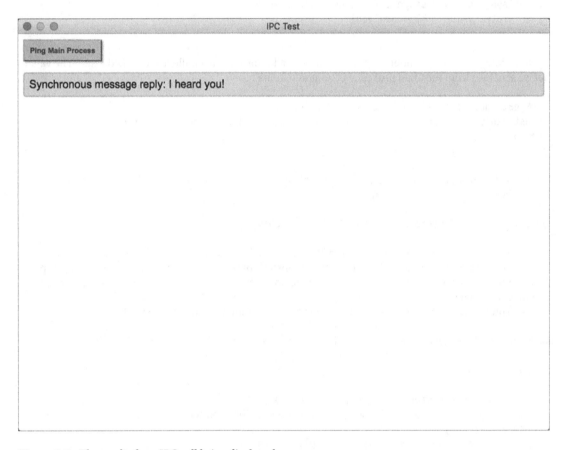

Figure 6-3. *The result of our IPC call being displayed*

This is the basics of using synchronous IPC within Electron. Now, let's explore using IPC messaging in an asynchronous fashion.

Asynchronous IPC Messaging

Often, the event that we trigger by sending our IPC message might take a noticeable amount of time for the method to finish and the response returned to the renderer process. This will leave our renderer process nonfunctioning. Certainly not the best user experience for your application. For these situations, we can use the asynchronous IPC methods instead.

Let's add two more elements to our HTML file, the result of this can be seen in Figure 6-3:

```
<button id="sendAsyncMsgBtn">Ping Main Process Async</button>
<p id="asyncReply">Awaiting async response</p>
```

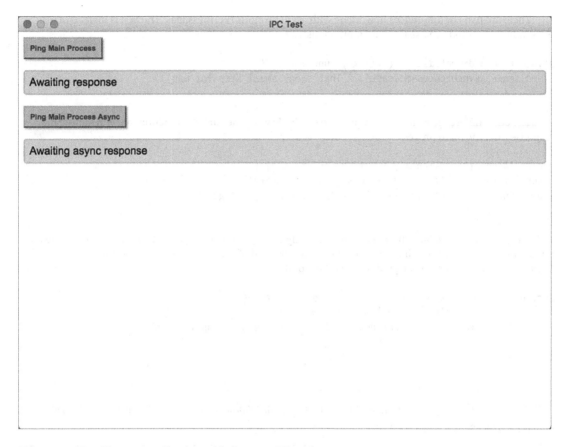

Figure 6-4. Our Electron appli*cation with the async UI ready*

Switching to our renderer.js file, we will get the reference to our new button:

```
const asyncMsgBtn = document.getElementById('sendAsyncMsgBtn')
```

then like before, we will create an event listener for the button click:

```
asyncMsgBtn.addEventListener('click', function () {

})
```

There are two key differences in working with asynchronous IPC messages. The first is instead of using the sendSync method, we use the send method instead.

```
asyncMsgBtn.addEventListener('click', function () {
  ipc.send('asynchronous-message', ''That's one small step for man')
})
```

The other difference is that we now need to explicitly write the callback function that will handle the response from the Main process.

```
ipc.on('asynchronous-reply', function (event, arg) {
  const message = `Asynchronous message reply: ${arg}`
  document.getElementById('asyncReply').innerHTML = message
})
```

The IPC code in the Main process changes slightly as well in the main.js file. The actual listener does remain the same, but the method to respond changes. Instead of calling the returnValue method on the Event object, we now use event.sender.send to respond.

```
ipc.on('asynchronous-message', function (event, arg) {
  if (arg === 'That's one small step for man') {
    event.sender.send('asynchronous-reply', ', one giant leap for mankind.')
  }
})
```

■ **Note** If we are using a different channel name for our asynchronous response, this allows us to have multiple IPC messaging flows occurring.

Go ahead and save the files and run the application. You should be able trigger both styles of IPC messaging (Figure 6-5).

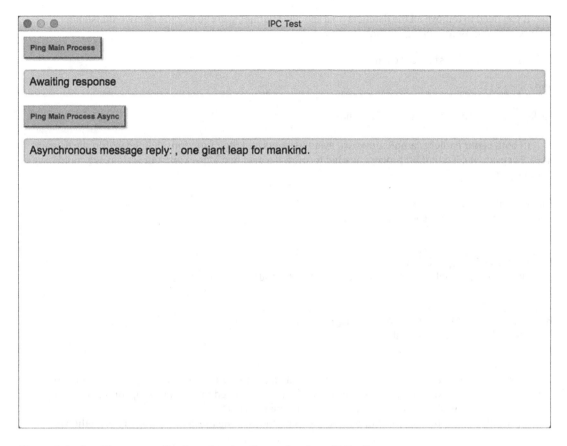

Figure 6-5. Our Electron application, showing the results of our IPC call

Managing Event Listeners

Much like we probably heard as a child about cleaning up after yourself, the same holds true for any event listener or IPC listener we might create within our Electron application. The IPC modules have the same syntax for either the sync or async process. If we want to remove a single listener from the method on the Main process, the syntax is:

```
ipcMain.removeListener( channel name, function)
```

and from the Renderer process:

```
ipcRenderer.removeListener( channel name, function)
```

The function should be the reference to the function that was executed by the on method.

If you need to remove all the listeners on a specific channel, you can use the removeAllListeners method to do so. Here is the basic syntax:

```
ipcMain.removeAllListeners(channel)
```

and

```
ipcRenderer.removeAllListeners(channel)
```

In both of our earlier examples, our two event listeners had their functions defined within the listener itself. For example, if our Main process needed to know if a user had logged into our system, we could have this event shell:

```
function userDidLogin() {
  ipcRenderer.on('userLogin', this.handleLoginSuccess);
}

function userDidLogout() {
  ipcRenderer.removeListener('userLogin', this.handleLoginSuccess);
}

function handleLoginSuccess(event, args) {
  console.log('data', args.data);
}
```

This could be tied to changing a Menu Item based on the user's login status, or some other method. For this example, once we have had the state change, there is no need to keep listening for that event. By removing it, that is one less thing our application must concern itself with.

Electron's IPC module provides one more useful methods along these same lines. That method is:

```
ipc.once(channel, listener)
```

This method is available for both the Main and Renderer process. The method will listen on the specific channel. Once it has received the event, it will execute the listener function, then remove itself from the IPC listeners.

Summary

Although the IPC module does not have a lot of methods – just variations of sending and receiving – it is the backbone for our Electron processes to coexist. You will use this module to possibly start a third-party Node library in the Main process from a user action in the Renderer process. In our next chapter, we will be leveraging them quite a bit to work with Electron's dialog module.

CHAPTER 7

Working with the Dialog Module

The Electron dialog module provides us with the ability to display native system-level dialogs, including file open, file save, and various alerts. If you have written traditional web apps, you will know that these types of dialogs are not all available to you. In this chapter, we will look at the three dialog types and many of the parameters we can control.

The Dialog module is restricted to the Main process, meaning to interact with it we will either need to call its methods from a menu event, via the Inter-Process Communication (IPC) module from the Renderer process, or by using the Remote module (as seen in a previous chapter).

Getting Started

Let's clone a fresh copy of Electron so we have a clean starting point for exploring interacting with the Dialog Module.

```
git clone https://github.com/electron/electron-quick-start dialog-example
```

Next, change your active directory to electron-quick-start.

```
cd dialog-example
```

Now, we need to install the dependencies:

```
npm install
```

Finally, reset Git with

```
git init
```

The File Open Dialog

Unlike using the File API to open and read a file, as we would in a traditional web app, in Electron we will use a combination of the Dialog module and Node's FS module. The basic method to display a File Open dialog is dialog.showOpenDialog.

We will begin by opening the index.html file and replace the content within the <body> tag with

```
<button id="select-directory">Choose a directory</button>
<textarea id="selectedItem"></textarea>
```

This will give us control to trigger our File Open Dialog, and a container to display the results of the interaction. For a touch of style, add this CSS (within the <head> tag) as well:

```
<style>
  button {
    color: rebeccapurple;
    font-family: sans-serif;
    font-weight: bold;
    padding: .5rem;
    background-color: #ccc;
    box-shadow: 2px 2px 2px #ccc;
    display: block;
    margin: 1em;
  }

  textarea {
    width: 90%;
  }
</style>
```

Next, switch to the renderer.js file. Here we need to attach an event listener to the button to communicate to the Main process. Since we are going to be using the IPC module, we need to import it.

```
const ipc = require('electron').ipcRenderer
```

Now, we need the reference to the button

```
const selectDirBtn = document.getElementById('select-directory')
```

Finally, we can define our event listener for this button:

```
selectDirBtn.addEventListener('click', function (event) {
  ipc.send('open-directory-dialog')
})
```

We will use the synchronous IPC call, since the application is basically 'frozen' while the dialog is being displayed.

Turning to the main.js file, we need to write the companion listener for the IPC event we just made. Again, we need to import the IPC module into our code. Additionally, the Dialog module will be needed as well. These should go at the beginning of the code:

```
const ipc = electron.ipcMain
const dialog = electron.dialog
```

With both the IPC module and Dialog module defined, we can write the event listener. The event listener is simply:

```
ipc.on('open-directory-dialog', function (event) {})
```

Within this function, we will make our call to the Dialog module to display the File Open dialog. This method has three optional parameters, but two of them will almost always be used.

The first parameter is a reference to the BrowserWindow object. On macOS, it is common for dialogs to appear as connected sheets to the active window, and not appear detached. We will look at this parameter later in the chapter. For now, we can ignore it from our parameters.

The second parameter that can be passed into method is an object that contains the various dialog settings. We will explore these after we have our first dialog up and running. For this initial sample, we need to set the properties that the Open Dialog can have. Table 7-1 lists the attributes that can be set.

Table 7-1. *The Dialog Module showOpenDialog properties*

Property name	Dialog Action
openFile	Will allow files to be selected.
openDirectory	Will allow directories to be selected.
multiSelections	Will allow multiple items to be selected.
createDirectory	Will add a 'New Folder' button to the dialog (macOS only).
showHiddenFiles	Will display normally hidden system files.
promptToCreate	Will prompt for the creation of a file path if entered by the user (Windows only).

These properties can be combined and passed in as an array, or as a string if only one property is needed.

On Windows and Linux an open dialog cannot be both a file selector and a directory selector, so if you set properties to ['openFile', 'openDirectory'] on these platforms, a directory selector will be shown.

For our code, we will allow selecting a directory. Our options object is simply:

```
{
    properties: ['openDirectory']
}
```

The final parameter is the callback function, assuming you want to do something with the selection. This callback will be passed in either a string or an array of strings, each representing the file path to the selected item(s). For this sample code, we will simply take the result and use the IPC module to send it to the Renderer process. Here is the completed code:

```
ipc.on('open-directory-dialog', function (event) {
  dialog.showOpenDialog({
    properties: ['openDirectory']
  }, function (files) {
    if (files) event.sender.send('selectedItem, files)
  })
})
```

One final thing to add to our demo is to write the event listener for the 'selected-directory' IPC event in the Renderer.

```
ipc.on('selectedItem, function (event, path) {
  document.getElementById('selectedItem').innerHTML = `You selected: ${path}`
})
```

This function will then write out the path to our textarea.

Save the files and run our application using npm start.

Clicking the 'Choose a directory' button, then select a directory on your computer. The path information will then be sent from the Main process to the Renderer process and be displayed in the text area, as shown in Figure 7-1.

Figure 7-1. *The select directory style dialog*

Additional Open Dialog Properties

The showOpenDialog has several other properties that can be set within the options object. The first is the title property.

On Windows, this string will be displayed on the top of the dialog as shown in Figure 7-2.

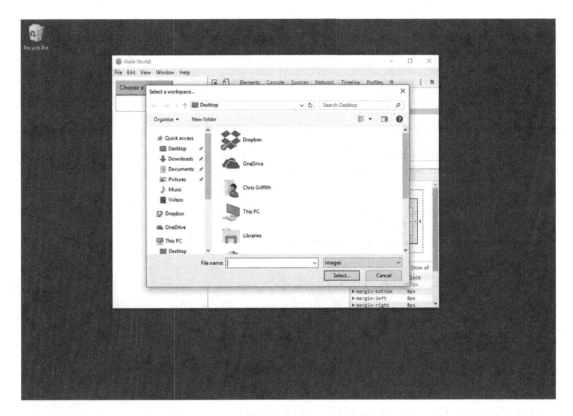

Figure 7-2. *The title property being displayed*

■ **Note**   The `title` property is ignored on macOS.

The next property that can be set allows you to define an initial path that the dialog will open to. This can be very useful to pre-navigate the user to the proper directory. You will need to pass a properly constructed path. If we wanted to have our dialog start at our Documents directory, the call would look like this.

```
dialog.showOpenDialog({
  title: 'Select a workspace...',
  properties: [ 'openFile'],
  defaultPath: '/Users/<username>/Documents/',
}, function (files) {
  if (files) event.sender.send('selectedItem, files)
})
```

Of course you will need to switch the path based on the platform. For example, here we define the user's document directory based on the platform. That's why you should prefer the use of dirname or ./, and use the path module rather than hard-code the default path.

```
let startPath = ''
if (process.platform === 'darwin') {
 let startPath  = '/Users/<username>/Documents/'
}
```

You can also change the label text on the default button by setting the buttonLabel property. This will override the default 'Open' label from the system dialog.

```
dialog.showOpenDialog({
  title: 'Select a workspace...',
  properties: [ 'openFile'],
  defaultPath: '/Users/<username>/Documents/',
  buttonLabel: "Select..."
}, function (files) {
  if (files) event.sender.send('selected-directory', files)
})
```

Selecting a File

Instead of selecting a directory, let's see how to select a specific file from the local file system. In the index. html file, let's add a new button after our Choose a directory button:

```
<button id="select-file">Choose an image file</button>
```

In the renderer.js file, get the reference to this button:

```
const selectFileBtn = document.getElementById('select-file')
and also add the event listener
selectFileBtn.addEventListener('click', function (event) {
  ipc.send('open-file-dialog')
})
```

Now, let's turn to the main.js file and add our initial code:

```
ipc.on('open-file-dialog', function (event) {
  let startPath = ''

  if (process.platform === 'darwin') {
    startPath = '/Users/<username>/Documents/'
  }

  dialog.showOpenDialog({
    title: 'Select a workspace...',
    properties: ['openFile'],
    defaultPath: startPath,
```

```
    buttonLabel: "Select...",
  }, function (files) {
    if (files) event.sender.send('selectedItem', files)
  })
})
```

This should look almost identical to the directory code from earlier. The only change is that the properties array is now set to openFile instead of openDirectory.

The last property you might want to include is to set a file filter. This allows you to control the files that the user can select from within the dialog. This is the array of objects that defines the display label and the allowable file extensions. When defining the extensions, you only need to include the extension and not the dot nor the wildcard element (e.g., '.jpg' and '*.jpg'). So, our code will now look like this:

```
ipc.on('open-file-dialog', function (event) {
  let startPath = '';

  if (process.platform === 'darwin') {
    startPath = '/Users/chrisgriffith/Documents/'
  }

  dialog.showOpenDialog({
    title: 'Select a file...',
    properties: ['openFile'],
    defaultPath: startPath,
    buttonLabel: "Select...",
    filters: [
      { name: 'Images', extensions: ['jpg', 'png', 'gif'] }
    ]
  }, function (files) {
    if (files) event.sender.send('selectedItem', files)
  })
})
```

On Windows, this information will be shown as a drop-down menu that will allow you to switch the filters (Figure 7-3).

Figure 7-3. *The Save as type option being displayed*

On macOS, this control is not shown, but the filter is still applied to the dialog. Please note we've changed the 'openDirectory' property to 'openFile' in this instance.

The BrowserWindow Parameter

We skipped the initial parameter that the showOpenDialog supports since it is optional. On macOS, it is quite common to have the Open dialog attach itself to the actual application window and not have it open in a separate window, as shown in Figure 7-4.

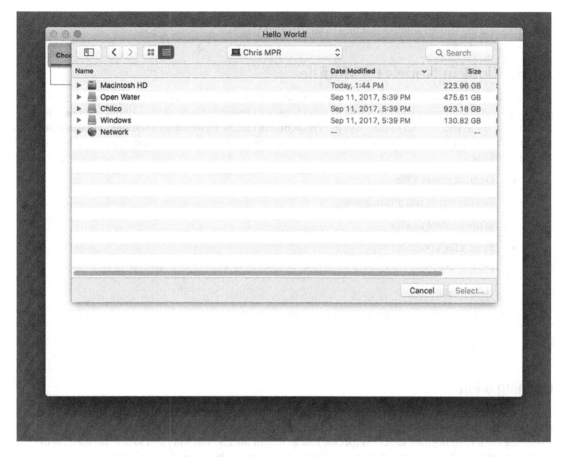

Figure 7-4. *The Open File dialog on macOS attached to the Application Window*

If you choose to not attach the dialog to the application window, note that the file dialog is not automatically centered, and you will need to programmatically position it. To attach a dialog to the application window, simply pass in the reference to the application window into the dialog's show method. Here is the basic code needed to display the dialog to select a file. Once the user has selected a file, the code will emit an IPC event to the renderer process with information on the selected files.

```
dialog.showOpenDialog(mainWindow, {
  title: 'Select a file...',
  properties: ['openFile'],
  defaultPath: '/Users/<username>/Documents/',
  buttonLabel: "Select...",
  filters: [
    { name: 'Images', extensions: ['jpg', 'png', 'gif'] },
    { name: 'Text', extensions: ['txt'] }
  ]
}, function (files) {
  if (files) event.sender.send('selected-directory', files)
})
```

Just remember, if your application is going to support multiple windows, you need to ensure that you are referencing the correct window instance to attach the dialog to.

A Brief Look at Node's FS Module

The reading and writing of files is handled using one of Node's core modules, FS (aka File System). This module provides both synchronous as well as asynchronous versions of each of its methods. As a rule, is it better to use the asynchronous option over the synchronous option. By doing so, we should not block our user interaction, since the code's execution thread will not be blocked. The basic functions available to us are the following:

- Open or create a file
- Get file status and information
- Write content to a file
- Read a file's contents
- Close a file
- Delete a file

To use the fs module, import it using the standard method:

```
const fs = require('fs')
```

Opening a File

For most operations, you will not need to manually open and close the file you are working with. The standard read and write commands will do this automatically for you. However, if you are working with streaming content or needing to access specific blocks within the file, you will need to use this method to properly work with that file. Each of the parameters for the fs module is described in Table 7-2.

```
fs.open(path, flags[, mode], callback)
```

Table 7-2. *The FS Module's open method's parameters*

Parameter	Description
path	This string is the full file path and file name.
flags	Controls the interactions with the file (see Table 7-3).
mode	Optional parameter that defines the permissions.
callback	This function receives two arguments: the error code and the file descriptor.

The FS module's flag's parameter supports several different access settings to the file, and these are listed in Table 7-3.

Table 7-3. *FS Modules' access flag values*

Flag	Description
r	Opens the file for reading.
r+	Opens the file for reading and writing.
rs	Opens the file for reading, synchronous mode.
rs+	Opens the file for reading and writing, synchronous mode.
w	Opens the file for writing. If the file does not exist, it will be created. If the file does exist, it will be overwritten.
wx	Opens the file for writing. If the file does exist, the function will fail.
w+	Opens the file for reading and writing. If the file does not exist, it will be created. If the file does exist, it will be overwritten.
a	Open file for appending. The file is created if it does not exist.
a+	Open file for reading and appending. The file is created if it does not exist.
ax	Opens the file for appending. If the file does exist, the function will fail.
ax+	Open file for reading and appending. If the file does exist, the function will fail.

Getting File Information

If you need to get information about a file, use the `fs.stats` method. This is quite useful in determining if the file is a real file or if it is a directory. Here is a snippet that takes in a file path, then outputs to the console, the file information:

```
fs.stat(filePath, function (err, stats) {
    if (err) {
        return console.error(err)
    }
    console.log(stats)
    console.log("Got file info successfully!")

    // Check file type
    console.log("isFile ? " + stats.isFile())
    console.log("isDirectory ? " + stats.isDirectory())
})
```

gives us:

```
fs.Stats
atime: Mon Mar 13 2017 15:13:31 GMT-0700 (PDT)
birthtime: Mon Mar 13 2017 15:09:16 GMT-0700 (PDT)
blksize: 4096blocks: 8
ctime: Mon Mar 13 2017 15:13:12 GMT-0700 (PDT)
dev: 16777220
gid: 1859252656ino: 30007351
mode: 33188
mtime: Mon Mar 13 2017 15:13:12 GMT-0700 (PDT)
```

```
nlink: 1
rdev: 0
size: 603
uid: 224974590

Got file info successfully!
isFile ? true
isDirectory ? false
```

Writing a File

To write a file to the user's file system, simply use the `fs.writeFile` method. The parameters for this module are shown in Table 7-4.

```
fs.writeFile(file, data[, options], callback)

fs.writeFile(fileName, content, function (err) {
    if(err){
        console.log("An error occurred creating the file "+ err.message)
    } else {
        console.log ("The file has been successfully saved")
    }
})
```

Table 7-4. *The FS Module's parameters*

Parameter	Description
path	This string is the full file path and file name.
flags	Controls the interactions with the file (see Table 7-3).
mode	Optional parameter holds details about encoding, mode, and flag. By default, the values of encoding are utf8, mode is octal value 0666, and flag is 'w'.
callback	This function receives two arguments: the error code and the file descriptor.

Reading Files

To read a file from a user's computer, it can be done in two variations: reading the complete file or partially reading the file. The more common method will be reading the complete file. Here is a code snippet to do this:

```
fs.readFile(filepath, 'utf-8', function (err, data) {
    if(err){
        alert("An error occurred reading the file :" + err.message)
        return
    }
    //Display the file contents
    console.log("The file content is : " + data)
})
```

If you want to read the file in synchronous mode, use fs.readFileSync() instead. If you need to perform a partial read of a file, refer to the documentation for the fs module, available at <nodejs.org/api/fs.html>.

Deleting a File

If you need to delete a file on the user's computer, then you will use the fs.unlink() method. Since these commands are based on the standard POSIX functions (a standard command set for manipulating files and directories), the delete function is referred to as unlink. As a good measure, you should use the fs.existsSync () method to test if the file exists before attempting to delete it.

```
if ( fs.existsSync(filePath) ) {
  fs.unlink(filepath,function(err){
    if(err){
        console.log("An error ocurred updating the file"+ err.message)
        return
    }
    console.log("File succesfully deleted")
 })
}
```

Watching for Updates

Another useful method available in the fs module is the fs.watch() method.

```
fs.watch(fileName, {
  persistent: true
}, function(event, filename) {
  console.log(event + " event occurred on " + filename)
})
```

Working Directories

In all the previous examples, we were working with just files. The fs module also supports working with directories as well. To create a new directory, use the fs.mkdir() method.

```
fs.mkdir(myDir, function(err){
    if (err) {
        console.log('mkdir err:'+err)
    }

    console.log('New Directory Created')
})
```

Reading the Directory Contents

Often, reading the entire contents of a directory is needed. To perform this action, use the fs.readdir() or fs.readdirSync() methods. The result of calling either method will be an array for files and directories contained within the parent directory. If we read the electron-quick-start directory using this code:

```
fs.readdir('./', function(err, files){
    if (err) {
        console.log('readdir err:'+err)
        return
    }
    console.log(files)
})
```

we will get the following array back:

```
[".git", ".gitignore", "LICENSE.md", "README.md", "index.html", "main.js", "node_modules",
"package.json", "renderer.js"]
```

Deleting a Directory

When you need to remove a directory from the user's computer, the fs.rmdir() or fs.rmdirSync() methods can be used. Simply pass in the path to the directory to the methods. It will not prompt the user about the action.

```
fs.rmdir(myDir, function(err){
    if (err) {
        console.log('rmdir err:'+err)
        return
    }
    console.log('deleted the directory')
})
```

For more about this module, refer to the Node documentation as there are many other methods you should be aware of.

The File Save Dialog

The showSaveDialog method is like the openFileDialog, just with fewer parameters. Let's add a new button to our index.html:

```
<button id="save-file">Save</button>
```

and in the render.js file add this code:

```
const saveFileBtn = document.getElementById('saveFile')

saveFileBtn.addEventListener('click', function (event) {
  ipc.send('save-file-dialog')
})
```

Finally, in the main.js, we will add our IPC listener:

```
ipc.on('save-file-dialog', function (event) {})
```

Let's explore the parameters we can set in the showSaveDialog. Just like its companion, the first parameter is the reference to the application window. This parameter is optional; if it is included then the dialog will appear as an attached sheet (Figure 7-5).

Figure 7-5. *The dialog with the sheet option enabled*

The Save Dialog has four options that can be set: title, defaultPath, buttonLabel, and filters. These parameters should be familiar from the File Open dialog.

```
ipc.on('save-file-dialog', function (event) {
  let startPath = '';

  if (process.platform === 'darwin') {
    startPath = '/Users/<username>/Documents/'
  }
```

117

```
dialog.showSaveDialog({
    title: 'Save file...',
     defaultPath: '/Users/<username>/Documents/highscores.txt',
      buttonLabel: "Save",
      filters: [
      { name: 'Text', extensions: ['txt'] }
    ]
  }, function (file) {
    console.log(file)

  })
})
```

There are a few minor differences to be aware of. The first difference is the defaultPath string. If you simply pass in just a path, the dialog will default to use 'Untitled' as the filename. If you want to send this dialog with a suggested filename, include it as part of the defaultPath.

The second difference is that the file will inherit the extension from the last time in the FileFilter array (if one is set). So, if you do not set the default name, you might want to take care to set the preferred extension via the filters. Note, if the Hide Extension option is enabled, the filename will not show the extension, regardless of the FileFilter setting.

The result of this method will be the full file path that the user selected.

```
/Users/<username>/Documents/highscores.txt
```

The actual writing of the file would be done via the Node FS module]. For this simple example, we will save a small text string as our high score data. Here is the complete File Save dialog

```
ipc.on('save-file-dialog', function (event) {
  let startPath = "";

  if (process.platform === 'darwin') {
    startPath = '/Users/<username>/Documents/'
  }

  dialog.showSaveDialog({
    title: 'Save file...',
    defaultPath: startPath +'highscores.txt',
    buttonLabel: "Save",
    filters: [
      { name: 'Text', extensions: ['txt'] }
    ]
  }, function (file) {
    console.log(file);
    if (file) {
      let theData = "Chris,10000"
      FS.writeFile(file, theData, function (err) {
        if (err === null) {
          console.log('It\'s saved!');
```

```
      } else {
        //ERROR OCCURRED
        console.log(err);
      }
    });
  }
 })
})
```

The Message Dialog

In addition to the tandem File Open and File Save methods, the Dialog API also supports displaying a Message Dialog (Figure 7-6). These dialogs are often referred to as Alert Dialogs.

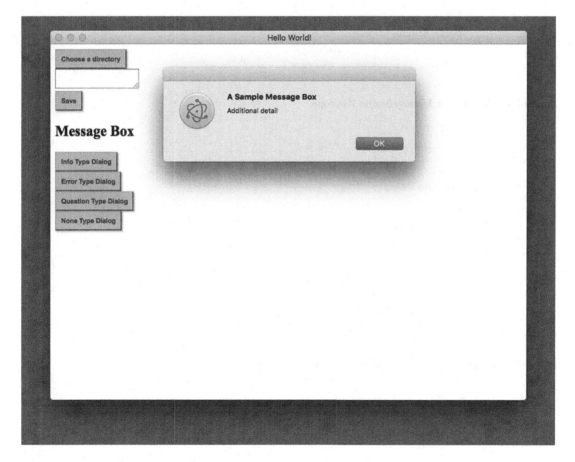

Figure 7-6. *A sample Message Dialog*

The showMessageBox method also follows the same general parameter sequence: browserWindow, options, and the callback function. There are four variations of the MessageBox; info, error, question, and none. These are defined by setting the type property in the options object. On macOS, there is no difference in display of these MessageBox types, but on Windows, the icon will change to reflect the type (see Figures 7-7 through 7-10).

Figure 7-7. *The Info type MessageBox on Windows*

Figure 7-8. *The error type MessageBox on Windows*

Figure 7-9. *The Warning type MessageBox on Windows*

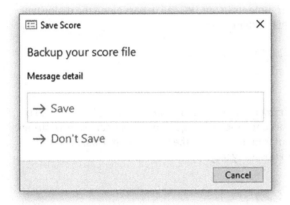

Figure 7-10. *The none type MessageBox on Windows*

Let's extend our Electron Dialog sample to support displaying these types. In our index.html, we will add four buttons, one for each type:

```
<h2>Message Box</h2>
<button id="info">Info Type Dialog</button>
<button id="error">Error Type Dialog</button>
<button id="question">Question Type Dialog</button>
<button id="none">None Type Dialog</button>
```

In our renderer.js file, we will get the references to each of the buttons:

```
const infoDialogBtn = document.getElementById('info')
const errorDialogBtn = document.getElementById('error')
const questionDialogBtn = document.getElementById('question')
const noneDialogBtn = document.getElementById('none')
```

then create the click EventListeners for each button:

```
infoDialogBtn.addEventListener('click', function (event) {
  ipc.send('display-dialog', 'info')
})

errorDialogBtn.addEventListener('click', function (event) {
  ipc.send('display-dialog', 'error')
})

questionDialogBtn.addEventListener('click', function (event) {
  ipc.send('display-dialog', 'question')
})

noneDialogBtn.addEventListener('click', function (event) {
  ipc.send('display-dialog', 'none')
})
```

We will use the fact that we can send additional arguments in our IPC call to pass along the dialog type we want to display. In the main.js file we can create this starter listener.

```
ipc.on('display-dialog', function (event, dialogType) {
  console.log(dialogType)
})
```

Let's expand out the properties in the options parameter for our dialog. The first property to set will be defining the custom button labels. This property will accept either a string for the label or an array of strings for labels. On macOS, the order of the button is laid out from the right to the left. On Windows, the buttons are laid out vertically. So, setting our dialog buttons to this array to:

```
dialog.showMessageBox({
        buttons: ['Save', 'Cancel', 'Don\'t Save']
})
```

This will cause our dialogs to look like this (without the title or description, as they haven't been added yet) in Figure 7-11.

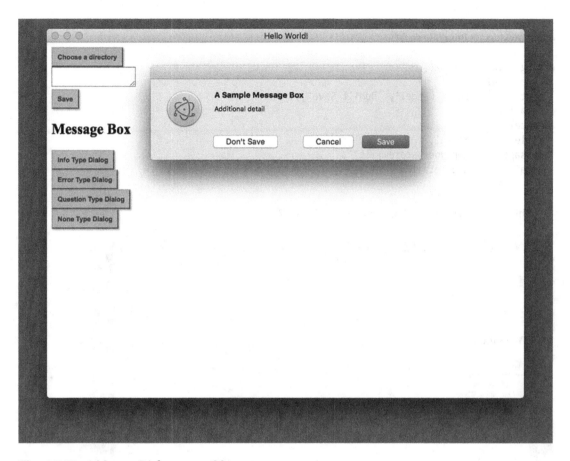

Figure 7-11. *A Message Dialog on macOS*

Another thing to note, on Windows: if this array contains the string 'Cancel' or 'No', then it will automatically be positioned along the bottom of the dialog.

The next property you can set is the defaultId. This integer will tell the dialog which item in the button array to set as the default button. Since we want the Save button to be the default action, we can set this value to 0, although, without this parameter, the default value would also be 0.

```
defaultId: 0
```

The canceled property is only used on the Windows platform, and only if the buttons array does not contain either 'Cancel' or 'No'. Since Windows message dialogs also contain a close button in the upper right, this is the index value we can assign to the element. If your buttons array does contain either string, that button will return the same value as the displayed Cancel or No button.

With our buttons defined, we can turn our attention to the text in the dialog. The dialog method has three separate text elements: title, message, and detail.

The title property is only used on Windows, and it is displayed along the top of the dialog box.

The next display property is the message string. This is text that is displayed in a larger font and bold on the preceding Mac OSX example.

The final text display property is the detail string. This is what is shown in the body of the dialog. Here is our showMessageBox code so far:

```
dialog.showMessageBox({
  type: dialogType,
  buttons: ['Save', 'Cancel', 'Don\'t Save'],
  defaultId: 0,
  cancelId: 1,
  title: 'Save Score',
  message: 'Backup your score file?',
  detail: 'Message detail'
})
```

This code will create a dialog that looks like Figure 7-12.

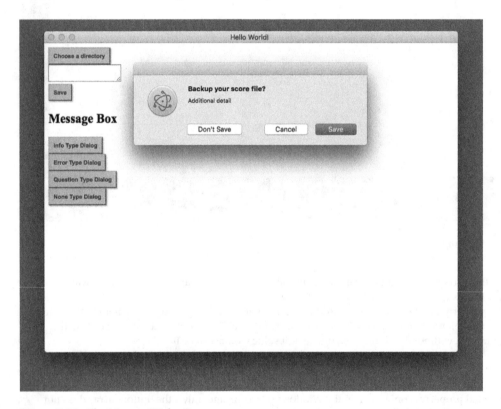

Figure 7-12. *The Message Dialog Box*

Custom Icons

On Mac, the icon that is displayed with each dialog type is the application icon. If you want to have a custom icon, say a warning icon with your app icon overlaid over it, see what is shown in Figure 7-13.

Figure 7-13. *A sample custom icon*

First, we need to import the nativeImage module from Electron in our main.js file.

```
const nativeImage = electron.nativeImage
```

This module will allow us to work with the icons in a more convenient fashion. Here we will reference the custom icon:

```
let warningIcon= nativeImage.createFromPath('images/warning.png') [Please suggest using the
path module here]
```

Then in the dialog options, we can set the icon property to this value:

```
ipc.on('display-dialog', function (event, dialogType) {
dialog.showMessageBox({
    type: dialogType,
    buttons: ['Save', 'Cancel', 'Don\'t Save'],
    defaultId: 0,
    cancelId: 1,
    title: 'Save Score',
    message: 'Backup your score file?',
    detail: 'Message detail',
    icon: warningIcon
  }, function (index) {
    console.log(index)
  });
})
```

So, now when we display our dialog, our custom icon is displayed instead of the default icon (Figure 7-14).

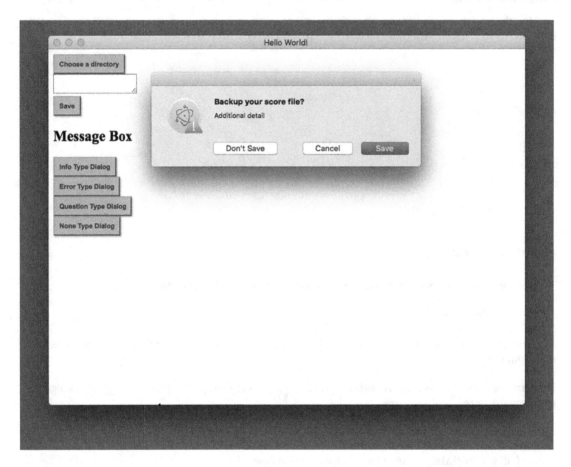

Figure 7-14. *The dialog using our custom icon*

You might consider writing your dialog method to be more generic in nature, switching out icons, labels, and button text as needed via input parameters.

Handling the Response

The callback function will accept the index value of the response from the dialog.

```
ipc.on('display-dialog', function (event, dialogType) {
  console.log(dialogType)
  dialog.showMessageBox({
    type: dialogType,
    buttons: ['Save', 'Cancel', 'Don\'t Save'],
    defaultId: 0,
    cancelId: 1,
    title: 'Save Score',
    message: 'Backup your score file?',
    detail: 'Message detail',
    icon: warningIcon
  }, function (index) {
    console.log(index)
  })
})
```

Depending on how you structure your code, you might handle the response within this function, or send back an ipc message to the Renderer process to handle it.

Error Dialogs

Although the showMessageBox does have an error type, there is an additional method we can call for when the app has yet to emit its ready event. This is the showErrorBox method; see Figure 7-15 for a sample of this. This method takes in two parameters: a title and its content. Custom icons are not supported at this time.

```
dialog.showErrorBox('Frak!', 'Cyclons reported on the port hanger deck!')
```

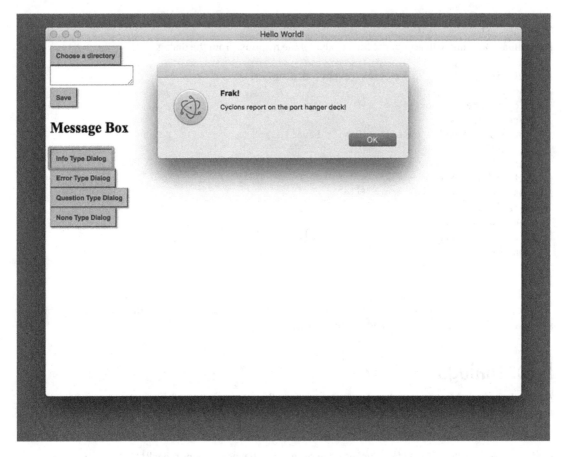

Figure 7-15. *The Error message dialog. It will use the application's icon by default.*

This method does not support custom icons nor changing buttons options (there is a default 'OK' button that will dismiss the box but cannot be customized). Also, note there is no callback function, since there is only the single response that can occur.

Summary

In this chapter, we explore the File Save and File Open dialogs and their display options. We also looked at the Message dialog as well. The variations of this method were examined, so you can display the proper type per the platform's user interface guidelines. Finally, we demonstrated the simple Error dialog method.

CHAPTER 8

WebContents, Screens, and Locales

The development team at GitHub has added many good features to Electron. There are a few features that we would like to make you aware of and experiment with in this chapter.

First, we'll take a look at a property of the BrowserWindow called webContents, which has many events and methods but we'll be focusing on a few items with which we think you should become familiar: capturing events, managing windows, and capturing a window as an image or pdf file. After that, we'll take a look at the screens module and learn how to detect the screens attached to your user's system. Finally, we'll review how to detect the system's locale so you can display the correct language in your application for your users.

Let's get started by setting up the Electron Quick Start project so we have a clean place to start.

Getting Started

As with each of these examples, we are using the Electron Quick Start example. We will use git clone to create a new copy of the quick start in a new folder, in this case named `webcontents-screens-locale-example`. First, open terminal and navigate to the folder where you would like to place your code.

```
git clone https://github.com/electron/electron-quick-start webcontents-screens-locale-example
```

Next, change your active directory to electron-quick-start.

```
cd webcontents-screen-locals-example
```

Now, we need to install the dependencies:

```
npm install
```

Finally, reset Git with

```
git init
```

Now that you have our example project installed, type `npm start` into your terminal application just to make sure the application loads and runs as expected.

Let's take a moment to modify this package.json file to match our own by updating some nodes.

1. Change the name node to "webcontents-screens-locale-example."

2. Change the version number to "0.0.1" since we are just starting out.

3. In the description let's use something like "A sample Electron application to demonstrate online detection."

4. Remove the repository node. If you decide to put your results in a repository you can change or re-add this node with the correct address.

5. Keywords can be "Electron," "webcontents," "screens," "locale," "example."

6. "author": Your name goes here.

7. Let's change the "license" node to "MIT."

Now that we have our webcontents-screens-locale-example project created and have made certain that it runs, let's start making some changes to the code.

Discovering Electron's WebContents

If you wanted to build a Web browser with GitHub Electron, you would use the Electron's webContents event emitter. A lot. Mind you, we don't suggest you build a browser with Electron. People have done it, but it sounds like a lot of work. Nevertheless, many of the events and methods inside the webContents object deal with things your application probably won't need except for a few items we'd like to draw to your attention.

The web contents can be accessed directly in the Main Process or as part of a BrowserWindow's instance. How you access the events and methods of webContents will depend upon what you are trying to accomplish. In this chapter, we will try to give you some guidance on how to access these events and methods.

The first thing we should do is take a look at what webContents look like when printed to the console. Open the main.js file in your favorite code editor and start by adding the line for the webContents constant along with the console log statement as it appears below at the top of your code:

```
const electron = require('electron')
// Module to control application life.
const app = electron.app
// Module to create native browser window.
const BrowserWindow = electron.BrowserWindow
const webContents = electron.webContents

const path = require('path')
const url = require('url')

console.log('webContents', webContents.getAllWebContents())
```

All we are doing here is creating a constant that gives us access to Electron's webContents object and then logging the contents of webContents object to the console using webContent's getAllWebContents() method. Save the file, and in your terminal application run the npm start command and take a look at the output (Figure 8-1).

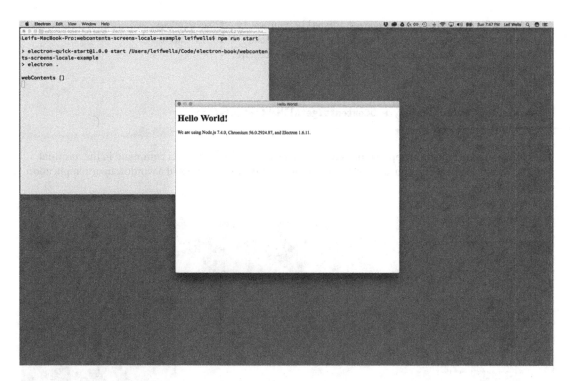

Figure 8-1. *Message in the console reveals webContents at startup is an empty array*

Well, that wasn't in any way exciting. The only output we are seeing is webContents []. Of course, we have done this on purpose so that we can show you that this early in the application startup process, webContents is an empty array. In other words, we won't see anything inside this array until we add a BrowserWindow object to the screen. Let's do that now.

At the bottom of the createWindow function, add the console log seen at here at the bottom of the createWindow method to your code.

```
function createWindow () {
  // Create the browser window.
  mainWindow = new BrowserWindow({width: 800, height: 600})

  // and load the index.html of the app.
  mainWindow.loadURL(url.format({
    pathname: path.join(__dirname, 'index.html'),
    protocol: 'file:',
    slashes: true
  }))

  // Open the DevTools.
  // mainWindow.webContents.openDevTools()

  // Emitted when the window is closed.
  mainWindow.on('closed', function () {
```

```
    // Dereference the window object, usually you would store windows
    // in an array if your app supports multi windows, this is the time
    // when you should delete the corresponding element.
    mainWindow = null
})

  console.log('webContents', webContents.getAllWebContents());
}
```

Quit the sample Electron application, save your file, and run the npm start command in the terminal again so we can look at what appears inside webContents after we have created a window in our application (Figure 8-2).

Figure 8-2. *New console log shows the webContents array after a window is created*

That is more like it, right? That is a lot of data! We'll print it out here so we can review what is there.

```
webContents []
webContents [ WebContents {
    webContents: [Circular],
    history: [],
    currentIndex: -1,
    pendingIndex: -1,
    inPageIndex: -1,
    _events:
    { 'navigation-entry-commited': [Function],
      'ipc-message': [Function],
      'ipc-message-sync': [Function],
      'pepper-context-menu': [Function],
      'devtools-reload-page': [Function],
      'will-navigate': [Function],
      'did-navigate': [Function],
      destroyed: [Object],
      'devtools-opened': [Function],
      '-new-window': [Function],
      '-web-contents-created': [Function],
      '-add-new-contents': [Function],
      move: [Function],
      activate: [Function],
      'page-title-updated': [Function] },
    _eventsCount: 15,
    _maxListeners: 0,
    browserWindowOptions: { width: 800, height: 600 } } ]
```

Of course, the first line is our first console log call that returns an empty array. The second line is where things get interesting. Inside the array is a WebContents object that is represented here in a naked kind of way. You can see that there is a history array that would hold objects representing the pages loaded by this window. The currentIndex, pendingIndex and inPageIndex are how the WebContents tracks the history. The next set of lines is an object that contains references to internal events that WebContents uses. Finally, at the bottom is the browserWindowOptions object that shows the options that were specified when our window was created. Let's test this out.

Inside our createWindow method, update the code with the following line in bold.

```
function createWindow () {
  // Create the browser window.
  mainWindow = new BrowserWindow({width: 800, height: 600, title: 'hello world'})
```

Now we can run the npm start command and see the title of our window in the console log output (Figure 8-3).

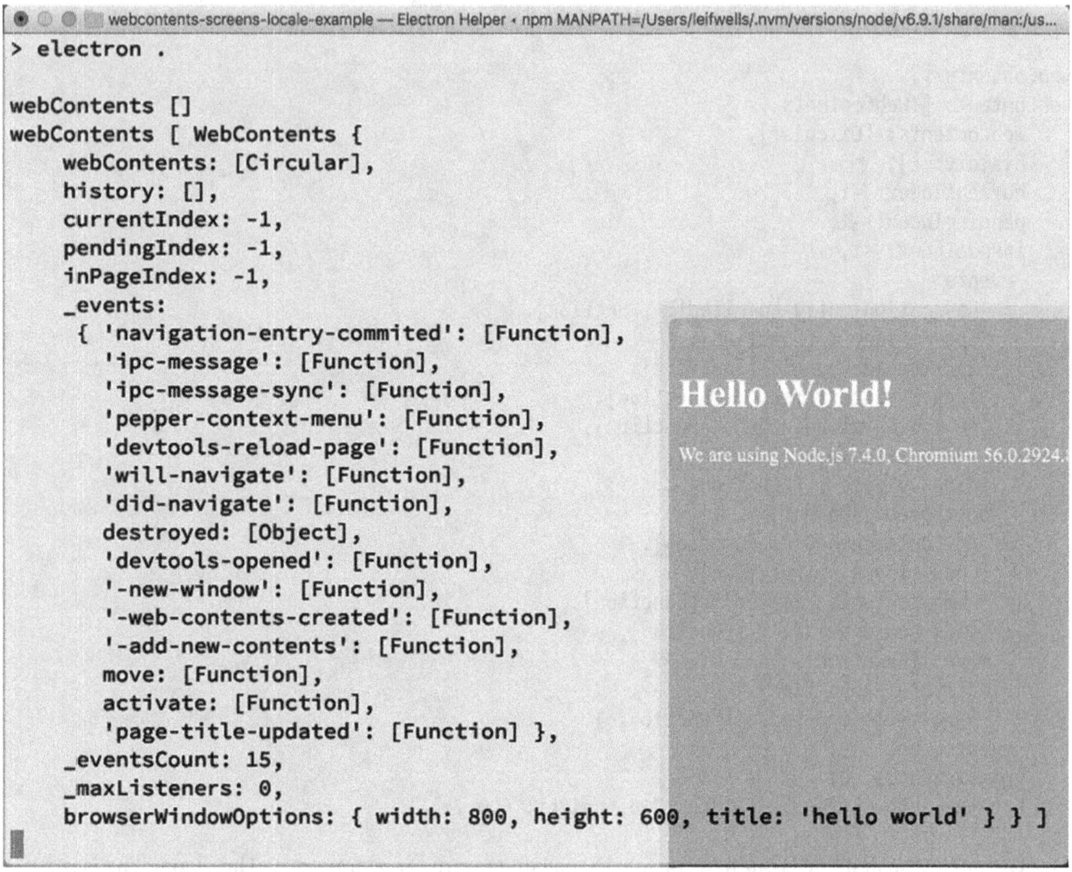

```
  ● ○ ●  ▓▓ webcontents-screens-locale-example — Electron Helper ‹ npm MANPATH=/Users/leifwells/.nvm/versions/node/v6.9.1/share/man:/us...
> electron .

webContents []
webContents [ WebContents {
    webContents: [Circular],
    history: [],
    currentIndex: -1,
    pendingIndex: -1,
    inPageIndex: -1,
    _events:
    { 'navigation-entry-commited': [Function],
      'ipc-message': [Function],
      'ipc-message-sync': [Function],                Hello World!
      'pepper-context-menu': [Function],
      'devtools-reload-page': [Function],          We are using Node.js 7.4.0, Chromium 56.0.2924.
      'will-navigate': [Function],
      'did-navigate': [Function],
      destroyed: [Object],
      'devtools-opened': [Function],
      '-new-window': [Function],
      '-web-contents-created': [Function],
      '-add-new-contents': [Function],
      move: [Function],
      activate: [Function],
      'page-title-updated': [Function] },
    _eventsCount: 15,
    _maxListeners: 0,
    browserWindowOptions: { width: 800, height: 600, title: 'hello world' } } ]
```

Figure 8-3. *The console output for the webContents array*

See how that works? In case you can't read it, the interesting part looks like this:

```
browserWindowOptions: { width: 800, height: 600, title: 'hello world' }
```

A Little Setup Before We Begin

To make this example more effective for the content we are presenting, we need to make some updates to our current code. This example is going to create two windows, and we could also create two separate methods. But let's be practical and update our current createWindow method to be a little more dynamic. Let's change createWindow to look like this:

```
function createWindow (fileStr, options) {
  // Create the browser window.
  let win= new BrowserWindow(options)

  // and load the index.html of the app.
  win.loadURL(url.format({
    pathname: path.join(__dirname, fileStr),
```

```
    protocol: 'file:',
    slashes: true
  }))

  // Open the DevTools.
  // win.webContents.openDevTools()

  // Emitted when the window is closed.
  win.on('closed', function () {
    // Dereference the window object, usually you would store windows
    // in an array if your app supports multi windows, this is the time
    // when you should delete the corresponding element.
    win = null
  })

  return win
}
```

Note the items in bold. Our createWindow method now takes two arguments: fileStr which is expected to be the name of the file our window will load, and options that is expected to be an object containing the setting for the window. Next, we create a variable named "win" for our new window, instantiate that window passing the options argument, load the URL for that window using the fileStr argument, and finally return the window.

Now to make this work, we need to make a change inside our "ready" event listener. Make the following change:

```
app.on('ready', () => {
  mainWindow = createWindow('index.html', { width: 800, height: 600, title: 'MAIN' })
})
```

Here, we are setting our mainWindow variable by passing arguments to the createWindow method. Nice. Now, there is one more thing to do to make this work. Open your index.html file and remove the text from inside the title tag in the header. The code should look like this:

```
<head>
    <meta charset="UTF-8">
    <title></title>
</head>
```

The reason we are clearing the title in the HTML header here is that currently, on the macOS, if there is a title in the header it does not get overwritten in the Electron window creation process. This does not occur on the Windows platform.

Let's run the npm start command in the terminal to make sure it works (Figure 8-4).

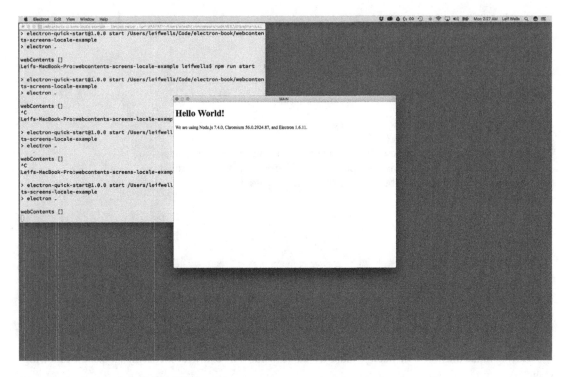

Figure 8-4. *Our updated Main Window*

Note that the title in the title bar is now "MAIN." Nice, right. A window created in a more dynamic way. One more change and we'll be ready to move on. First, at the top of our file, update the following line so we have a new variable named secondWindow.

```
let mainWindow, secondWindow
```

Now, let's update our "ready" listener to create another window:

```
app.on('ready', () => {
  mainWindow = createWindow('index.html', { width: 800, height: 600, title: 'MAIN' })
  secondWindow = createWindow('index.html', { width: 400, height: 400, title: 'SECOND' })
})
```

If we've done everything properly, we should see two windows. Let's check it out by running the npm start command (Figure 8-5).

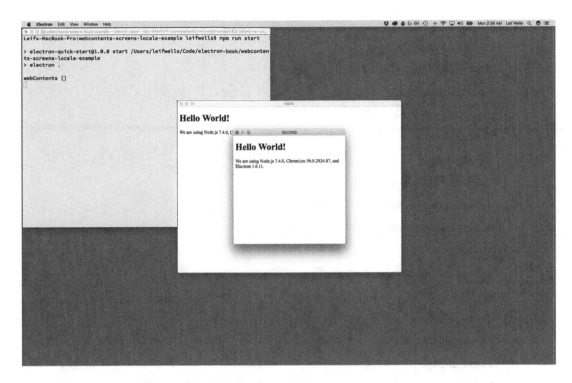

Figure 8-5. *Our main and second windows load*

That does it. Now we're ready to move on to adding a few event listeners to our project.

WebContents Events

So, now that you have a little idea of what the WebContents object represents and can set up the project to load two windows, let's start leveraging webContents to get a little more information. The BrowserWindow's WebContents object emits a couple of events that you might need to use in your application. To give you an idea of what those events are, here's an alphabetical list of them:

- "before-input-event"
- "certificate-error"
- "context-menu"
- "crashed"
- "cursor-changed"
- "destroyed"

- "devtools-closed"

- "devtools-focused"

- "devtools-opened"

- "devtools-reload-page"

- "did-change-theme-color"

- "did-fail-load"

- "did-finish-load"

- "did-frame-finish-load"

- "did-get-response-details"

- "did-get-redirect-request"

- "did-navigate"

- "did-navigate-in-page"

- "did-start-loading"

- "did-stop-loading"

- "dom-ready"

- "found-in-page"

- "login"

- "media-started-playing"

- "media-paused"

- "new-window"

- "page-favicon-updated"

- "paint"

- "plugin-crashed"

- "select-client-certificate"

- "select-bluetooth-device"

- "update-target-url"

- "will-attach-webview"

- "will-navigate"

- "will-prevent-unload"

Depending on what the application you are building does, not all of these events will be relevant to you. They are named very practically, so you can guess what they represent. We listed each of them here to give you an idea of how many events webContents emits, and if any of them peak an interest you should review the documentation to get a clear idea of what they do. Our assumption is that you will be creating an application that, for the most part, is self-contained and doesn't load a web application from the Internet. Under that assumption we are going to focus on a couple of events that you may find helpful: "did-start-loading," "did-get-response-details," "dom-ready," "did-finish-load," and "did-stop-loading."

If you wish to explore any of the other events available, feel free to use the resulting code from this exercise as a starting point for your investigations.

The "did-start-loading" Event

The first event we will look at is the "did-start-loading" event. This event is fired by the window's WebContent's object and happens, oddly enough, when the window begins loading. For various reasons, we may wish to capture this event on the Main Process in our application, perhaps to inform the user of this activity, or to trigger another activity. Let's create a listener inside our createWindow method to see how this works. Inside the main.js file, at the bottom of the createWindow method and before the return window line, add this event handler:

```
win.webContents.on('did-start-loading', event => {
    console.log('did-start-loading', event.sender.webContents.browserWindowOptions.title)
})
```

This is a pretty simple event listener typically used in debugging. Since we know that the event.sender is a BrowserWindow object and has a webContents property, we can log the browserWindowOptions' title property in the console. Run the npm start command to see this working (Figure 8-6).

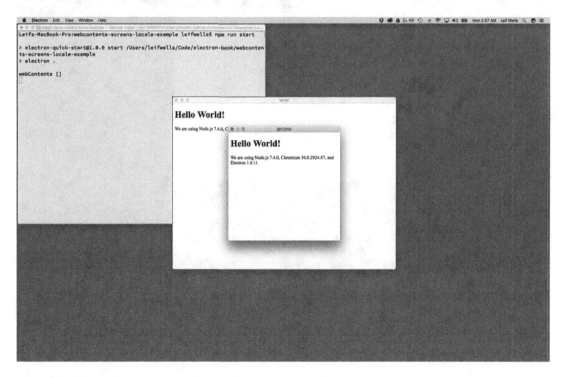

Figure 8-6. *The message we sent to the console was not received*

Hold on. That didn't work. What did we do wrong? It is good practice to place event listeners on any object before the event is fired. In this case, since the "did-start-loading" event is fired when window. loadURL() is called, we need to attach that event before that line. Move that line up in our code to appear immediately below the creation of the win variable:

```
function createWindow (fileStr, options) {
  // Create the browser window.
  let win = new BrowserWindow(options)

  win.webContents.on('did-start-loading', event => {
    console.log('did-start-loading', event.sender.webContents.browserWindowOptions.title)
  })
```

Now we can run the npm start command to see if the event is properly captured (Figure 8-7).

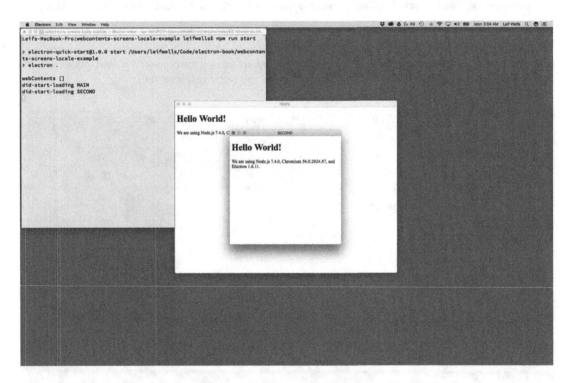

Figure 8-7. *Now the console messages appear in the terminal window*

Now we can see the console log along with the title we sent to the createWindow method. Awesome. Now we can add a couple of more events that may be important to capture in your application: "dom-ready," "did-finish-load," and "did-stop-loading." In the main.js file, just below the "did-start-loading" event listener, add listeners for "dom-ready," "did-finish-load," and "did-stop-loading" like below:

```
function createWindow (fileStr, options) {
  // Create the browser window.
  let window = new BrowserWindow(options)

  window.webContents.on('did-start-loading', event => {
    console.log('did-start-loading', event.sender.webContents.browserWindowOptions.title)
  })

  window.webContents.on('dom-ready', event => {
    console.log('dom-ready')
  })

  window.webContents.on('did-finish-load', event => {
    console.log('did-finish-load', event.sender.webContents.getTitle())
  })

  window.webContents.on('did-stop-loading', event => {
    console.log('did-stop-loading', event.sender.webContents.id)
  })

  // and load the index.html of the app.
  window.loadURL(url.format({
    pathname: path.join(__dirname, fileStr),
    protocol: 'file:',
    slashes: true
  }))

  // Emitted when the window is closed.
  window.on('closed', function () {
    // Dereference the window object, usually you would store windows
    // in an array if your app supports multi windows, this is the time
    // when you should delete the corresponding element.
    window = null
  })

  return window
}
```

We have included these events on purpose and each has a specific purpose. Notice how we have different console log calls in each listener. The listener of "dom-ready" is just logging the event name, while "did-finish-load" logs the sender's WebContent's title, and the "did-stop-loading" logs the sender's WebContent's id.

As a side note, try to remember the difference between these event names: "load" and "loading" in "did-finish-load" and "did-stop-loading." If you decide to use both events and one of them isn't being captured, you may have incorrectly used "did-finish-loading," for instance, instead of "did-finish-load." These two event names might catch you off guard.

Run the npm start command in the terminal and see what happens (Figure 8-8).

Figure 8-8. *Messages from the event listeners appear in the terminal window*

Interesting, right? Here's a printout of the console logs so we can review them.

```
did-start-loading MAIN
did-start-loading SECOND
dom-ready
dom-ready
did-finish-load index.html
did-stop-loading 1
did-finish-load index.html
did-stop-loading 2
```

Note first that there are two of each message logged. The first two messages help you understand why, of course, and that is because we are opening two windows. Now, let's take a moment to consider our new event listeners' console logs.

Were you expecting "dom-ready" to show up last? Or "did-finish-load"? As Web developers we are typically conditioned to keep an eye on the "dom-ready" event, but both "did-finish-load" and "did-stop-loading" occur after the "dom-ready" event is fired. And if the application that your BrowserWindow object is loading is complex - like an Angular or React application instead of the simple index.html file we are currently loading - there may be things that application may also be waiting for the "dom-ready" event to fire, as well. If your Main Process is waiting for the window to be ready before attempting to interact with it, you may wish to rely upon the "did-stop-loading" event.

Why isn't the "did-finish-load" event logging "MAIN" or "SECOND" instead of "index.html"? We were wondering that as well. In our investigations, it seemed that relying upon the getTitle method would be poor form since it is not showing the information we requested. At least we can see the ids appear to be correct in the "did-stop-loading."

Let's try something else in the "did-finish-load" listener and see if we can't do better. Change the following code in bold in the main.js file:

```
window.webContents.on('did-finish-load', event => {
  console.log('did-finish-load', BrowserWindow.fromId(event.sender.webContents.id).
getTitle())
})
```

Again, note that if you have not removed the title text inside the header of the HTML, that text may be captured instead of the text that was dynamically set.

What we are doing here is leveraging the BrowserWindow class' fromId method with the event sender's WebContent's id to get the window object so we can call getTitle() on it. I know that sounds like technical gymnastics, but if you want a consistent way to get the window title, this method may be helpful.

Run the npm start command and see it in action (Figure 8-9).

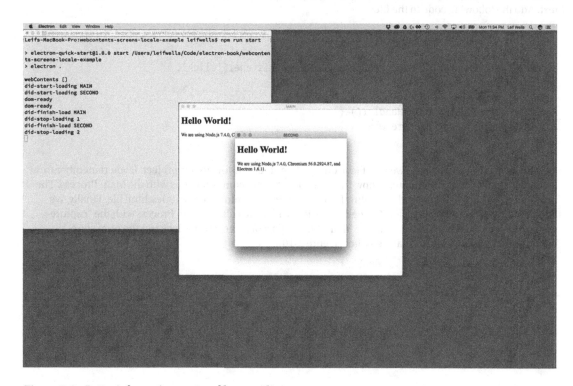

Figure 8-9. *Better information captured by event listeners*

The capturePage Method

The WebContents object has another nice feature that you may wish to take advantage of: the capturePage method. Capturing your application's screen is a feature that developers often are charged with creating. Luckily for us, the developers at Electron have made it easy for us to capture an image of our window, and Electron's Inter-Process Communication makes it easy to communicate between the Main and Renderer Processes, and Node.js makes it easy to save that image. This example will take a moment to set up, but we are certain you will find it rewarding.

Let's begin in the Renderer process. Open your index.html file. Remember, we are using this file as the basis for both our "MAIN" and "SECOND" windows, so changes in this file will appear in both windows. Inside the index.html code, make the following update just above the closing tag of the body element (</body>):

```
<div>
    <button id="captureButton">Capture PNG</button>
</div>
```

Basically, we just added a button to the window. Now, open the renderer.js file, which is where the JavaScript code for the Renderer Process is being kept. Right now there are just a few lines of commented text. Add the following code to the file:

```
const { ipcRenderer } = require('electron')

document.getElementById('captureButton').addEventListener('click',
captureButtonClickHandler)

function captureButtonClickHandler() {
    ipcRenderer.send('capture-window')
}
```

In the first line of our code we add Electron's ipcRenderer module to our project. If you remember from an earlier chapter, the ipcRenderer is how the Renderer Process communicates with the Main Process. The next line is the click listener for the "captureButton" element we added to the index.html file. Finally, we added the captureButtonClickHandler method inside, which we call the Main Process with the "capture-window" event. Before we move on to the Main Process part of this example, let's run the npm start command and take a look at what we've got (Figure 8-10).

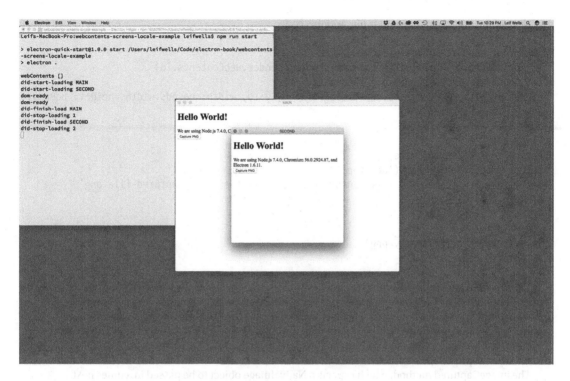

Figure 8-10. *The new button appears in both windows*

Two windows? Check. New button on each window? Check. We've passed inspection! Now open the main.js file and add the following code in bold to the top of the file:

```
const electron = require('electron')
// Module to control application life.
const app = electron.app
// Module to create native browser window.
const BrowserWindow = electron.BrowserWindow
const webContents = electron.webContents
const ipcMain = electron.ipcMain

const path = require('path')
const url = require('url')
const fs = require('fs')

// Keep a global reference of the window object, if you don't, the window will
// be closed automatically when the JavaScript object is garbage collected.
let mainWindow, secondWindow, windowToCapture
```

Here we are adding ipcMain, the Main Process module for Inter-Process Communication, along with "fs," the file system module from Node.js that gives us access to the computer's drive. Finally, we add the windowToCapture variable, which we will be using in a moment. Also, you may wish to delete the console. log() line here, as it is unnecessary.

Next, at the bottom of the main.js file, add this code:

```
ipcMain.on('capture-window', event => {
  windowToCapture = BrowserWindow.fromId(event.sender.webContents.id)
  let bounds = windowToCapture.getBounds()
  windowToCapture.webContents.capturePage({x: 0, y: 0, width: bounds.width, height: bounds.
height}, imageCaptured)
})

function imageCaptured(image) {
  let desktop = app.getPath('desktop')
  let filePath = desktop + '/' + windowToCapture.getTitle() + '-captured-file.png'
  console.log(filePath)
  let png = image.toPNG()

  fs.writeFileSync(filePath, png)
}
```

The first item here is the "capture-window" event listener, which sets the windowToCapture variable, creates a bounds object (an object that contains x, y, width, and height properties) by accessing the BrowserWindow's getBounds method. Finally, the listener calls the BrowserWindow's WebContents' capturePage method, passing 0 for x and y and then the bounds object's width and height. The second argument for the capturePage method is the name of the callback function, imageCaptured, which is invoked when capturePage completes its work.

The imageCaptured method, which expects a NativeImage object to be passed in, comes next. NativeImage is a handy object provided by Electron, which allows developers the ability to create application icons in the PNG and JPEG formats, to handle situations like this. Next, the method creates a variable named desktop, a string that represents the path to the computer's desktop folder, by calling app.getPath('desktop'). Best practice would be to present a dialog that allows the user to choose where to place this file, but we can take a shortcut here to save time. Check out the Dialogs chapter to get more information about Dialogs, and, as always, ask the user where they want files to be saved.

Once we have the desktop path, we combine it with the title of the window and add "-captured-file. png" to it. Please observe that the desktop path does not end in a trailing "/", which is why we've added it between the desktop path and the window title. And, then we call the NativeImage method toPNG(), which converts the image of our window into a variable named png. Now that we have the png and the path to where we'd like to save it, all we need to do is save the png file. This is where the FS module comes in. Using the writeFileSync method and passing the path and the png, we trigger a write function that will either work or throw an error.

As a side note, if you are planning on saving files with your Electron application, make sure you familiarize yourself with the Node.js FS module and the writeFileSync and writeFile methods. We are using writeFileSync here because it suits our purposes, but the writeFile method works asynchronously, which may be more useful for avoiding user interface blocking when saving large files.

Let's save our files and give the npm start command a go and see how it works. When the application loads, click the "capture image" button. An image should be saved to your desktop.

We chose to click on the button in the window named "SECOND," so these are our results (Figure 8-11).

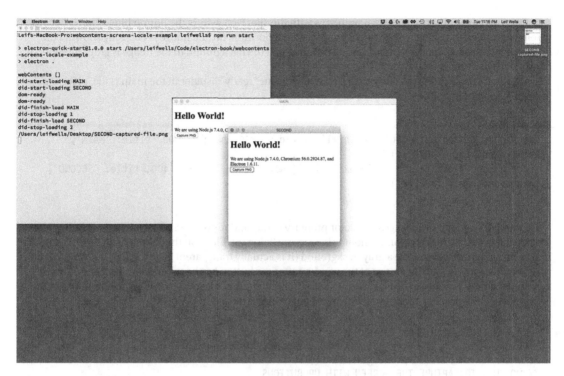

Figure 8-11. *Capturing the window. Note the saved file on the desktop.*

Awesome. Our code saved a file to the desktop and named it correctly. Open up the file so we can take a look at it (Figure 8-12).

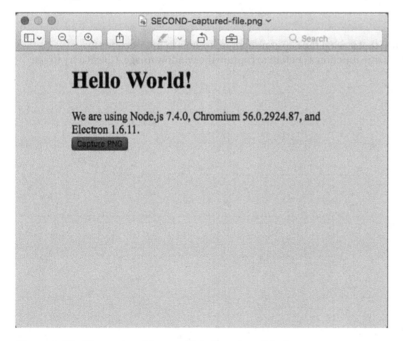

Figure 8-12. *The captured image. Note the color of the button.*

OK. This isn't right. There are two problems with this file. First, why is the button blue? That is because when we grabbed the image, the button was in the down position. So, the image is correctly showing the button, but that isn't what we want today. Also, notice that the background of the image is gray. Shouldn't it be white like it appears on the screen?

We can fix these problems fairly easily. First, inside our "ready" listener in the main.js file, place the following updates in bold:

```
app.on('ready', () => {
  mainWindow = createWindow('index.html', { width: 800, height: 600, title: 'MAIN',
  backgroundColor: '#FFF' })
  secondWindow = createWindow('index.html', { width: 400, height: 400, title: 'SECOND',
  backgroundColor: '#FFF' })
})
```

Here, we've added the background color property to our options object so that when the window is created it has a background color. Without this property being set, Electron thinks it doesn't have a color and makes the image appear to have a gray background (it is actually transparent).

Next, we want to grab the image of the window after the button has been released. There are a few ways to do this. We choose to use JavaScript's setTimeout method to trigger the capturePage method. In the "capture-window" listener, make the following changes in bold:

```
ipcMain.on('capture-window', event => {
  windowToCapture = BrowserWindow.fromId(event.sender.webContents.id)
  let bounds = windowToCapture.getBounds()
  // DO THIS TO CAPTURE THE SCREEN WITH UP BUTTONS
  setTimeout(() => {
  windowToCapture.webContents.capturePage({x: 0, y: 0, width: bounds.width,
  height: bounds.height}, imageCaptured)
  }, 500)
})
```

This code waits half a second (that is what the 500 argument represents in milliseconds for setTimeout()), and then calls the same function as before to capture the window image. Give it a try to see your results (Figure 8-13).

Figure 8-13. *Captured image of the window without the button down state*

Alright! That is more like it! Great job!

The printToPDF Method

Like the capturePage method, the WebContents' printToPDF method can be equally helpful. It is basically the same setup as the capturePage exercise. Let's get started.

Open your index.html file and add the following code in bold to add a second button:

```
<body>
    <h1>Hello World!</h1>
    <!-- All of the Node.js APIs are available in this renderer process. -->
    We are using Node.js <script>document.write(process.versions.node)</script>,
    Chromium <script>document.write(process.versions.chrome)</script>,
    and Electron <script>document.write(process.versions.electron)</script>.
    <div>

        <button id="captureButton">Capture PNG</button>
        <button id="printButton">Print to PDF</button>

    </div>
</body>
```

Then, in the renderer.js, update this line at the top of the file with the code in bold which will add a new variable named windowToPrint.

```
let mainWindow, secondWindow, windowToCapture, windowToPrint
```

Now, add the following code in bold to listen to the click event and broadcast an event over Inter-Process Communication to the Main Process:

```
const { ipcRenderer } = require('electron')

document.getElementById('captureButton').addEventListener('click',
captureButtonClickHandler)
document.getElementById('printButton').addEventListener('click', printButtonClickHandler)

function captureButtonClickHandler() {
    ipcRenderer.send('capture-window')
}

function printButtonClickHandler() {
    ipcRenderer.send('print-to-pdf')
}
```

Now, open the main.js file and add the following code to the bottom of the file:

```
ipcMain.on('print-to-pdf', event => {
  windowToPrint = BrowserWindow.fromId(event.sender.webContents.id)

  windowToPrint.webContents.printToPDF({}, pdfCreated)
})

function pdfCreated(error, data) {
  let desktop = app.getPath('desktop')
  let filePath = desktop + '/' + windowToPrint.getTitle() + '-printed.pdf'

  if(error) {
    console.error(error.message)
  }
  if(data) {
    fs.writeFile(filePath, data, error => {
      if(error) {
        console.error(error.message)
      }
    })
  }
}
```

Just like in the capturePage section of this chapter, we are listening for an event over IPC, and this time it is the "print-to-pdf" event we broadcast from the Renderer Process. We create a BrowserWindow object by leveraging the Event's WebContents object's id property and then call that BrowserWindow object's Webcontents' printToPDF method. The first argument for the printToPDF method is an object that holds any custom options you may like to set, options like margins of the page, the size of the page, and whether the background of the window should be captured. We are sending along an empty object, which means we are accepting the default options for this PDF file. Finally, like before, we use the FS module to write the file to the desktop. Save your files and run the npm start command in the console to see your results, which should look like the following screenshots (Figures 8-14 and 8-15).

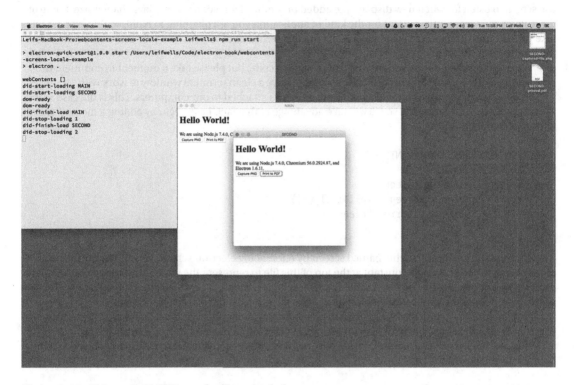

Figure 8-14. *Using printToPDF saved a file to the desktop*

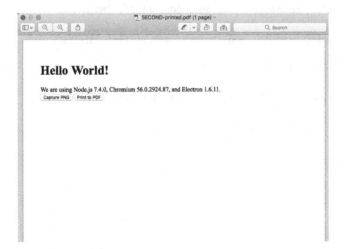

Figure 8-15. *The PDF that was created using printToPDF*

Getting Information about Screens

Another practical feature that your Electron may need to access is Electron's screen module. The screen module gives you information about the screen or screens attached to the user's computer. You can also use screen to listen for when new displays are added or removed, or when the displays change size. Some of these items may seem unimportant for the kind of application you are planning to build, so this exercise will take you through the process of using one of the practical features of screen: using the screen module to set the location of a window.

We are going to continue working with this chapter's code, but please take a moment to comment or remove any of the console logs in your code so we can have a clean terminal window to work with.

As developers, we often work using multiple monitors attached to our computers. This is the case with the computer we are using here, so we will take advantage of that fact. Let's begin by adding a method to the bottom of our main.js file.

```
// SCREEN FUNCTIONS AND EVENTS
function getScreenInfo() {
  let screen = electron.screen
  let currentScreens = screen.getAllDisplays()
  console.log('screens', currentScreens)
}
```

This method creates a variable named screen by referencing electron.screen, which is important to remember. If we had created a constant at the top of this file to represent the screens module, we would have received an error stating that electron.screens isn't available until after the application is ready. This makes sense: it is not until the application has initialized that it can access the computer's screen.

Next, we use the getAllDisplays method to create the currentScreens variable. Then, we log the contents of the currentScreens variable so we can take a look at what they look like in the terminal window.

Now we need to call this method. Inside our "ready" listener for our application, update the code in bold to call getScreenInfo():

```
app.on('ready', () => {
  getScreenInfo()
  mainWindow = createWindow('index.html', { width: 800, height: 600, title: 'MAIN',
backgroundColor: '#FFF' })
  secondWindow = createWindow('index.html', { width: 400, height: 400, title: 'SECOND',
backgroundColor: '#FFF' })
})
```

Let's take a look at our results by running the npm start command in the terminal (Figure 8-16).

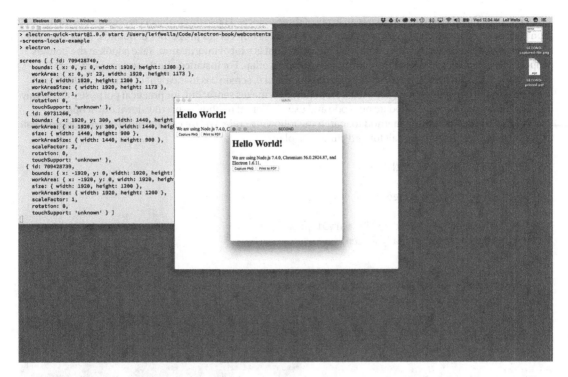

Figure 8-16. *Information about the screens appears in the terminal window*

That's a lot of data in the terminal window. Let's print it out here so we can review it together.

```
screens [ { id: 709428740,
    bounds: { x: 0, y: 0, width: 1920, height: 1200 },
    workArea: { x: 0, y: 23, width: 1920, height: 1173 },
    size: { width: 1920, height: 1200 },
    workAreaSize: { width: 1920, height: 1173 },
    scaleFactor: 1,
    rotation: 0,
    touchSupport: 'unknown' },
  { id: 69731266,
    bounds: { x: 1920, y: 300, width: 1440, height: 900 },
    workArea: { x: 1920, y: 300, width: 1440, height: 900 },
    size: { width: 1440, height: 900 },
    workAreaSize: { width: 1440, height: 900 },
    scaleFactor: 2,
    rotation: 0,
    touchSupport: 'unknown' },
  { id: 709428739,
    bounds: { x: -1920, y: 0, width: 1920, height: 1200 },
    workArea: { x: -1920, y: 0, width: 1920, height: 1200 },
    size: { width: 1920, height: 1200 },
    workAreaSize: { width: 1920, height: 1200 },
    scaleFactor: 1,
    rotation: 0,
    touchSupport: 'unknown' } ]
```

First, note that the screen variable is an array of three objects. Those three objects represent the three monitors, or screens, attached to this computer. Each of these objects has properties of bounds, workArea, size, workAreaSize, scaleFactor, rotation, and touchSupport. That is a lot of information. Take a look at the bounds property of each object. Note that the coordinates do not overlap. For instance, the three x properties are 0, 1920, and -1920. That means that screen 1 is in the middle at 0, screen 2 is to the right of screen 1 at 1920, and screen 3 is to the left of the screen 1 at -1920. Hopefully that makes sense. But, for practical purposes, this is way too much information, so let's update our code and use a different method to narrow down our scope.

Update the getScreenInfo method to match the following code. We are commenting out our original call to getAllDisplays and adding a call for getPrimaryDisplay.

```
// SCREEN FUNCTIONS AND EVENTS
function getScreenInfo() {
  let screen = electron.screen

  let primaryScreen = screen.getPrimaryDisplay()
  console.log('prime', primaryScreen)
}
```

Now, let's give the npm start command a try and see what we get (Figure 8-17).

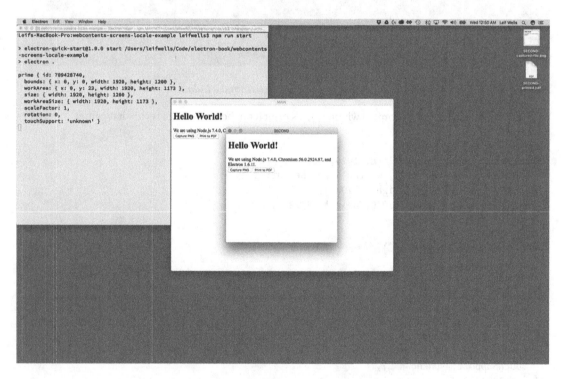

Figure 8-17. *Information about the primary display appears in the terminal window*

OK, so, the getPrimaryDisplay method returns on screen. Nice. Same properties as the objects we received from the getAllDisplays, only this object represents the screen the user has designated as their main screen (or, in this case, the screen where the macOS dock is located). Let's use this information to position our second screen.

First, inside our getScreenInfo method, let's comment two lines and return the bounds of the getPrimaryDisplay so we can use it later. Make the following updates to the method:

```
// SCREEN FUNCTIONS AND EVENTS
function getScreenInfo() {
  let screen = electron.screen

  return screen.getPrimaryDisplay().bounds
}
```

Now, we need to put that information to use. Inside the "ready" listener, make the following changes in bold:

```
app.on('ready', () => {
  let screenBounds = getScreenInfo()

  mainWindow = createWindow('index.html', { width: 800, height: 600, title: 'MAIN',
backgroundColor: '#FFF' })

  let newX = screenBounds.width - 400
  let newY = screenBounds.height - 400
  secondWindow = createWindow('index.html', { x: newX, y: newY, width: 400, height: 400,
title: 'SECOND', backgroundColor: '#FFF' })
})
```

What we are doing here is placing the secondWindow into the bottom right corner of our primary screen by using a little Math and updating our window options. First, we create a variable named screenBounds and call the getScreenInfo method to set it. Then we take the width property of screen bounds and, since we know that the width of the second window is 400 pixels, we subtract the window's width. Then, we do the same with height. That gets us the new x and y coordinates that we use to position our second window. It is important to remember on macOS, when the dock is locked on the screen and window cannot overlap the dock when it is resized, and therefore the bounds will never equal that of the primary screen. Also, remember from the BrowserWindow chapter that we must use both the x and y properties with setting the options for a window; otherwise the properties are ignored.

Run the npm start command and see where the second window displays (Figure 8-18).

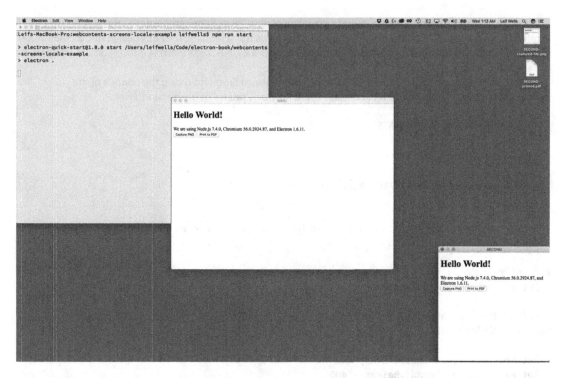

Figure 8-18. *The second window appears in the bottom corner*

Finding Locales

The final practical feature we will review in this chapter is Electron's Locales feature. Locales are used to discover the language settings on the computer being used. Internationalization, or i18n is so named because the word begins with an "I," ends in an "n," and has 18 characters in between; and localization, or l10n, is important because these days, an Electron application can easily be distributed through the Internet to users all around the world. Wouldn't it be nice to display text and menu items in the language preferred by the user? Of course, you would since you like your users and want them to enjoy using your application.

How you implement your i18n features will be up to you. The Web application you are displaying in your Renderer Process probably has modules available to implement i18n, but you still need to detect it. Sure, you can check the window.navigator.userLanguage in the Renderer Process, but to create the application's menus are created in the Main Process. Discovering the locale of the system your application is running on in the Main Process is essential.

For now, let's add the following line in bold to our "ready" listener.

```
app.on('ready', () => {
  console.log(app.getLocale())

  mainWindow = createWindow('index.html', { width: 800, height: 600, title: 'MAIN',
  backgroundColor: '#FFF' })

  let newX = screenBounds.width - 400
  let newY = screenBounds.height - 400
```

```
secondWindow = createWindow('index.html', { x: newX, y: newY, width: 400, height: 400,
  title: 'SECOND', backgroundColor: '#FFF' })
})
```

Now, run the npm start command and take a look at your terminal window (Figure 8-19).

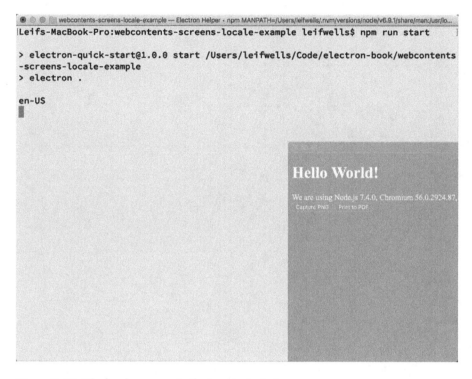

Figure 8-19. *The locale appears in the terminal window*

On this computer, the log entry in the terminal window says en-US, which, of course, means that this computer has been set up to display English and things like currency and units of measurement based on how people who live in the United States would see them. In the Electron documentation, you will find a long list of languages that can be discovered using getLocale(). Now that you know how to access the locale, there is absolutely no reason to not get internationalization running for your application.

Summary

In this chapter, we took a look at webContents, screen, and Locales. We learned how to access the webContents object's methods like getTitle() on BrowserWindow objects. We created listeners for important webContents events. We learned how to create an image and PDF file from a window using the webContents object's capturePage() and printToPDF() methods. We learned how to get information on all the displays attached to the user's computer and how to identify the primary display. And, finally, we learned how to discover what locale the user's computer has been set up to use. We hope that you found this information helpful.

CHAPTER 9

The Dock Icon on macOS

The dock is the row of applications that appear at the bottom of your main screen in macOS (Figure 9-1). The dock allows you to see icons for applications you commonly use; applications that are active; and, of course, the lovely trash can. The dock has an option to be hidden, which is a setting some users may choose. When the dock is hidden, you can get the dock to appear by moving your mouse to the area it normally sits. Application icons that appear in the dock can bounce when the application needs your attention. They can also inform you of useful events. For instance, the Mail application icon will show you how many unread email messages there are in your inbox.

Figure 9-1. *The dock*

Each of these dock features are expected features of your application, and the folks at GitHub have made these features part of Electron. This chapter focuses on features only available with macOS applications. If you are never intending to create applications for macOS, we'll understand if you choose to skip this chapter.

Getting Started

As with each of these examples, we are using the Electron Quick Start example. We will use git clone to create a new copy of the quick start in a new folder, in this case named `electron-dock-example`.

1. Open terminal and navigate to the folder where you would like to place your code:

    ```
    git clone https://github.com/electron/electron-quick-start electron-dock-example
    ```

2. Change your active directory to electron-quick-start:

    ```
    cd electron-dock-example
    ```

3. Install the dependencies:

   `npm install`

4. Reset Git:

   `git init`

Now that you have our example project installed, type npm start into your terminal application just to make sure the application loads and runs as expected.

Let's take a moment to modify this package.json file to match our own by updating some nodes.

1. Change the name node to "electron-dock-example."

2. Change the version number to "0.0.1" since we are just starting out.

3. In the description let's use something like "A sample Electron application to demonstrate macOS dock features."

4. Remove the repository node. If you decide to put your results in a repository you can re-add this node with the correct path.

5. Keywords can be "Electron," "macOS," "dock," "example.".

6. "author": Your name goes here.

7. Let's change the "license" node to "MIT."

Now that we have our electron-dock-example project created and have made certain that it runs, let's start making some changes to the code.

The Application's Dock Icon

At this point you have the quick start project installed in the electron-dock-example folder and have tested it to make sure it works. Alright, then, let's get started with the simplest of features: setting the dock icon for your application.

The first thing we need to do is create a few icons. We know we're terrible for asking a developer to create graphics. But we're really not asking all that much. We need three icons for this exercise. Apple has guidelines for application icons located at https://developer.apple.com/macos/human-interface-guidelines/icons-and-images/app-icon/ (Figure 9-2).

Figure 9-2. *Apple's Human Interface Guidelines Web site*

As a side note, if this URL works when you read it, great. Unfortunately, Apple enjoys changing their guidelines web site often. If the link does not work, do a search on the site for "app icon," and that should get you to a page like this one.

Another side note: you haven't given Apple's Human Interface Guidelines site a visit? If you are building applications for Apple's operating systems, you really should spend some time with this documentation. You could save yourself some heartache.

The guidelines state that graphics for application icons can range in sizes from 16px x 16px to 1024px x 1024px, and you should create graphics for all these sizes for your published application. For our purposes, we need three graphics at 1024px x 1024px. They can be simple, single-color graphics as long as you can tell the difference between each of them.

If you are afraid of making graphics, visit the book's page on apress.com to access the graphics created for this exercise: 1.png, 2.png, and 3.png. Create a new folder on the root of the project named "assets" and place the files there.

Open your favorite code editor and select the main.js file. Inside the createWindow method, find the line where the BrowserWindow object is invoked and add the icon property to the argument object like we show here:

```
function createWindow () {
  // Create the browser window.
  mainWindow = new BrowserWindow({width: 800, height: 600, icon: path.join(__dirname,
  'assets/1.png')})
```

Now, run the npm start command. The result is shown in Figure 9-3.

Figure 9-3. *Setting the icon property when creating a BrowserWindow object does not set the icon on macOS.*

Wait. That's not our icon, is it? No. That definitely isn't our icon. What did we do wrong? Nothing, really. If you are working on a Windows or Linux machine, you've done nothing wrong. This is how you set the icon for a window on those platforms, but not the icon in the Mac OS X dock. Let's leave this code as it is.

Now let's change the code to set the icon in the macOS dock for real. We get access to the dock through Electron's app module. At the bottom of the createWindow method, place this line of code app.dock.setIcon(path.join(__dirname, 'assets/2.png')) inside the if statement testing whether you are on macOS like it appears below. In this line of code, we are accessing the app module's dock object and setting the icon.

```
// Emitted when the window is closed.
  mainWindow.on('closed', function () {
    // Dereference the window object, usually you would store windows
    // in an array if your app supports multi windows, this is the time
    // when you should delete the corresponding element.
    mainWindow = null
  })
  if (process.platform === 'darwin') {
    app.dock.setIcon(path.join(__dirname, 'assets/2.png'))
  }
}
```

Run the npm start command and take a look at your dock. If you are using the graphics we provided, you should see a yellow smiley face staring back at you from the dock, as shown in Figure 9-4.

Figure 9-4. *The application icon has been set using app.dock.setIcon*

Making the Dock Icon Bounce

Now that we have our icon appearing in the dock, let's make it dance. One of the most important things the dock icon can do is to get the user's attention by bouncing. A bouncing dock icon can be seen even if the dock is hidden. There are two types of bouncing: informational and critical. The default bouncing type is informational, which means that the icon will bounce for one second. A bounce set for critical will make the icon bounce until either the application becomes active or the bouncing has been canceled.

Let's make our icon bounce. Add the following line of code in bold to your createWindow method:

```
app.dock.setIcon(path.join(__dirname, 'assets/2.png'))
app.dock.bounce()
```

Run the npm start command in your terminal and see what happens.

Hang on. Nothing happens. You haven't done anything wrong. The point of this step in our exercise is that the icon will not bounce if the application is focused. There is no reason for the dock to try to get your attention if the application is active. So, to test bouncing out we need to change some code and rely upon the speed of your reflexes.

First, let's make the icon bounce inside a setTimeout method. Change the line we just added with the following code:

```
app.dock.setIcon(path.join(__dirname, 'assets/2.png'))
setTimeout(() => {
    app.dock.bounce()
}, 5000)
```

This code essentially says to make the icon bounce after five seconds.

Second, to see the application's icon bounce in the dock, we need to make sure that the application is not focused. As in, we need to make sure that our application isn't the application in the foreground. This is where your reflexes come in. When you run the npm start command this time, as soon as the application is visible, click on your desktop. This will make the macOS Finder come to focus. Then you can see your icon bounce. Give it a try.

How did that work for you? Did you see your application's icon bounce high once? Awesome, right?

Let's update our code so we don't have to speed click anymore. One of the events we have access to for our window is the blur event. That is, the event that is emitted when the application goes out of focus. We can use that event to trigger our bounce call.

Update your code:

```
app.dock.setIcon(path.join(__dirname, 'assets/2.png'))
mainWindow.on('blur', () => {
  setTimeout(() => {
    app.dock.bounce('critical')
  }, 5000)
})
```

So, instead of the bounce call being made after five seconds immediately after the application is launched, the call will be made five seconds after the blur event is fired. We've also added the `'critical'` argument to our bounce call. This means that when the icon starts bouncing, it won't stop until the application becomes focused again.

This change makes our example more like a real application scenario: our application becomes inactive (you'll still have to activate the Finder by clicking the desktop), and an activity inside our application needs the user's attention (in this case, the timer is triggered). When you run the `npm start` command in the terminal and click the desktop, after five seconds the icon will bounce and continue to bounce. Click on the application or the dock icon to activate the application. The icon stops bouncing. Click on the desktop again, and after five seconds the icon will begin bouncing again. Give it a try.

Earlier we mentioned canceling a bouncing dock icon, so we should mention that you typically will not need to manually cancel a bouncing dock icon. Getting the user's attention typically results in the user activating the application, which automatically cancels a bouncing dock icon. Nevertheless, there is one scenario where canceling a bouncing icon could be necessary. Suppose your application is reliant upon a connection to the network, and while your application is in the background the network connection is severed. After the change in connection is detected, the application will make the dock icon bounce using the critical argument so the dock icon will bounce until the application comes to the foreground. Suppose the application continued to detect the connection status and the connection is restored. In this case, when the connection is reestablished the app.dock.cancelBounce method is called to stop the bouncing. If you choose to use cancelBounce, be aware that you will need to capture the id of the dock icon when you create it and pass that id as an argument for the cancelBounce method. While we won't be using the cancel method in this example, we wanted to inform you of how to cancel a bouncing dock icon when necessary.

Changing the Dock Icon

Now let's take one more step that can be helpful. Remember that third image we put into our assets folder? Let's put that to use. Make the following updates to your code using the code in bold:

```
app.dock.setIcon(path.join(__dirname, 'assets/2.png'))
mainWindow.on('blur', () => {
  setTimeout(() => {
    app.dock.setIcon(path.join(__dirname, 'assets/3.png'))
    app.dock.bounce('critical')
  }, 5000)
})
mainWindow.on('focus', () => {
  app.dock.setIcon(path.join(__dirname, 'assets/2.png'))
})
```

These changes allow us to change the icon when we make the icon bounce. See where we set the icon to the 3.png file? Changing the icon is another way to let the user know the application needs their attention, but it can also be used to show that the application has entered a specific condition. For instance, when the Cisco AnyConnect Secure Mobility Client application, a virtual private network (VPN) application, connects to a network, the application icon can change from a normal icon to one that indicates you are connected to the VPN (Figure 9-5).

Figure 9-5. *Images captured of different dock icons used by a popular VPN application*

Give this code a try by entering npm start into your terminal; click the desktop; and in five seconds you will see our red, sad face icon bouncing in the dock.

Dock Icon Badges

Great. Now we know how to set the application icon in the dock and make it bounce. What else can we make it do? How about show a badge? You've seen badges before. On macOS, they appear as a red dot atop your dock icon, typically showing a number. The Mail application will show a badge to indicate how many unread messages are in your inbox. Slack will show a badge to indicate you have new messages in one of your channels.

The Electron team have made it fairly simple to add a badge to your application icon. The app.dock.setBadge method takes a string argument to set the text in your badge. Let's give this a try by updating our code:

```
app.dock.setIcon(path.join(__dirname, 'assets/2.png'))
mainWindow.on('blur', () => {
  setTimeout(() => {
    app.dock.setBadge('!')
    app.dock.setIcon(path.join(__dirname, 'assets/3.png'))
    app.dock.bounce('critical')
  }, 5000)
})
mainWindow.on('focus', () => {
app.dock.setBadge('')
  app.dock.setIcon(path.join(__dirname, 'assets/2.png'))
})
```

This code sets the badge to show with an exclamation point inside our 'blur' event listener and resets it inside the 'focus' event listener. Note that we pass an empty string - app.dock.setBadge('') - to reset the badge and make the red dot disappear. You can experiment with other text if you like, but Apple's guidelines suggest keeping it simple and to use one character or a number. If your application needs to let the user know that there are hundreds of messages waiting for them, for instance, you may wish to make the badge text "99+", or do what the folks at Slack do and set the badge to "*".

Let's take this example one step further and change the badge text based on reading the current badge text. Update the code to match the following code:

```
app.dock.setIcon(path.join(__dirname, 'assets/2.png'))
mainWindow.on('blur', () => {
  setTimeout(() => {
    let badgeString = app.dock.getBadge()
    if(badgeString === '') {
      app.dock.setBadge('1')
    } else {
      app.dock.setBadge((parseInt(badgeString) + 1).toString())
    }
    app.dock.setIcon(path.join(__dirname, 'assets/3.png'))
    app.dock.bounce('critical')
  }, 5000)
})
mainWindow.on('focus', () => {    app.dock.setIcon(path.join(__dirname, 'assets/2.png'))
})
```

Inside the "blur" event listener we are setting a badgeString variable to be equal to the text of the current badge using the app.dock.getBadge method. Then we change the badge based on that text in the if...else statement. If the app.dock.getBadge returns an empty string, we set the badge to a string containing the number 1. Otherwise, we run app.dock.setBadge((parseInt(badgeString) + 1).toString()) that updates the badge by converting the current badge string to a number adding 1 to that number and then converting that number to a string. Keep in mind that setBadge expects an argument and that argument must be a string.

The expected behavior for this updated code is that we will start off without a badge showing, and every time the application receives a blur event, the badge count will update by one. Run the npm start command in the terminal and see this code in action! When the application is not the focused application, your dock should have an icon that looks like Figure 9-6.

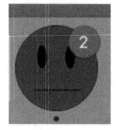

Figure 9-6. *Our dock icon as it appears with the application in the background and with a badge set to 2*

Did it work as expected? Great. If not, make sure your blur and focus listeners are properly set as they are in the code sample above. You may debug your code by adding some console.log statements to make it clear that your listeners are working. Remember, the results of console.log statements placed in the Main Process appear in the terminal window.

Summary

Dock icons do more than just show macOS users that your application is running. They bounce to get the user's attention. They change to indicate a change in application state. They give users more information about the application by showing badges. These application features are expected if you are building an application for macOS, so knowing how to properly use the dock icon is important.

CHAPTER 10

Shell

Electron's shell functionality assists developers with helpful ways to interact with the desktop environment. The methods within shell are designed as shortcuts to assist us in identifying and opening that files our application cannot (and should not) open itself. Your application can open files in the background, which is usually how you can use shell. But you may wish to allow your users to open files themselves by giving them access to a File ➤ Open menu. You may wish to open files with your application for various reasons: to open saved preference files saved by the application, to open a user's files saved earlier by the application, or to load data for your application saved as flat files (JSON or text files). Also, keep in mind that the Renderer Process of your application is essentially a Web browser, so you can load any HTML files. When your Electron application creates or references files or URLs, the people who use your applications expect the application to assist them with locating and opening those files or URLs. With shell, Electron makes these tasks easy for developers and users.

Best Practice: While Electron's shell functions are available in both the Main and Renderer processes, we recommend that you use it in your Main process so that you can better control its use. Use Inter-Process Communication (IPC) as a bridge between your Renderer process and Main process to make these functions work.

In this chapter, we'll start with the Electron Quick Start project and add the Electron shell methods beep, showItemInFolder, openItem, and openExternal.

Getting Started

As with each of these examples, we start off using the Electron Quick Start project. We will use git clone to create a new copy of the quick start in a new folder, in this case named electron-shell-example.

1. Open terminal and navigate to the folder where you would like to place your code:

   ```
   git clone https://github.com/electron/electron-quick-start electron-shell-example
   ```

2. Change your active directory to electron-quick-start:

   ```
   cd electron-shell-example
   ```

3. Install the dependencies:

   ```
   npm install
   ```

4. Reset Git:

   ```
   git init
   ```

© Chris Griffith, Leif Wells 2017
C. Griffith, L. Wells, *Electron: From Beginner to Pro*, https://doi.org/10.1007/978-1-4842-2826-5_10

Now that you have our example project installed, type npm start into your terminal application just to make sure the application loads and runs as expected.

Let's take a moment to modify this package.json file and match our own by updating some nodes.

1. Change the name node to "electron-shell-example."

2. Change the version number to "0.0.1" since we are just starting out.

3. In the description let's use something like "A sample Electron application to demonstrate shell features."

4. Remove the repository node. If you decide to put your results in a repository you can change or re-add this node with the correct address.

5. Keywords can be "Electron," "shell," and "example."

6. "author": Your name goes here.

7. Let's change the "license" node to "MIT".

Now that we have our electron-shell-example project created and have made certain that it runs, let's start making some changes to the code.

Making the System Alert Sound

Let's begin with the most simple of the shell methods, shell.beep – which prompts the computer to make the system beep sound. Open the main.js file in the root of the project and add this line to the top of your file:

const { shell } = require('electron')

This syntax, using the module name shell inside curly braces, gives you access to Electron's shell package and now you can add the methods by referencing the shell variable. Let's give that a try.

At the bottom of your createWindow method, add the shell.beep call:

```
function createWindow () {
  // Create the browser window.
  mainWindow = new BrowserWindow({width: 800, height: 600})

  // and load the index.html of the app.
  mainWindow.loadURL(url.format({
    pathname: path.join(__dirname, 'index.html'),
    protocol: 'file:',
    slashes: true
  }))

  // Open the DevTools.
  // mainWindow.webContents.openDevTools()

  // Emitted when the window is closed.
  mainWindow.on('closed', function () {
    // Dereference the window object, usually you would store windows
    // in an array if your app supports multi windows, this is the time
    // when you should delete the corresponding element.
    mainWindow = null
  })
  shell.beep()
}
```

Let's test this out by opening the Terminal application and entering npm start to load our application. Did you hear the beep? Cool, right? OK, maybe not so cool, but it works. If you did not hear the beep, please make sure that your computer's sound is not muted or that you don't have headsets that you are not wearing plugged in. We'd use shell.beep if we wanted to get the user's attention along with something like making the dock icon bounce. Using the system's beep can be annoying, so be responsible and use it sparingly.

Let's take shell.beep one step further and add it to the renderer.js file, too, like so:

```
// This file is required by the index.html file and will
// be executed in the renderer process for that window.
// All of the Node.js APIs are available in this process.

const { shell } = require('electron')

shell.beep()
```

Now, run npm start in Terminal and you should hear two beeps: one from the Main process and one from the Renderer process. Like we said earlier, we don't believe using shell.beep in the Renderer process is a good idea - we like keeping our system integration in the Main process - but we wanted to make sure you know how to do it if you found a proper use case.

Showing Files in the Operating System

Let's move on to something more practical like revealing a file in the user's operating system. This is a fairly practical feature that your application may need. Suppose as part of a process in your application a file is generated, and you would like to present that file in its containing folder. This is the method you would use to make that happen.

Before we start, make sure that you remove both of the shell.beep calls we just created because, like we just said, beeping can be annoying.

First, let's create a new text file so we can test out this method. In your code editor, create a new file on the root of the project and name it test.txt and place some text inside of it, say, "shell is swell."

Now that we have a test file we can use shell.showItemInFolder. In your main.js file, update the code inside the createWindow method to look like this:

```
let filePath = app.getAppPath() + '/test.txt'
shell.showItemInFolder(filePath)
```

In this code we're using the Main process app package's getAppPath method to get the application path so that we can locate our test.txt file. We add '/' and the file name so that the filePath variable becomes a string representing the file we would like to use. The leading '/' is important because getAppPath does not end in a "/" and without it, the path will be incorrect and the file will not be found. We pass the filePath variable in the next line as the path argument for our showItemInFolder method.

Before you start the application again, make sure to check if the folder you want to open isn't already open so you aren't disappointed in the results. Now, when you run npm start from Terminal, you will see the folder and file, as shown in Figure 10-1.

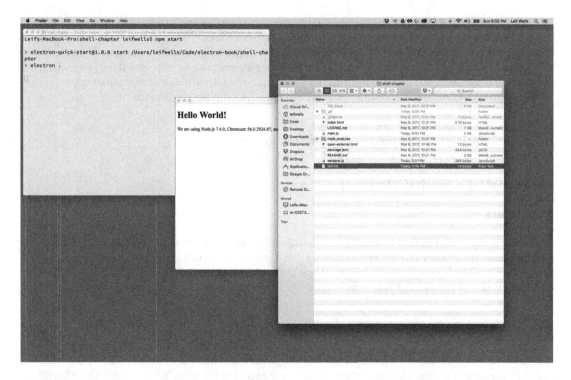

Figure 10-1. *This image shows shell.openItemInFolder opening a folder and highlighting a file in the Mac OS X Finder*

Please notice that the correct folder is open and the correct file is selected, highlighting it to the user. Mission accomplished!

Opening Files with the Operating System

Now that we've located a file in our operating system, let's build off that feature to open that file using shell. openItem method. This method allows you to open files in the assigned application for the file type. For instance, suppose your application creates a text file for the user. To open that file for the user, you would use shell.openItem. We're going to continue using the test.txt file for this example, and in our system the file will open in the default text editor on Mac OS X.

Update your code with the following highlighted updates:

```
let filePath = app.getAppPath() + '/test.txt'
shell.openItem(filePath)
```

Now, run npm start in Terminal and you will see this method in action (Figure 10-2).

Figure 10-2. *This image shows shell.openItem opening a text file with the system's default text editor, TextEdit*

Notice that our Electron application has opened our text file with TextEdit. This is useful for common system text and image files, files that already have an assigned default application. One common file type that shell.openItem doesn't work well with is HTML files. That is where shell.openExternal comes in. Best practice for opening a file with an external application should require user interaction. If the user hasn't used the File ➤ Open menu item or a specific button in your Renderer Process, let the user know a file will be opened.

Opening HTML Files with the Operating System

Opening HTML files in Electron is a little tricky. You see, Electron is essentially a browser so opening an HTML file using shell might be a little confusing: are we opening the HTML file in Electron or in a browser? If you open an HTML file in your current Chromium window, your application will disappear while you could provide a back button, and restarting your application from the point you left may be difficult. So, shell.openItem doesn't open HTML files. We need to use shell.openExternal and it will open in your default browser.

Before we start this example, we need to create another file on the project root, this time naming it test. html and entering the text "test html file" into the file. In this example, we're not actually using a file coded in HTML, just a file with the .html file extension.

Now we can update the main.js file to match the following following code:

```
let filePath = 'file:///' + app.getAppPath() + '/test.html'

shell.openExternal(filePath)
```

In this code we've added two lines. In the first line we're creating the variable filePath but this time we are creating a string in the URL format prefixing it with "file:///" so that our browser understands that this file is on our file system and not on a server somewhere on the Internet. If we want to open a URL online, we could set this string to a typical URL like https://electron.atom.io/ or any real address.

Best Practice: An Electron application has full access to the user's system just like any desktop application. As a Web developer, working with the imbedded security of a browser may make you ill-prepared to work in the desktop environment. Follow security guidelines for desktop application development for the platforms on which your application will be running. Do no harm.

Run the npm start command in Terminal to see the file opened by your browser. See how our simple HTML file is opened and displayed in Chrome, our default browser (Figure 10-3).

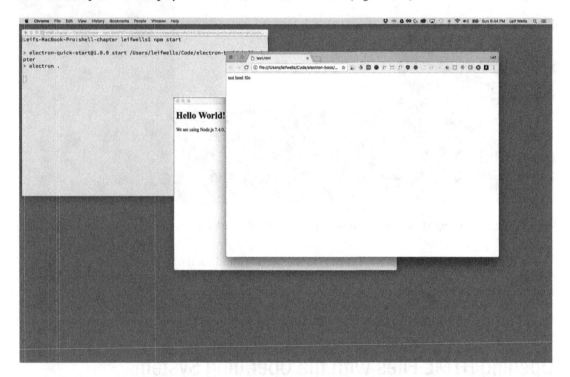

Figure 10-3. *This image shows the result using shell.openExternal to open an HTML file*

There are some caveats to this scenario, though. If you are going to use shell to open HTML file, we recommend that you limit the HTML file to use simple syntax and be careful of using external CSS and image files without doing proper testing in multiple browsers on target platforms. Each browser handles "file:///" addresses a little differently, so if you keep things simple this might work for you.

Summary

In this chapter we took a look at a few of the methods that are part of Electron's shell package: shell.beep - a simple command to make the system beep sound occur; shell.openItemInFolder - the method that allows your application to display a file in the user's operating system; shell.openItem - the method to use when you want your application to open a file with the default application for that file type; and shell.openExternal - the method that opens files and Internet URLs. These shell methods could be necessary for any application. We recommend using shell in the Main process to keep your system integration in one place.

CHAPTER 11

■ ■ ■

Online/Offline Detection

These days, developers tend to assume that the people using their applications are always online. One could even assume that just because someone is using a desktop or laptop computer, they will be within reach of an Ethernet cable or Wi-Fi signal. Reality teaches us that this assumption isn't correct and that as a developer of desktop applications we need to plan accordingly.

Using the cloud to store the artifacts of a user's activities is a normal condition of modern web applications. You would assume correctly that if the user has logged into your application, then they are online. But when you deploy code to the desktop using Electron, the application code is inside the executable file and not on a server. If you are relying upon a connection to the Internet, detecting whether that connection is live is a fundamental task.

In this chapter, we will create a sample application that checks to see if the computer that the application is running on is online and inform the user that a change has occurred. Through the process of creating this sample, we will look at various techniques of online detection and create a solution that utilizes both the main and the renderer processes. A typical Node developer may try to put everything inside the Main Process. A typical web developer may try to put everything inside the Renderer Process. In this chapter, we believe that you will see that if you leverage the features of both processes, you will achieve a much more elegant solution.

Getting Started

As with each of these examples, we are using the Electron Quick Start example. We will use git clone to create a new copy of the quick start in a new folder, in this case named `online-detection-example`. First, open the terminal and navigate to the folder where you would like to place your code.

```
git clone https://github.com/electron/electron-quick-start online-detection-example
```

Next, change your active directory to `online-detection-example`.

```
cd online-detection-example
```

Now, we need to install the dependencies:

```
npm install
```

Finally, reset Git with

```
git init
```

Now that you have our example project installed, type `npm start` into your terminal application just to make sure the application loads and runs as expected.

© Chris Griffith, Leif Wells 2017

C. Griffith, L. Wells, *Electron: From Beginner to Pro*, https://doi.org/10.1007/978-1-4842-2826-5_11

Let's take a moment to modify this package.json file to match our own by updating some nodes.

1. Change the name node to "online-detection-example."

2. Change the version number to "0.0.1" since we are just starting out.

3. In the description let's use something like "A sample Electron application to demonstrate online detection."

4. Remove the repository node. If you decide to put your results in a repository, you can change re-add this node with the correct address.

5. Keywords can be "Electron," "online," "detection," "sample."

6. "author": Your name goes here.

7. Let's change the "license" node to "MIT."

Using the Renderer Process to Detect Online Status

Typically, in any web application you would use an event listener to detect changes in online status. It would look something like this:

```
window.addEventListener( 'online', updateOnlineStatus )
window.addEventListener( 'offline', updateOnlineStatus )
```

This example code is waiting for the window object to emit either an online or offline event, and when either of these events occur the updateOnlineStatus function is called. It is a fairly simple technique to assemble, so let's get started.

First, we'll set up our HTML and CSS files. Inside our index.html file let's change the body tag to the following code:

```
<body>
    <div class="container">
    <header>
        <h1>Are You Online?</h1>
            <div class="button-holder">
                <button id="checkStatusButton" type="button">Check Status</button>
            </div>
    </header>
        <section class="main">

                    <h2 id="h2-online">You are Online</h2>
                    <h2 id="h2-offline">You are NOT Online</h2>

        </section>

            <footer></footer>
    </div>
</body>
```

This code separates the *body* tag into three sections: header, main, and footer. Inside the header tag we are placing an h1 for the title and a button with the id of "checkStatusButton." We will leave the footer empty of content, but we will style it in our CSS.

The section tag is where our main content will reside. It holds three h2 elements with id attributes. Those ids will be used to show or hide these h2 elements depending upon the current online status.

Now that we have the basic structure created for our example, we need to create CSS for layout and styling. First, we need to create a CSS file, then we will add a link to our index.html file so it will be used.

First, in the root of your project, create a new file and name it "index.css."

Here's code for the index.css file:

```
html,
body {
        padding: 0;
        margin: 0;
}

body {
        font-family: 'Helvetica Neue', Helvetica, sans-serif;
}

header {
        position: absolute;
        width: 100%;
        height: 20px;
        top: 0;
        left: 0;
        padding-left: 15px;
        padding-top: 5px;
        background-color: #CCC;
        border-bottom: 1px solid #999;
}

header h1 {
        font-size: 12px;
        font-weight: bolder;
        margin: 0;
        padding: 0;
}

.button-holder {
        position: absolute;
        right: 25px;
        bottom: 5px;
        width: auto;
        height: auto;
        padding-top: 5px;
}

section {
        width: 100%;
        margin-top: 30px;
}
```

```
section h2 {
        display: none;
        font-size: 48px;
        font-weight: 100;
        margin: 0;
        padding: 0;
        text-align: center;
}

footer {
        position: absolute;
        left: 0;
        bottom: 0;
        width: 100%;
        height: 10px;
        padding-bottom: 5px;
        border-top: 1px solid #999;
        background-color: #CCC;

}
```

We are keeping the CSS simple here, but the highlights are the following:

- The `.button-holder` tag positions the button to the right side in the header.

- `section` and `section h2` are used to style our main section.

- `footer` gives us a nice gray bar.

Now that we have our CSS file, let's link to it in our project. Open the index.html file and add the following highlighted code to the head tag:

```
<head>
    <meta charset="UTF-8">
    <title>Are You Online?</title>
    <link rel="stylesheet" type="text/css" href="index.css">
 </head>
```

If we run our project now, it looks like Figure 11-1.

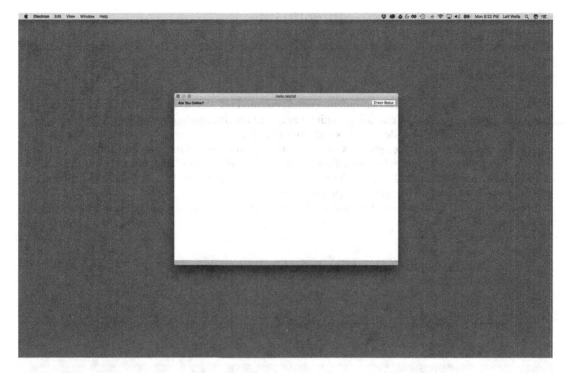

Figure 11-1. *The example's empty UI*

Notice that you don't see anything in the main container. That is because our CSS for section h2 tag is using display: none; so that all of them are hidden. Now we can add some JavaScript to detect whether our application is online and reveal the appropriate h2 element.

Open the renderer.js file. It currently has commented lines at the top of the file. We'll delete those comments and enter the following code:

```
const updateOnlineStatus = () => {

    if( navigator.onLine ) {
        document.body.style.backgroundColor = 'green'
        document.getElementById( 'h2-checking' ).style.display = 'none'
        document.getElementById( 'h2-online' ).style.display = 'block'
        document.getElementById( 'h2-offline' ).style.display = 'none'
    } else {
        document.body.style.backgroundColor = 'red'
        document.getElementById( 'h2-checking' ).style.display = 'none'
        document.getElementById( 'h2-online' ).style.display = 'none'
        document.getElementById( 'h2-offline' ).style.display = 'block'
    }
}
```

```
window.addEventListener( 'online', updateOnlineStatus )
window.addEventListener( 'offline', updateOnlineStatus )
document.getElementById( 'checkStatusButton' ).addEventListener('click', updateOnlineStatus)

updateOnlineStatus()
```

At the top of this code block is our updateOnlineStatus method. This is where all the action takes place. The status variable is created by checking whether `navigator.onLine` method returns a string of `'online'` or `'offline'`. From there the code branches with code that changes the styles of the corresponding h1 tags to make the correct message appear as well as the background color of the body tag. At the bottom of this code block we have the event listeners. There is one each for the "online" and "offline" events that call our updateOnlineStatus method, and one for the "click" event on the header button. Finally, we call the updateOnlineStatus method that gets our application going.

Now, if you look at the bottom of our index.html file you will see that the renderer.js file is already being referenced:

```
<script>
    // You can also require other files to run in this process
    require('./renderer.js')
</script>
```

If we launch our application using npm start (and you are online), you should see Figure 11-2.

Figure 11-2. *The example's UI showing the computer is online*

And if you disconnect from your Internet, you should see Figure 11-3.

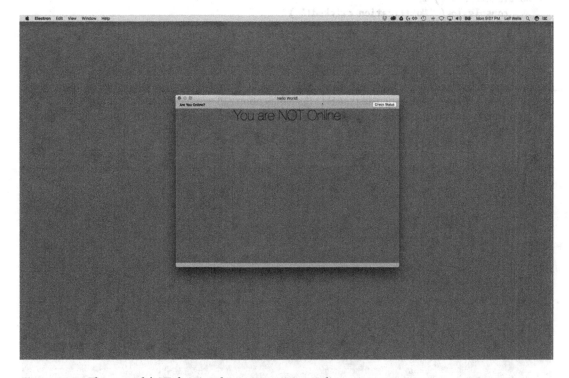

Figure 11-3. *The example's UI showing the computer is not online*

We can take this sample one step further by adding an additional feature: Notification. The Notification API is part of the HTML specification and an excellent choice of a UI element for informing the user of important information. Using a Notification also allows us to inform the user of a change in online status when our application is not in the foreground.

We can create a Notification to our code at the bottom of our updateOnlineStatus method:

```
const updateOnlineStatus = () => {
    let status = navigator.onLine ? 'online' : 'offline'
    console.log( status )
    if( navigator.onLine ) {
        document.body.style.backgroundColor = 'green'
        document.getElementById( 'h2-checking' ).style.display = 'none'
        document.getElementById( 'h2-online' ).style.display = 'block'
        document.getElementById( 'h2-offline' ).style.display = 'none'
    } else {
        document.body.style.backgroundColor = 'red'
        document.getElementById( 'h2-checking' ).style.display = 'none'
        document.getElementById( 'h2-online' ).style.display = 'none'
        document.getElementById( 'h2-offline' ).style.display = 'block'
    }
```

```
    let note = new Notification( 'You are ' + status , { body: 'You are now ' + status })
    note.onclick = () => {
        console.log( 'Notification clicked!' )
    }
}
```

The new code for this method begins with a let note, which creates a variable as a Notification object that has an argument that is a simple bit of text. The next lines create a console message when the notification is clicked. This is a simple example of using the HTML5 Notification API, which comes with Chromium.

Now when you turn on or off your Internet access, you will see a notification in the upper-right corner of your screen (Figure 11-4).

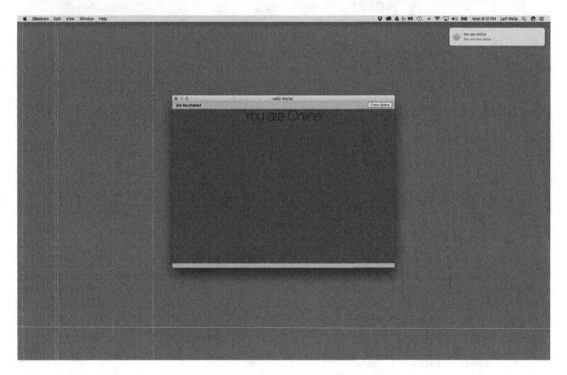

Figure 11-4. *A notification has appeared in the upper-right corner of the screen*

Pros and Cons of the Renderer-Only Solution

This example works great! It uses the Window and Notification APIs available in our Chromium-based Renderer Process and works reliably when we manually change our own Internet access.

But there is one major drawback to this solution: LieFi. This is the condition that many people get into when they are able to connect to a router, but the router is not connected to the Internet. You see that you have a 5-bar connection, but you can't load anything from the Web. Your connection is a lie. If you are not worried about this condition, feel free to use and improve upon this sample. Otherwise, let's take a look at a solution that uses the Main Process.

The Main Process-Only Solution

Since our Renderer-Only Online/Offline detection may not be enough to satisfy our requirements, we should try using the Main Process. We need a way to get Node to check if there is an active link to the Web. To do this, we need to add a module to our project. Luckily, GitHub user @sindresorhus has created a module named is-online (`https://github.com/sindresorhus/is-online`). If you don't know, @sindresorhus is the person who hosts Awesome Electron (`https://github.com/sindresorhus/awesome-electron`), a page of helpful Electron links. Take a look when you get the chance. The is-online module pings root servers and if it gets a response within 2 seconds, it knows your application is really online. No lies here. We will need to create an interval, a loop of code that gets called at a set period, to call is-online. Finally, we will need to tell our renderer process what the current status is so it can be displayed using Electron's Inter-Process Communication (IPC). So let's get started.

To install is-online, we need to run the following command in your terminal application from the root of our project:

```
npm install is-online --save
```

Take a look at your `package.json` file at the root of your project. There should be a new dependencies node and it should look like this:

```
"dependencies": {
    "is-online": "^7.0.0"
}
```

At the time of this writing, version 7.0.0 was available. You may see a higher version number, but that is good. Now we can start using is-online in our Main Process. Open the main.js file in the root of the project and add the following highlighted lines of code to the top of the file:

```
const electron = require('electron')
// Module to control application life.
const app = electron.app
// Module to create native browser window.
const BrowserWindow = electron.BrowserWindow

const path = require('path')
const url = require('url')

const ipcMain = electron.ipcMain
const isOnline = require('is-online')

let checkIsOnlineInterval
let currentOnlineStatus
```

The first line gives us access to Electron's Inter-Process Communications API, which we will be using to send messages from the Main Process to the Renderer Process. The second line allows us to use the is-online module. The third line creates a variable `checkIsOnlineInterval` that will be used to create an interval in which we will check online status. The fourth line creates the `currentOnlineStatus` variable that will be used to hold the current connection status.

At the bottom of the `main.js` file we will insert the following method:

```
function checkIsOnline() {
  isOnline().then( online => {
    console.log( "Online? " + online )
    mainWindow.webContents.send( 'update-online-status' , { online: online })
    if( currentOnlineStatus !== online ) {
        if (process.platform === 'darwin') {
            app.dock.bounce( 'informational' )
        }
    }

    currentOnlineStatus = online
  })
}
```

This is the function we will be calling to find out if we are online. The isOnline function returns a Promise and inside the then method we make a IPC call, `'update-online-status'`, to the renderer process along with an argument object that holds the reference to our online status.

In the next if statement we want to notify the user if the status is offline by bouncing the application icon in the dock if you are on the macOS platform:

app.dock.bounce('informational')

The dock is a reference to the collection of icons typically found at the bottom of the screen on the macOS computer, so this is obviously a Mac-only feature. This line of code uses the app reference created at the top of our file and accesses that object's dock object's bounce method. You can pass the argument "informational," like we've done here, or "critical." With the "informational" argument, the icon is only bounced for a second. With "critical" the icon will bounce until the application is activated or app.dock. cancelBounce(id) is called. We'll look at that scenario in another chapter.

Finally, we set the currentOnlineStatus variable to match the online status so that we may refer to it later.

Now we need to create an interval so that we may call the checkIsOnline repeatedly. Place the following code at the bottom of your main.js file:

```
function startCheckingOnlineStatus() {
    checkIsOnlineInterval = setInterval(checkIsOnline, 10000 )
}
```

The setInterval method creates an interval that calls the checkIsOnline method. For our purposes here, we are setting the time between checks to 10000, which translates to 10 seconds. Now that we have created the method for creating the interval, we have to call it to get it started. Place the following highlighted code at the bottom of our createWindow method:

```
function createWindow () {
  // Create the browser window.
  mainWindow = new BrowserWindow({width: 800, height: 600})

  // and load the index.html of the app.
  mainWindow.loadURL(url.format({
    pathname: path.join(__dirname, 'index.html'),
    protocol: 'file:',
    slashes: true
  }))
```

```
// Open the DevTools.
mainWindow.webContents.openDevTools()

// Emitted when the window is closed.
mainWindow.on('closed', function () {
  // Dereference the window object, usually you would store windows
  // in an array if your app supports multi windows, this is the time
  // when you should delete the corresponding element.
  mainWindow = null
})

startCheckingOnlineStatus()
}
```

Now, when the main window is created the interval is also created.

■ **Note**   Inside our checkIsOnline method, we make a console call:

```
console.log( "Online? " + online )
```

It is important to remember that when we create console messages in the Main Process, these messages do not appear in the Chromium DevTools console window. These messages will appear in the terminal window where you called npm start to launch your application.

Let's enter npm start into our terminal window to start the app and see how it works. You should see messages in the terminal window every 10 seconds (Figure 11-5).

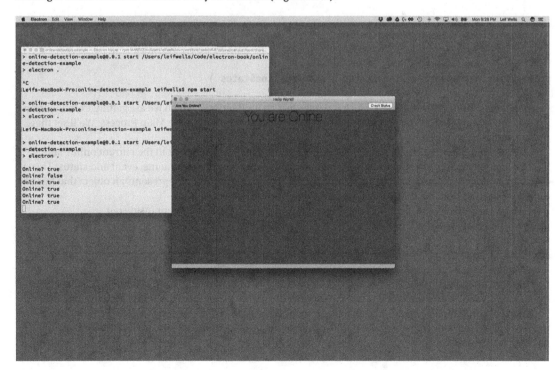

Figure 11-5. *Messages from the Main Process are appearing in the terminal window*

Great! Since users of your application will never see a terminal window, we need to do a little work in the code for our renderer process so we can better inform them of any changes in the online status.

Update the following highlighted lines in the renderer.js file:

```
const { ipcRenderer } = require('electron')
let onlineStatus

const updateOnlineStatus = ( event, status ) => {
    if( status.online ) {
        document.body.style.backgroundColor = 'green'
        document.getElementById( 'h2-checking' ).style.display = 'none'
        document.getElementById( 'h2-online' ).style.display = 'block'
        document.getElementById( 'h2-offline' ).style.display = 'none'
    } else {
        document.body.style.backgroundColor = 'red'
        document.getElementById( 'h2-checking' ).style.display = 'none'
        document.getElementById( 'h2-online' ).style.display = 'none'
        document.getElementById( 'h2-offline' ).style.display = 'block'
    }

if( this.onlineStatus !== undefined && this.onlineStatus !== status.online ) {
        let note = new Notification('You are ' + (status.online ? 'online' : 'offline'),
                        { body: 'You are now ' + (status.online ? 'online' : 'offline')})
        note.onclick = () => {
            console.log( 'Notification clicked!' )
        }
    }

    this.onlineStatus = status.online
}

ipcRenderer.on('update-online-status', updateOnlineStatus )
```

On the top line of this new code block is a reference to ipcRenderer, which we are getting from Electron. The ipcRenderer will allow the Renderer Process to receive messages from the Main Process. We'll set that up in a moment.

In the second line we create a variable onlineStatus that will be used to hold the current online status.

The updateOnlineStatus method is created next. It is expecting two arguments, event and status. The event argument is sent by default by the Main Process. The status argument represents an object that has an online property, a Boolean that indicates whether the application is online.

We set the onlineStatus variable in the next block of code in the if statement inside our updateOnlineStatus method:

```
if( this.onlineStatus !== undefined && this.onlineStatus !== status.online )
```

We don't need to update the user if the online status has not changed. This if statement is asking if our onlineStatus variable exists and if it is not the same as the online property of the status argument; and if so, we need to update the screen. The status argument is also used when creating the Notification, so we need to update the code there as well. At the bottom of the updateOnlineStatus method we update our onlineStatus variable.

At the bottom of this code block we set up the listener for the IPC call from inside the checkIsOnline method in the Main Process (main.js):

```
ipcRenderer.on('update-online-status', updateOnlineStatus )
```

This means that the ipcRenderer object is waiting for the 'update-online-status' event and when it occurs the updateOnlineStatus method will be called.

Of note, we commented out those last three lines. We'll be using them again in the next section of this chapter, but for now we do not need them.

Now enter npm start into our terminal window to start the app and see how these updates work.

Pros and Cons of a Main Process-Only Approach

As you can see, doing all the online detection in the Main Process works well. We are able to avoid the Lie-Fi effect and let the Renderer Process know of any changes in online status. But there is an issue with this approach: the interval. Typically, running an interval every 10 seconds forever is not advisable, but as this is the only way we are doing the detection, the shorter the time frame the better. Also, we are waiting until 10 seconds before checking. And if we extend the times between checks, that is all the more chances for us to miss a change in online status.

Let's try to see if we can combine the Renderer Process scenario with the Main Process scenario to make a better solution to online detection.

The Combined Approach

As we've seen so far, both the approaches to online detection we've tried so far have had some problems. We cannot trust the Renderer Process-Only solution because it couldn't prevent Lie-Fi, the condition where a computer may be connected to a router, but that router does not have a connection to the Internet. The Main Process-Only solution uses a timer, which makes detection less reliable due to the time between detection events. So, let's combine approaches to make a superior solution.

Most of the changes required for our new solution occur inside our renderer.js file. First, we will add a new method to the file just below the updateOnlineStatus method:

```
constcheckOnlineStatus = () => {
    document.body.style.backgroundColor = 'white'
    document.getElementById( 'h2-checking' ).style.display = 'block'
    document.getElementById( 'h2-online' ).style.display = 'none'
    document.getElementById( 'h2-offline' ).style.display = 'none'

    ipcRenderer.send('check-online-status')
}
```

This new method does two things: it changes the UI state to a checking state, one that has a white background and shows the text "Checking...", and then the method sends a 'check-online-status' IPC message to the Main Process.

Below the new checkOnlineStatus method are lines we commented in the previous solution. Let's uncomment and change them to look like this:

```
window.addEventListener( 'online', checkOnlineStatus )
window.addEventListener( 'offline', checkOnlineStatus )
document.getElementById( 'checkStatusButton' ).addEventListener('click', checkOnlineStatus,
false )
```

As you can see, we changed the handlers for these event listeners to use the new checkOnlineStatus method. This means that with each of these events, we will be asking the Main Process to check the status as opposed to going ahead and changing it. Even though the window's online or offline events are accurate, instead of letting the Renderer Process go ahead and react to the status change, this code informs the Main Process that there has been a status change and allows it to run detection as well, making the Main Process central in the detection of online status.

Finally, let's add a call at the bottom of our code:

```
checkOnlineStatus()
```

By adding this code, we are kicking off our new detection routine immediately as the Renderer Process starts preventing any time gap in Main Process detection.

Now we can move back to our main.js file. Changes here, too, are fairly simple. At the bottom of the file, we need to listen for the check-online-status IPC call:

```
ipcMain.on('check-online-status', checkIsOnline )
```

With this listener, the Main Process triggers the checkIsOnline method that detects the online status and then informs any parts of our application listening for the update-online-status event.

Give it a try by running npm start and make sure you take your computer online/offline to see how quickly the detection works.

Summary

Our goal in this chapter was to create an online detection solution. We added code that allowed the Renderer Process to handle online/offline detection using the navigator.onLine method available in Chromium. We then investigated using a Node module, is-online, to detect online status from within the Main Process. Finally, we combined the two approaches to create a better solution. Along the way, we hope that we revealed that evaluating a solution to a problem with an Electron application requires a developer to look beyond the traditional, typical front-end or back-end web developer roles, and better solutions can be found by leveraging both the Main and Renderer Processes to create a more complete result. You can create powerful Electron applications utilizing your knowledge and skills of Node, HTML/CSS/Javascript, and available open source projects.

■ ■ ■

CHAPTER 12

Advanced BrowserWindow

In an earlier chapter, we discussed how to create windows using the BrowserWindow object. But we've often found that simply creating windows is not enough. An effective application may need to create more than one window and instigate communication between windows. We thought that a great way to teach you the basics of these concepts would be to implement a simple splash screen example.

In this chapter, we will reinforce the creation of windows using the BrowserWindow object, create a frameless and non-resizable window, retrieve and display the version of the application, integrate communication between these windows using inter-process communication (IPC), and set up a simulation for a slow starting application.

Loading an Application

Users typically start Electron applications, like any other desktop applications, by clicking or double-clicking on an icon in their computer's system interface. Everyone has experience with this interaction: you find the application icon, you click it, and your application appears on the screen. But what happens between when the user clicks and the application appears? Most likely, a lot happens: the application code is initialized; user authorization is checked; user preferences are loaded; and data is acquired via an online service or local database, processing that data for display. Any and all of these tasks can take many seconds.

It is important to remember how a BrowserWindow object gets displayed using the default parameters. When Chromium is ready, the blank window frame will appear then, and as soon as the application is ready Chromium will render the application UI. Since our starter code doesn't really do anything taxing to the CPU, we don't even notice it. If the application you're building is very simple, this may not be a problem. If not, your users may experience something that appears like the application is broken while waiting for the application to render. And if we've learned anything from mobile development over the past 10 years, it's that users don't like waiting for applications to start, even on their desktop computers. This is where a splash window comes in.

Splash Window

Every application can use a splash window. With desktop applications, a splash window is similar to a mobile application's splash window in that it gives the user immediate feedback that the application is loading and provides cover for any system information gathering, user preferences, and any pre-loading of data. Some applications use a splash window as a starting point: click here to load a recent file. Other applications just show the splash window as a branding exercise. Either way, it is good to know how to get started creating a splash window.

© Chris Griffith, Leif Wells 2017
C. Griffith, L. Wells, *Electron: From Beginner to Pro*, https://doi.org/10.1007/978-1-4842-2826-5_12

Installing the Quick Start

As with each of these examples, we are using the Electron Quick Start example. We will use git clone to create a new copy of the quick start in a new folder, in this case named splash-window-example. First, open terminal and navigate to the folder where you would like to place your code.

```
git clone https://github.com/electron/electron-quick-start splash-window-example
```

Next, change your active directory to splash-window-example.

```
cd splash-window-example
```

Now, we need to install the dependencies:

```
npm install
```

Finally, reset Git with

```
git init
```

Now that you have our example project installed, type npm start into your terminal application just to make sure the application loads and runs as expected.

Setting Up a Splash Window

Now that you have created your splash-window-example project and installed dependencies, we should update some code to make this project uniquely ours.

In your code editor, find the package.json file in the root of your project and open it to make the following changes in bold:

```json
{
  "name": "splash-window-example",
  "version": "1.0.1",
  "description": "An example app using a splash window",
  "main": "main.js",
  "scripts": {
    "start": "electron ."
  },
  "repository": "",
  "keywords": [
    "Electron",
    "splash",
    "window",
    "example"
  ],
  "author": "Your Name Here",
  "license": "CC0-1.0",
  "devDependencies": {
    "electron": "~1.6.2"
  }
}
```

Best Practice: When you use a starter project to build your application, it is important to remember that the original author's information is in the package.json file. Since you are not going to be committing code back to the starter project, it is important for you to update this information to avoid problems. And try to remember to keep information like version and description in your package.json file up to date.

Changes to the package.json aren't necessary, but we like to start with this first because when we forget to do it we end up doing it later anyway. First we updated the name value to splash-window-example. Next we updated the version to 1.0.1 (but you can use any number you'd like). We've updated the keywords array with the words Electron, splash, window, and example. Finally, we changed the author value. In the code snippet above it says "Your Name Here," but you can enter your name.

Creating the Splash Window File

Our next step will be to create the file and code needed to create our splash window. Since the quick start code already uses the index.html file as the starting point for the application's user interface, we will continue using it but update the main.js file to open the splash window first. But before we do that, let's create some new code.

In the root of your project use your code editor to create a file named splash.html and place the following code inside it.

```html
<!DOCTYPE html>
<html>
  <head>
    <meta charset="UTF-8">
    <title></title>
  </head>
  <body>

  </body>
</html>
```

Yeah, this is really basic HTML but we have to start somewhere, right? Now, open up the main.js file that is on the root of your project. This starting point of your application is we need to modify it to open our new splash window file. Near the top of the file, find the line that says `let mainWindow` and place the following code in bold beneath it.

```js
let mainWindow
let splashWindow

function createSplashWindow() {
  splashWindow = new BrowserWindow({
    width: 320,
    height: 240,
    frame: false,
    resizable: false,
    backgroundColor: '#FFF',
    alwaysOnTop: true,
    show: false
  })
```

```
splashWindow.loadURL(url.format({
  pathname: path.join(__dirname, 'splash.html'),
  protocol: 'file',
  slashes: true
}))

splashWindow.on('closed', () => {
  splashWindow = null
})

splashWindow.once('ready-to-show', () => {
  splashWindow.show()
})
}
```

On the first line, we create the splashWindow variable that we can reference from anywhere in our main.js file. The createSplashWindow method is the next piece of code. In the first section, we are creating a BrowserWindow object using the width, height, frame, resizable, backgroundColor, alwaysOnTop, and show properties. Let's evaluate these properties so that we understand why we are setting these properties with these values.

First, we are setting the width and height to arbitrary numbers – your typical size of 320 by 240 pixels. These numbers may change depending on the design of the content you may be placing inside your splash window. For now, since our splash window will be basically blank, we'll go with this size. The next property, frame, is the property that sets the frame around the window. For our styling purposes, we're going to set frame to false so there will not be a border around our splash window. The resizable property controls whether the user can resize our splash window. Combined with having no frame, this is a visual indication to the user that this window doesn't expect any interaction. Finally, we have the alwaysOnTop and show properties. We want the splash window to appear above all of our other windows, so we need alwaysOnTop to be set to true. If we did not use the alwaysOnTop setting, or if we set it to false, the next window we created would appear over our splash window. Setting the show property to false gives us the ability to display our splash window once it is ready. Later in this method we use the 'ready-to-show' event to show our splash window.

In the next section of our createSplashWindow method we load the splash.html file into our BrowserWindow object using BrowserWindow's loadURL method. This method uses the path module that is loading earlier in our code (not represented in the snippet above).

The last two sections of code inside createSplashWindow are event listeners. We listen for the closed event occurring from the splashWindow so we can remove the splashWindow from memory by setting it to null. Since we have set our splash window to be created with the show property set to false, this is where we make our splash window visible.

Now that you've created the createSplashWindow method, we need to call it. In the code, find the line where the 'ready' event listener is set and change createWindow to the following:

```
app.on('ready', createSplashWindow)
```

Open up your terminal application, navigate to your project folder and run the npm start command to get a visual idea of where we are so far (Figure 12-1).

Figure 12-1. *Our initial splash window*

OK, so it's not very exiting – the programmer's equivalent of ghosts roasting marshmallows in a blizzard. This is the reason designers are on our projects. Let's add a little magic to our splash window display.

Showing the Version in Our Splash Window

Something commonly displayed in a splash window is the version of your application. While we could simply put some text in our HTML file to display the version, that would mean that we would have to remember to update that item to keep it in sync with the real version number. In our project we track the version inside package.json file. Keeping the version number in one place is a good idea, so let's use Electron to grab that version number and display it inside our splash window.

The first thing we need to do is retrieve our version number. Open up the main.js file found at the root of your project. At the top of the file where several modules are created, add the code in bold below.

```
const electron = require('electron')
// Module to control application life.
const app = electron.app
// Inter-Process Communication (IPC)
const ipcMain = electron.ipcMain
// Module to create native browser window.
const BrowserWindow = electron.BrowserWindow
```

We added a comment here to remind us that this code adds the IPC module to our main.js file. Now, scroll to the bottom of the file where you see the comment included in the following snippet and add:

```
// In this file you can include the rest of your app's specific main process
// code. You can also put them in separate files and require them here.

//SPLASH WINDOW: REQUEST FOR VERSION
ipcMain.on('get-version', event => {
  console.log('app version: ', app.getVersion())
  event.sender.send('set-version', app.getVersion())
})
```

In the earlier chapter covering IPC, we covered how this works, but let's review this code here as a reminder. Inside the main.js file we added the ipcMain module, which is required to allow the Main Process to send and receive messages to and from the Renderer process. In the second snippet we added an event listener for the 'get-version' event. When we receive that event, we get the version using the getVersion method on our app object and send the version back to the sender. That version number is the string that appears in the package.json file. Remember, we changed that earlier in the chapter. Inside the listener we also have a console.log command that displays our version number in the terminal window.

Now that our code is set to get the version and display the version number in the terminal window, we need to get the splash window to trigger the event. Open the splash.html file and add the following code just below the closing body tag (</ body>):

```
<script>
    const { ipcRenderer } = require('electron')

    ipcRenderer.send('get-version')

</script>
```

Inside the script tag we imported the ipcRenderer module and sent the 'get-version' event to the Main Process.

Now that we've set up code to get the version number, let's take a look at what that looks like (Figure 12-2).

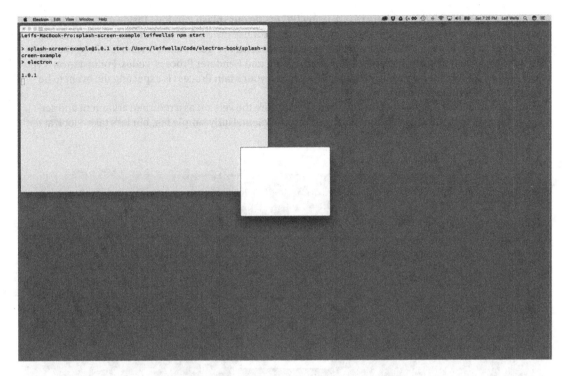

Figure 12-2. *The application version number appears in the terminal window*

Notice that you can see "1.0.1" in the terminal window. Yay! If you want to experiment further, you can quit your application, open the package.json file, and change the version value and test your application again.

Now let's make the version number appear inside the splash window. Open the splash.html and add a paragraph tag inside the body tag to the file like it is below, and update the code inside the script tag to listen for the 'set-version' event.

```
<html>
  <head>
    <meta charset="UTF-8">
    <title></title>
  </head>
  <body>
      <p>version <span id="versionSpan"></span></p>
  </body>
  <script>
    const { ipcRenderer } = require('electron')

    ipcRenderer.on('set-version', (event, arg) => {

      const versionSpan = document.getElementById('versionSpan')
      versionSpan.innerHTML = arg
    })
    ipcRenderer.send('get-version')

  </script>
</html>
```

As you can see here, this is where we are using IPC inside our splash window. Inside our script tag, we create the constant ipcRenderer, the IPC module required for use inside the Renderer Process. We use the ipcRenderer to first listen for the 'set-version' event, then to send the 'get-version' event. It is important to note that these event name strings match in both the Main and Renderer Process' codes. For instance, if you send a 'get-version' event from your Renderer Process and your Main Process is expecting the event to be 'my-get-version', your communication will fail.

Inside our listener for the 'set-version' event, we capture the version as a returned argument and set code in the span with the id of 'versionSpan' with the argument. Fairly simple fair, but let's take a look at the result (Figure 12-3).

Figure 12-3. *The version number is displayed in the splash window*

Nice! As we said earlier, a designer would hate your new splash window, but we have the information we wanted: a splash window that displays the version number of our application. But we are far from being finished. We need to display the main application window now, right?

Loading the Main Window

Now that our simple splash window is appearing when we start our application, we need to show our main window. Open up the main.js file and add the following code listed in bold.

```
splashWindow.once('ready-to-show', () => {
  splashWindow.show()
  createWindow()
})
```

All we are basically doing here is calling the createWindow method inside our splashWindow's 'ready-to-show' event listener. Let's see what happens when we run the npm start command now (Figure 12-4).

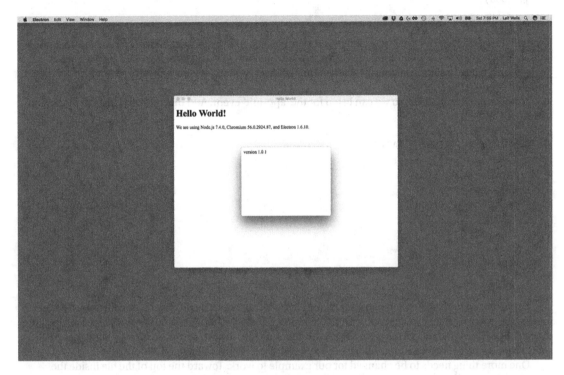

Figure 12-4. *The splash window appears above the main window*

That's great. We're done. Let's pack up and go home.

OK, so, maybe that wasn't all that great after all. First, our splash window stays there on top of our main window, immovable and in the way. Second, both windows appear to load immediately and at the same time. That's mostly because these windows are very simple and don't require a lot of CPU power to push to the screen. We need to update our code to make our splash window and main window behave like we wish.

Setting Up the Main Window

To make our splash window example work as we would like we need to set up our simple main window to fake as though our application takes a few seconds to load so that we can see how a splash window really works. So, let's get started.

To start off, let's update the renderer.js file to simulate the application loading something. Think of this like the time it would take to load data from a local or online database. To demonstrate this, we will add a timer to the main window.

Open your renderer.js file and add the following code.

```
// This file is required by the index.html file and will
// be executed in the renderer process for that window.
// All of the Node.js APIs are available in this process.
const { ipcRenderer } = require('electron')
```

```
setTimeout(() => {
    ipcRenderer.send('app-init')
}, 5000)
```

As a reminder, our renderer.js file is the Javascript file linked to the index.html. It controls Electron's Renderer Process. The code we just added is fairly simple. Just like in our splash.html file, we've added the ipcRenderer constant so we can send messages through Electron's IPC feature. Below our ipcRenderer declaration we have a simple Javascript timeout function, setTimeout, which waits five seconds to send an 'app-init' event to the Main Process.

Now open the main.js file so we can listen for the 'app-init' event. Add the following code to the bottom of the file.

```
// MAIN WINDOW: FINISHED LOADING
ipcMain.on('app-init', event => {
  if (splashWindow) {
    setTimeout(() => {
      splashWindow.close()
    }, 2000)
  }

  mainWindow.show()
})
```

Earlier we added the ipcMain constant to our file, so we can use it again here. This code is our listener for the 'app-init' event that we just set up in the renderer.js file. The first thing you see is that we are checking to see if the splashWindow exists before setting another time out for two seconds before closing the splashWindow using the close method. Finally, we make a call to show the mainWindow.

One more thing needs to be changed for our example to work. Toward the top of the file inside the createWindow method you need to make the following change in bold so the main window doesn't automatically show.

```
function createWindow () {
  // Create the browser window.
  mainWindow = new BrowserWindow({width: 800, height: 600, show: false})
```

So, before we test our new code, let's review what it is doing. First, the Main Process creates and shows the splash window. When the splash window is shown, the main window (the Renderer Process) is loaded, which triggers a five-second timer that then fires off a 'app-init' event, which when captured in the Main Process shows the main window, and creates a two-second timer that dismisses the splash window.

At this point, a window shot is pointless as what you will experience when running this code is animated windows. So, run the npm start command and see your splash window in action.

Summary

In this chapter, we created an example application that uses a splash window to create the impression with users that our application has started to cover for any startup activities that may slow down rendering of the main application window. To create our splash window, we used BrowserWindow's frameless, resizable, and alwaysOnTop parameters to make the splash window appear differently than your main application window. We used IPC to get the version number and display it in our splash window as well as have our main window tell our Main Process when it is ready. And, finally, we used a timer to momentarily hold our splash window on screen before making it disappear.

CHAPTER 13

■ ■ ■

Debugging Your Electron Application

Hopefully, the only debugging that you have had to do, so far, while exploring this book, has been to fix a simple typo. But, there will come a time as you begin to develop your Electron application that you will need to debug your code in a more complex fashion. In this chapter, we will look at some of the tools and techniques available to you.

Chromium's Dev Tools

You should already be familiar with the primary tool that you can use to debug your Renderer process, the built-in Dev Tools from Chromium. By default, the electron-quick-start code base has these tools enabled. To display the DevTools, simply call

```
mainWindow.webContents.openDevTools()
```

This command will then open a copy of the DevTools within our application's window, as shown in Figure 13-1. These are the same tools that you have probably used when debugging in Google Chrome.

© Chris Griffith, Leif Wells 2017
C. Griffith, L. Wells, *Electron: From Beginner to Pro*, https://doi.org/10.1007/978-1-4842-2826-5_13

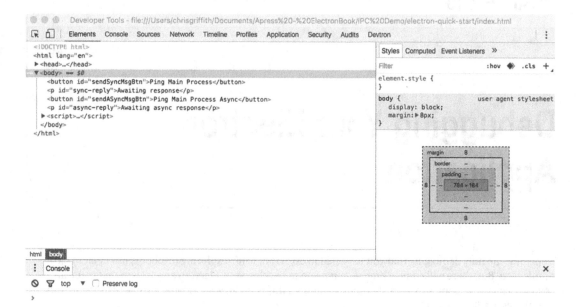

Figure 13-1. *Chrome Dev Tools*

We can inspect individual HTML elements and explore the CSS styles for them as well. The familiar JavaScript console is available, allowing us to examine our JavaScript code's outputs.

There are two other related Electron commands you should be aware of. If you want to close the instance of the DevTools, you can simply call

```
mainWindow.webContents.closeDevTools()
```

But, rather than manage the hiding and showing of the DevTools while you are developing, often an additional set of menu items is added that is specific to debugging. This is a technique we use when developing our Electron project. It is nothing fancy, just a top-level menu named Debug and single menu item that allows us to toggle the display of the DevTools. The actual command is simply this:

```
mainWindow.webContents.toggleDevTools()
```

Here is the menu snippet for our Debug menu that you can insert into your menu definition:

```
{
  label: 'Debug',
  submenu: [
    {
      label: 'Toggle Developer Tools',
      accelerator: (function () {
        if (process.platform === 'darwin') {
          return 'Alt+Command+I'
        } else {
          return 'Ctrl+Shift+I'
        }
      })(),
```

```
    click: function (item, focusedWindow) {
      if (focusedWindow) {
        focusedWindow.toggleDevTools()
      }
    }
  }
]
}
```

We are passing the reference to the active BrowserWindow to our click function with the focusedWindow parameter. This parameter will allow us to toggle the DevTools on the correct window if our Electron application has multiple windows.

For more on using Chrome's DevTools, see `https://developer.chrome.com/devtools` for a detailed tutorial on using them.

Debugging the Main Process

While the Chrome DevTools allows us to debug the Renderer Process, debugging the Main Process requires some additional changes to do so. Since the Main Process is our Node process, it executes without being directly exposed. To debug any code that is running within this process, we must rely on external debuggers that support the V8 debugging protocol. Two common tools that support this are VS Code and node-inspector.

Debugging the Main Process in VS Code

One of the easiest methods to debug Electron's Main Process is to use the built-in debugging tools in VS Code. VS Code has built-in debugging support for Node.js and can debug JavaScript, TypeScript, and any other language that gets transpiled to JavaScript.

■ **Note**　For those unfamiliar with the term transpiling, it is the process of taking one language and re-creating it in another. Examples are writing in CoffeeScript and producing standard JavaScript.

To use this, we need to add a debug configuration to our project. First, we need to create a .vscode directory if one does not already exist, at the top level of our project. Within this directory, create a launch.json file. This file will contain the debug configurations that VS Code will use to connect to our instance of our Electron app.

```
{
  "version": "0.2.0",
  "configurations": [
    {
      "name": "Debug Electron Main Process",
      "type": "node",
      "request": "launch",
      "cwd": "${workspaceRoot}",
      "runtimeExecutable": "${workspaceRoot}/node_modules/.bin/electron",
      "program": "${workspaceRoot}/main.js"
    }
  ]
}
```

For Windows, use "${workspaceRoot}/node_modules/.bin/electron.cmd" for a runtimeExecutable.

With VS Code set up to debug our Main Process, let's try it out. Add a breakpoint in your main.js file by double-clicking in the left gutter on the line you want the breakpoint to be added, as shown in Figure 13-2. Next, switch to the Debug view in VS Code (Shift-Cmd-D).

Figure 13-2. *VS Code's Debug Panel*

Next, make sure the Debug Electron Main Process configuration is selected from the drop-down menu in the debug pane, as shown in Figure 13-3.

Figure 13-3. *The Debug Target option menu*

Then click the green debug button next to that menu. VS Code will then launch Electron for you and once a breakpoint is reached, give you the ability inspect your code's state, as shown in Figure 13-4. In earlier version of VS Code, there were reported issues using this. The suggested workaround was to uncheck both the Exceptions breakpoint options. According to the filed issue on Github (`https://github.com/Microsoft/vscode/issues/16321`), this problem has been resolved. But there is nothing more frustrating than not being able to debug to a bug.

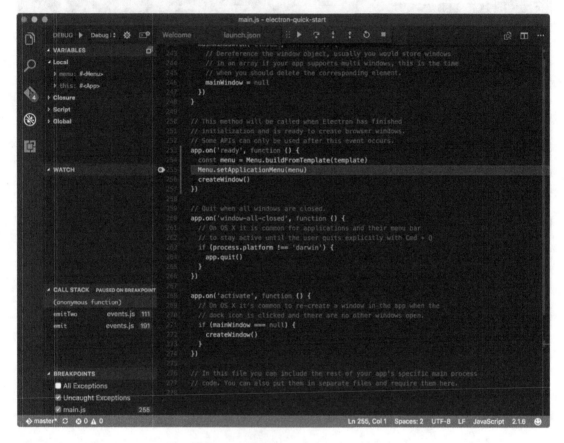

Figure 13-4. *The debugger in VS Code for the main process*

For more information on debugging with VS Code, visit `https://code.visualstudio.com/Docs/editor/debugging`.

Debugging the Main Process in node-inspector

If your background is more of a NodeJs developer, rather than a front-end developer, you might be more familiar using a tool like node-inspector, as shown in Figure 13-5. To use this solution with Electron, we need to perform several installation steps.

First, we need to install the node-gyp required tools. For those unfamiliar with node-gyp, it is a cross platform command-line tool written in Node.js for compiling native add-on modules for Node.js. Detailed instructions for this installation can be found at: https://github.com/nodejs/node-gyp#installation

Next, we can install node-inspector itself. This package wraps the node-inspector package to work with Electron.

```
npm install node-inspector --save-dev
```

Now, the next installation is the node-pre-gyp package. This package is an interface between npm and node-gyp, and allows the use of C++ addons from third party binaries.

```
npm install node-pre-gyp
```

With both packages installed, let's go ahead and recompile the node-inspector v8 modules for Electron.

```
$ node_modules/.bin/node-pre-gyp --target=VERSION --runtime=electron --fallback-to-build
--directory node_modules/v8-debug/ --dist-url=https://atom.io/download/atom-shell reinstall
$ node_modules/.bin/node-pre-gyp --target=VERSION --runtime=electron --fallback-to-build
--directory node_modules/v8-profiler/ --dist-url=https://atom.io/download/atom-shell
reinstall
```

■ **Note**　You will need to update the target argument to be your Electron version number.

Now, we need to be able to run Electron with the debug port enabled. This is done with a command-line switch, --debug=[port]. With this switch, Electron will listen for the V8 debugger protocol messages. The default port is 5858. You can either launch Electron directly from the command line using

```
electron --debug=5858 .
```

or you can edit the scripts in package.json file to include this switch:

```
"scripts": {
  "start": "electron --debug=5858 ."
}
```

If you want to pause execution on the first line of JavaScript, use the –debug-brk switch instead

```
electron --debug-brk=5858 .
```

With Electron running, open another terminal window to be able to start the node-inspector server.

```
ELECTRON_RUN_AS_NODE=true path/to/electron.app|exe node_modules/node-inspector/bin/
inspector.js
```

Now, open http://127.0.0.1:8080/debug?ws=127.0.0.1:8080&port=5858 in Chrome. You may have to click pause if starting with --debug-brk to force the UI to update.

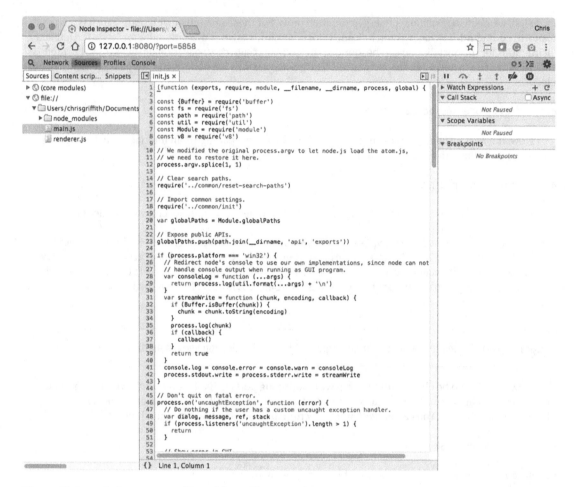

Figure 13-5. *node-inspector working with our Electron app*

You can now use the node-inspector to debug your application.

Chrome DevTools Extensions

Chrome's DevTools can be extended using add-on extensions. This can be quite useful, as you will probably be building your Electron application with an additional framework like React or Angular. The following DevTools Extensions are tested and guaranteed to work in Electron:

- Ember Inspector
- React Developer Tools
- Backbone Debugger
- jQuery Debugger
- AngularJS Batarang

- Vue.js devtools

- Cerebral Debugger

- Redux DevTools Extension

To use one of these extensions, visit `http://electron.atom.io/docs/tutorial/devtools-extension/` for the steps for their installation.

Devtron

There is also a dedicated DevTools extension just for Electron known as Devtron. This extension was built to focus on some Electron-specific needs, like monitoring IPC messages and linting. Installing Devtron is on a project-by-project basis. For our look at what this extension can do, we will use the sample app we built when exploring Electron's IPC system. With your command line's working directory set to that project, type in the following command:

```
npm install devtron --save-dev
```

This will install the package for use as a development-only dependency. Go ahead and launch our Electron application using npm start.

To use Devtron with your Electron application, you will need to be able to access Chrome's DevTools, as shown in Figure 13-6. The DevTools extension should be now loaded and available as an option along the top of the DevTools window.

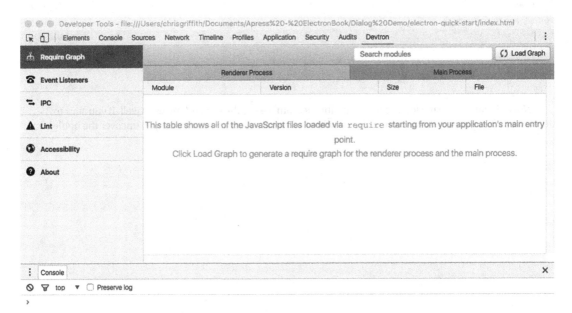

Figure 13-6. *Devtron's user interface*

Let's explore the five sections in Devtron

Require Graph

As your Electron application grows in complexity, you will be relying on the use of more and more libraries. The Require Graph pane, shown in Figure 13-7, allows you to view and trace the loading order of your JavaScript files. To see the output of this inspection, click the Load Graph button.

Figure 13-7. *The Require Graph interface*

Not only can we see the load order of our libraries, but we see the dependencies as well. If you start to encounter startup time issues or rendering slowdowns, using this graph might help you uncover the bottleneck.

Event Listeners

Devtron enables you to explore the events and listeners that your app has registered, as shown in Figure 13-8. Unfortunately, it will only listen on the core Electron APIs, meaning that none of your custom listeners will be tracked, like a button press in the UI. But as you build out your application, you will begin to interact more with these core events to provide your user a more native application experience, and you will want to ensure they are properly registered and active.

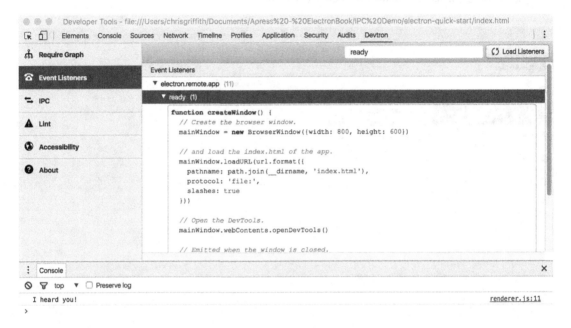

Figure 13-8. *Devtron's Event Listener interface*

Here we see our application's createWindow function that is call from the electron.remote.app ready event.

IPC Monitor

During our exploration of using Electron's IPC module, we tracked the messages using simple console logging. Devtron's IPC monitoring panel allows you to track and inspect the IPC messages (both synchronous and asynchronous), as shown in Figure 13-9. Since the IPC messaging traffic can be quite heavy in a complex application, you need to manually enable the event recording. Click the Record in the toolbar to start the recording. If you have any IPC messages you can trigger, go ahead and trigger them. Each IPC channel is logged, along with the arguments that are passed.

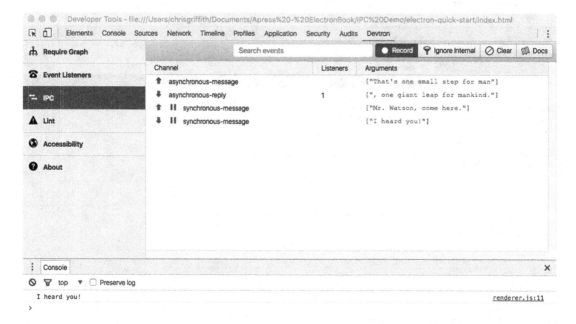

Figure 13-9. *Devtron's IPC monitoring interface*

Here we see the results of triggering our sample sync and async IPC messages from our sample IPC application in Chapter 6.

Linter

Devtron also provides some application-level linting that you can invoke. While it does not go deep into your code and check for application-specific issues, the Devtron linter will check your application for some common issues like handling various error events, as shown in Figure 13-10.

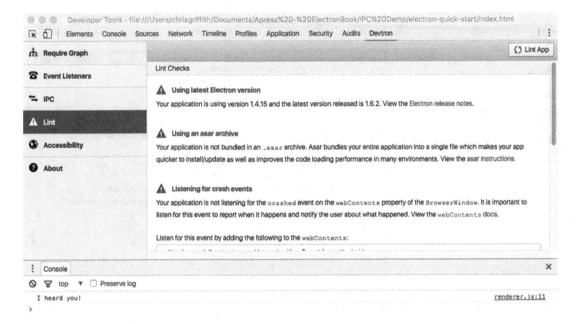

Figure 13-10. *Devtron Lint Check interface*

For our simple IPC demo application, the linter reported:

- We were not using the most current version of Electron.

- We had bundled our app into an asar archive.

- We do not handle the crashed event.

- We do not handle the unresponsive event.

- We do not handle the uncaughtException event.

While not an issue for our demo, when building a releasable application, these are items that your code should address.

Accessibility

Devtron will also perform a basic accessibility audit of your application. Click the Audit App button to have Devtron scan your app for common accessibility issues, as shown in Figure 13-11.

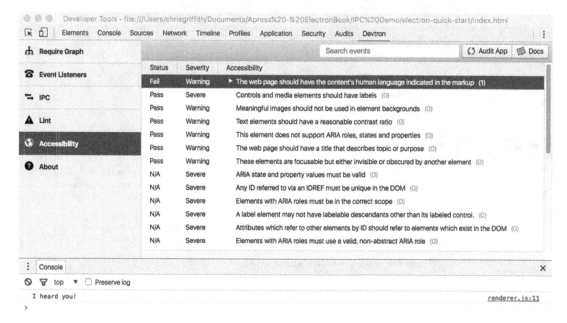

Figure 13-11. *Devtron's Accessibility interface*

For example, we failed the accessibility requirement to have the content's human language indicated. This is an easy fix to perform. In the index.html, replace <html> with <html lang="en">. To learn more about what each of these issues refers to, use the docs button to view a detailed guide on the rule Devtron uses.

As you can see, Devtron can provide some useful tools when debugging your Electron application.

Spectron

Most commercial grade applications will employ some form of automated testing for their application. Spectron is a framework that allows you to write your integration tests for your Electron app. It is built using a combination of ChromeDriver and WebdriverIO, so both the Main Process and Renderer Process can be tested.

To install Spectron, simply navigate to your project's main directory and run

```
npm install spectron --save-dev
```

Spectron supports working with continuous integration services like Travis or AppVeyor, and is compatible with many testing libraries like Mocha, Jasmine, and Chai. Now, writing the actual tests is beyond the scope of this book, but to learn more about Spectron, visit https://electron.atom.io/spectron/.

Summary

As developers, you are always striving to ship a product without any bugs or issues. In this chapter, we explored several techniques and tools you can use to debug the special nature of an Electron application. For those looking to leverage integration testing of their application, we introduce you to the Spectron module.

CHAPTER 14

■ ■ ■

Testing with Spectron

"Testing is Hard."

This is something you may have heard before. Experienced developers have heard it a number of times over their careers. Testing, be it unit testing or end-to-end testing, seems to have fluctuated in and out of vogue with many developers over the years. But testing has always been important. The ability to test an application in an automated way is an invaluable asset to individual developers and Enterprise teams alike.

Since you are reading this chapter, we will assume you have already decided that testing your Electron application is a great idea. We agree. And, so it would seem, the developers on the Electron team agree, as well, because Spectron, a test harness for Electron, was created to assist Electron developers with their testing practice. Spectron allows developers a practical way to load their application and test your implementation of the Electron API as well as your own code. Spectron has a robust API that allows developers to test properties of windows created, the webContents object, and anything else you would like to use from the Electron API to test your application.

As we have stated in earlier chapters, we are focused on providing examples of code for Electron; so in this chapter we will not be discussing testing of your web-standard application, the code that runs in the Renderer Process. The assumption is that you will be unit testing your own code externally to Electron, which is advisable (having more automated tests is always a good thing). This chapter will focus on testing the Main Process and then adding some simple code to our Renderer Process as an example of a Renderer to Main Process test.

In this chapter, we will set up Spectron and use Mocha and Chai to run a few simple tests on elements of the Electron API and on custom methods. We will use Spectron as our test runner, the library that controls our tests. Mocha is the testing framework, the library that gives us a defined structure for our tests, which we will use for our tests. You will see methods named "describe," "beforeEach," and "it," which are the fundamental methods of Mocha. Chai is the assertion library we will use inside Mocha's "it" methods and is the meat of our tests. Chai assists us by validating the conditions that we are testing. You will see how these three libraries work as we move through this exercise.

Getting Started

As with each of these examples, we are using the Electron Quick Start example. We will use git clone to create a new copy of the quick start in a new folder, in this case named spectron-test-example. First, open the terminal and navigate to the folder where you would like to place your code.

```
git clone https://github.com/electron/electron-quick-start spectron-test-example
```

Next, change your active directory to the new directory:

```
cd spectron-test-example
```

Now, we need to install the dependencies:

```
npm install
```

Finally, reset Git with this command:

```
git init
```

Now we need to install Spectron, the testing harness that will allow us to run tests on Electron projects. We'll install Spectron into our project as a developer dependency using the `--save-dev` setting. Type this command into your terminal and hit enter:

```
npm install --save-dev spectron
```

Spectron is very flexible in that it allows you to use any number of testing frameworks to run your tests. For this chapter, we will be adding Mocha and Chai. From the Mocha Website at `https://mochajs.org/` Mocha is described as "a feature-rich JavaScript test framework running on Node.js and in the browser." We've checked with many Node developers who recommend Mocha as an industry standard. If you've done some testing in the past, you may have already installed Mocha globally. We'll install Mocha in the project as a developer dependency by running the following command in the terminal application:

```
npm install --save-dev mocha
```

If you'd like, you may choose to install Mocha globally with this command:

```
npm install -g mocha
```

Chai is an assertion library, a tool that verifies that the assumptions used in testing Node and browser corrections are correct. In testing, assertions will look like `expect(1).toEqual(1)`, except where you see the first number 1, a test would provide an application's condition, then along with the expected condition (the second number 1). In between the conditions, in this case toEqual, is a phrase that expresses the test for those conditions. Chai allows developers to more easily test their code and has three different assertion styles: expect, should, and assert. These styles make Chai very flexible for developers. We'll be using expect in our testing, which you will see later. Install Chai into the project as developer dependencies using this command:

```
npm install --save-dev chai
```

Now that you have our example project installed, type `npm start` into your terminal application just to make sure the application loads and runs as expected.

Let's take a moment to modify this package.json file to match our own by updating some nodes.

1. Change the name node to "spectron-test-example."

2. Change the version number to "0.0.1" since we are just starting out.

3. In the description let's use something like "A sample Electron application to demonstrate testing using Spectron."

4. Remove the repository node. If you decide to put your results in a repository, you can change re-add this node with the correct address.

5. Keywords can be "Electron," "Spectron," "Testing," "Mocha," "Chai."

6. "author": Your name goes here.

7. Let's change the "license" node to "MIT."

Since we have the package.json open, let's add one more important element that will assist us in running our tests. In the "scripts" section, add the "test" line in the package.json file as you see below:

```
"scripts": {
    "start": "electron .",
    "test": "mocha"
},
```

This is a really simple line that calls Mocha, which will run our tests. We invoke this script by typing npm test into our terminal application. Of course, you could just type mocha into the terminal and get the same result, but the practice of creating a script item is enforced here because often testing requires more steps than just invoking Mocha.

We aren't ready to run our test script yet, but before moving forward, now would be a good time to run the npm start command again to make sure that our application starts and everything is working.

Adding a Test File

Now that we have our application set up, let's get our testing set up. When you invoke Mocha this way, Mocha expects to find a test file, named test.js by default, in the current working folder. Add a new file to the root of our project and name it "test.js". In your own projects you can move the file to another folder, but if you do, you will need to change the "test" script in the package.json file to reflect that change. For instance, mocha / testing/test.js would be the required change if you moved the test file into a folder named "testing."

Add the following code to the "test.js" file:

```
const electron = require('electron')
const Application = require('spectron').Application
const expect = require('chai').expect

describe('SPECTRON EXAMPLE', function() {
  this.timeout(10000)
  global.app = null

  before(() => {
    app = new Application({
      path: electron,
      args: ['.'],
    })
    return app.start()
            .then(() => {
              app.client.waitUntilWindowLoaded()
                app.browserWindow.show()
                return app
              })
  })

  after(() => {
    if(app && app.isRunning()) {
      return app.stop()
    }
})})
```

At the top of our file we require the modules required for testing to work. First, we create an electron variable. Next, we add Spectron's Application module, which will allow us to create a link to our application. We use the electron variable to create the path to the install location of Electron (inside our node_modules folder) when we use our Application variable to create our test application. The next line creates an expect variable giving us the expect style support from Chai.

The rest of the code is typical testing boilerplate using describe, before and after, to control our test. The describe function is the main structure of the test. When we run our test, the test title 'SPECTRON EXAMPLE' will appear in the terminal as a visual cue. You will see how it works. Inside the describe we first create a timeout variable for Mocha and Spectron that sets the amount of time they will wait for tests to run. We have set this variable to 10000, which translates to 10 seconds. When testing your application in the future, you may need to adjust this time higher if, for instance, your application loads a lot of data from the Internet. Next, we create a global variable called app that we create inside the beforeEach method and use throughout the tests. We create our application using the Application module we added earlier. Note the path property inside the argument being passed to Application, which we mentioned earlier. The args property at the bottom of the before you see we run app.start which starts our application. This means that before any test runs, we start our application. This is what is called "stand up," or standing up our application.

In the after method we test to see if the application exists and that the application is still running, and if so, we stop it. This is called "tear down," or tearing down our application.

It is important to understand what this means to us from an experiential aspect. When we run tests, what we will see is the application's window open and then close fairly quickly. The tests we will be running are very fast, so the application will only appear for a moment.

There are two monumentally important items to remember about this code. First, note the structure within the before method. See how it is using Promises to run the app.start process? We will be using this type of syntax throughout our tests. Second, note that we are using the arrow syntax, which is, () =>, in our before and after methods. This modern JavaScript syntax assists us in providing easier scoping for our code. But, look at the describe method. It is not using an arrow function. It is actually using an anonymous function. Why is that? Because there is a bug in Spectron that will make your testing not work. So, please remember this and avoid the hours of pain we experienced.

Now that we have our structure set up, let's add an actual test. Inside the describe method and below and outside of the after method, add the following code:

```
it('should open a window', () => {
    return app.client.waitUntilWindowLoaded()
        .getWindowCount()
          .then( count => {
            expect(count).to.equal(1)
          })
  })
})
```

Here we are testing to see if a window is opened by our application. If you remember from earlier examples that are based on electron-quick-start, opening a window is the first thing that happens. Note the title "should open a window." Coupled with the title in the describe method, it should read like a sentence: "SPECTRON EXAMPLE" "should open a window." This is standard testing practice and will make more sense once you see the test running.

Notice the structure inside our it method. Since we are building a Promise chain, the first line begins with return. Here we use the app.client.waitUntilWindowLoaded method from the Spectron API to wait for the application to load before we begin our test. The app, of course, is the Application instance we created earlier in our before method. The app.client is a reference to the client property of the Application instance, which is an instance of WebDriverIO, a great library that allows developers to control browsers and mobile applications. Finally, the waitUntilWindowLoaded does exactly what it name says: waits for the window to load. This is a helpful best practice that will avoid a test trying to run before the application is fully loaded.

In the next line, the getWindowCount method is called, which returns a Promise that is captured inside our then method's code. Then the actual test is performed using the expect style of testing provided by Chai. Note the syntax of the expect chain. Chai's syntax makes testing a little easier. It reads like a sentence. *"Expect (the count) to equal 1."* Makes sense?

Before we run our test, please take note that we have not changed our application's code as of yet. We know that the application runs because we set it up and tested it using the npm start command. We will need to modify our application's code, but for now we are ready to run our test. In the terminal, enter the following command:

```
npm test
```

Figure 14-1 shows the results of our test inside the terminal.

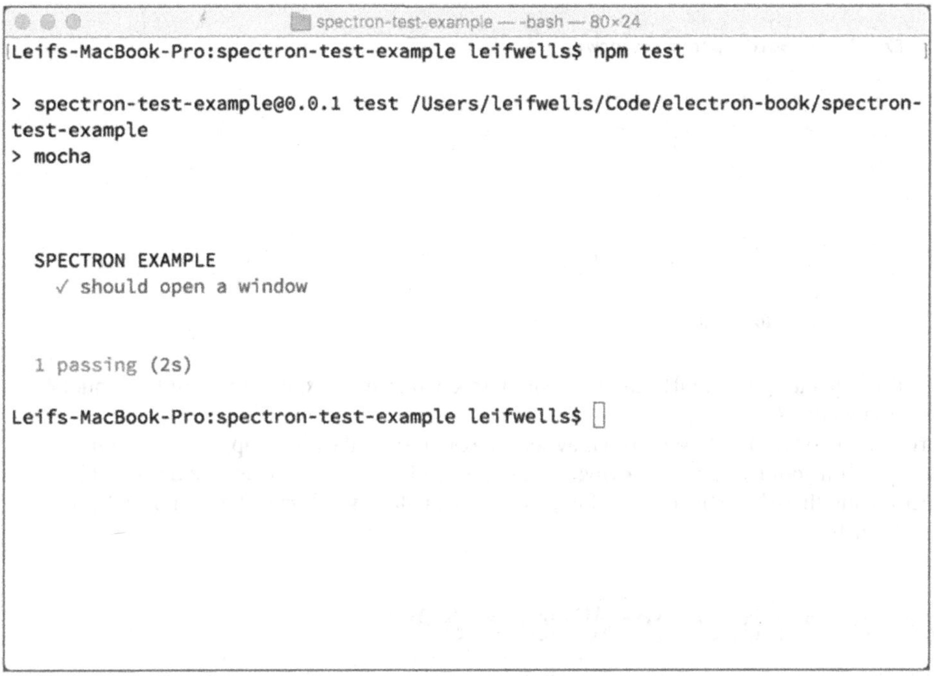

```
● ● ●                    spectron-test-example — -bash — 80×24
Leifs-MacBook-Pro:spectron-test-example leifwells$ npm test

> spectron-test-example@0.0.1 test /Users/leifwells/Code/electron-book/spectron-
test-example
> mocha



  SPECTRON EXAMPLE
    ✓ should open a window


  1 passing (2s)

Leifs-MacBook-Pro:spectron-test-example leifwells$ 
```

Figure 14-1. *Our first passing test*

Note, again, how the results appear in the terminal and can be read like sentences. The green check and the end results of "1 passing (2s)" in green means we have successfully passed our single test.

We should break our test so we can see it fail. In the expect line, change the 1 to 2 like so:

```
expect(count).to.equal(2);
```

Now, run npm test again and you should see results like those in Figure 14-2, although you will probably have to scroll up to see it. Notice how the structure of the output has changed to give you information about why the test failed.

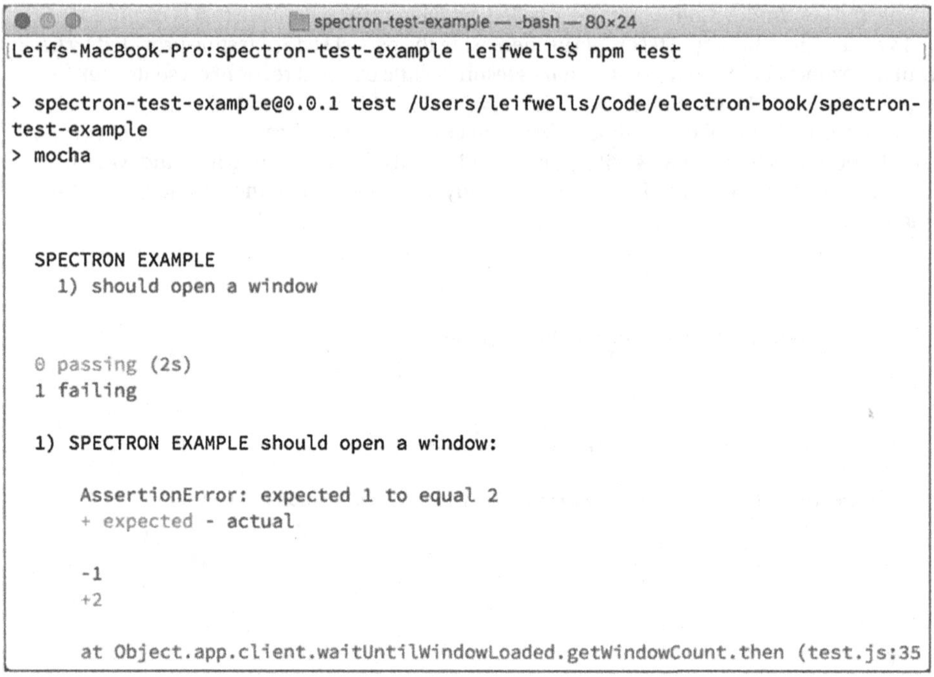

```
●  ●  ●                    spectron-test-example — -bash — 80×24
Leifs-MacBook-Pro:spectron-test-example leifwells$ npm test

> spectron-test-example@0.0.1 test /Users/leifwells/Code/electron-book/spectron-
test-example
> mocha




  SPECTRON EXAMPLE
    1) should open a window


  0 passing (2s)
  1 failing

  1) SPECTRON EXAMPLE should open a window:

     AssertionError: expected 1 to equal 2
     + expected - actual

     -1
     +2

     at Object.app.client.waitUntilWindowLoaded.getWindowCount.then (test.js:35
```

Figure 14-2. *Our first test did not pass!*

"AssertionError: expected 1 to equal 2" matches the syntax of our test, "Expect (the count) to equal 2."
See how it all comes together?

One important note to Windows users: You may see an extra terminal window appear over your
application when you run your tests. It is annoying, but not harmful. There appears to be a bug in either
Electron or Spectron and there have been issues filed about it. Hopefully this bug will be removed by the
time this book is published.

Using Spectron's browserWindow API

Now that we have tested the existence of the application's window and set it to fail, revert that code so that
we have a passing test and we will add more tests.

```
expect(count).to.equal(1)
```

Add the following test below our first test. We've added the first test here to remind you what it should
look like as a passing test:

```
it('should open a working window', () => {
    return app.client.waitUntilWindowLoaded()
        .browserWindow.isVisible()
            .then(res => {
                expect(res).to.be.true
            })
```

```
        .browserWindow.isFocused()
          .then(res => {
            expect(res).to.be.true
          })
        .browserWindow.isMinimized()
          .then(res => {
            expect(res).to.be.false
          })
        .browserWindow.isDevToolsOpened()
          .then(res => {
            expect(res).to.be.false
          })
  })
```

Our "should open a working window" test makes sure that the window we create is visible, is focused, is not minimized and does not have Dev Tools open. Let's see how that works. First, we again are waiting until the application window has loaded with Spectron's `app.client.waitUntilWindowLoaded` call. After that, we have chained together several calls to the `browserWindow` API to get some information. First, we call `browserWindow.isVisible` that returns a promise in which we run our test. Next, we call `browserWindow.isFocused` to assess whether the window is focused. Next, `browserWindow.isMinimized` is called to test whether the window has been minimized on launch. And, finally, we use `browser.isDevToolsOpened` to make sure the Dev Tools aren't opened. Coinicidentally, this is a very practical test seeing as you might run these tests before checking your code into a repository. It would prevent you from committing code that displays the Dev Tools.

Let's run our tests and see the output in the terminal application. Save the test file and run the `npm test` command (Figure 14-3).

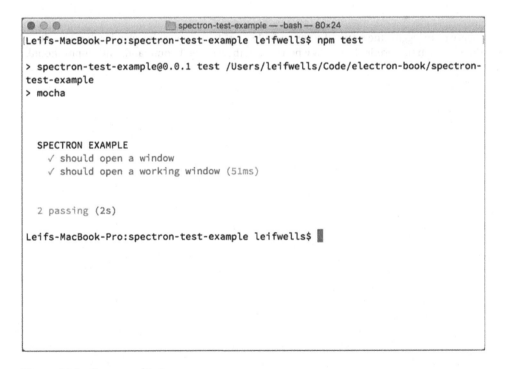

Figure 14-3. *Our second test passes*

Awesome! You passed two tests. But, sometimes testing can make you paranoid. Did we really pass these tests? Let's add a few console calls to the code so we can see them in the terminal window to relieve our stress:

```
it('should open a working window', () => {
    return app.client.waitUntilWindowLoaded()
            .browserWindow.isVisible()
              .then(res => {
                console.log('visible:', res)
                expect(res).to.be.true
              })
            .browserWindow.isFocused()
              .then(res => {
                console.log('focused:', res)
                expect(res).to.be.true
              })
            .browserWindow.isMinimized()
              .then(res => {
                console.log('minimized:', res)
                expect(res).to.be.false
              })
            .browserWindow.isDevToolsOpened()
              .then(res => {
                console.log('devTools:', res)
                expect(res).to.be.false
              })
  })
```

As you can see, we are logging the result (the res variable, "res" for response) received with each call. We should see this output in the terminal window when we run the npm test command. The output should look like that in Figure 14-4.

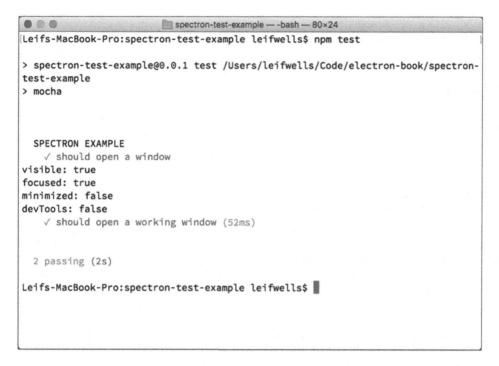

Figure 14-4. *Our second test passing with log messages*

Great. Now you know how you can use the console command to assist with debugging your tests. You may want to remove or comment the console calls as we move forward to our next task, testing the size of our browserWindow.

Another important note that can trip you up. Open your main.js file in the root of our project and uncomment (remove the two slashes in front of the line) of the following line and turn on the DevTools.

```
mainWindow.webContents.openDevTools()
```

Now, run the npm test command again and see what happens. There is not a lot of information in Figure 14-5 to make you understand what is actually making our test fail. Basically, there is a bug in Spectron (https://github.com/electron/spectron/issues/174) that makes the test throw errors when the DevTools are open.

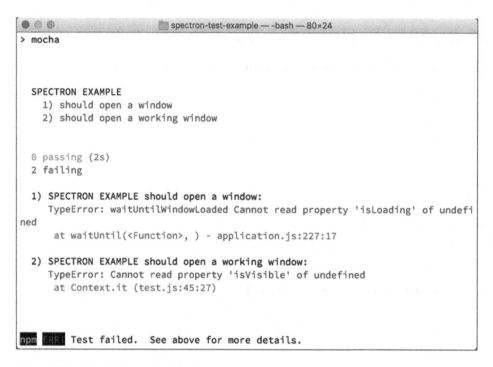

```
  ● ● ●                📁 spectron-test-example — -bash — 80×24
> mocha



  SPECTRON EXAMPLE
    1) should open a window
    2) should open a working window


  0 passing (2s)
  2 failing

  1) SPECTRON EXAMPLE should open a window:
     TypeError: waitUntilWindowLoaded Cannot read property 'isLoading' of undefi
ned
       at waitUntil(<Function>, ) - application.js:227:17

  2) SPECTRON EXAMPLE should open a working window:
     TypeError: Cannot read property 'isVisible' of undefined
       at Context.it (test.js:45:27)


npm ERR! Test failed.  See above for more details.
```

Figure 14-5. *Tests fail when DevTools are open*

Since end-to-end testing like this should be done with production-level code, you would never test with the DevTools open. So, hopefully, if you run into this, you'll remember our tip.

Testing the Size of the browserWindow

Another practical test would be to test the properties of the window we are opening. Your application may open a window that opens windows and dynamically sets their size based on the computer's screen size. If so, you will need to test that. In the following simplified test, we are going to check the bounds of the window, the left, top, width, and height of the window, to test if they are as expected.

Take a quick look inside your main.js file. Inside the createWindow method you will see this line:

```
mainWindow = new BrowserWindow({width: 800, height: 600})
```

From this line we can tell that our window will be 800 by 600 pixels in size. Inside your test.js file, add the following test below the previous test at the bottom of the code inside our describe method.

```
it('should open a window to correct size', () => {
    return app.client.waitUntilWindowLoaded()
            .browserWindow.getBounds()
            .then(res => {
              console.log('bounds:', res)
              expect(res.width).to.equal(800)
              expect(res.height).to.equal(600)
            })})
```

Again, we begin with applying the best practice of waiting for our window to load with `waitUntilWindowLoad`. After the window loads, the `browserWindow.getBounds` API call gets us the bounds object. The browserWindow part of that line represents the Application instance's browserWindow property, which is a reference to the window object that has been created. The getBounds method returns an object via a Promise, which, again, we capture in our then method. Then, we are console logging the results before testing the width and height, and then we are testing those values. Let's run the `npm test` command again to see if our test passes (Figure 14-6).

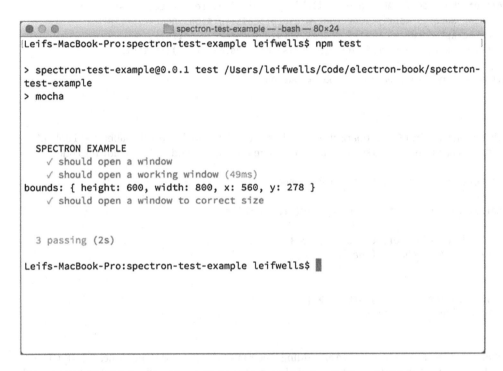

Figure 14-6. Our third test passing with log statement showing the bounds object

Notice the output from the console log command we added for the result listed in the terminal: `bounds: { height: 600, width: 800, x: 560, y: 278 }`. We added that line of code to reveal what the bounds object returned from the `browserWindow.getBounds` API call. It has four properties: x and y for the location of the upper left corner of the window, and `width` and `height` for the width and height of the window. These properties can be used many ways in our tests.

Testing Interactions in the Renderer Process

Testing our application, specifically the part of the project that runs in the Renderer Process, is the next part of our example. In your own Electron applications you will create an application using HTML, CSS, and JavaScript. Our example is built upon the electron-starter project, which is just an HTML file that doesn't really do much, so there isn't very much to test.

Make the Example Interactive

Let's start by updating our HTML. In the root of the project, open the index.html file and add a button to the bottom of the body tag like you see below.

```
<body>
    <h1>Hello World!</h1>
    <!-- All of the Node.js APIs are available in this renderer process. -->
    We are using Node.js <script>document.write(process.versions.node)</script>,
    Chromium <script>document.write(process.versions.chrome)</script>,
    and Electron <script>document.write(process.versions.electron)</script>.

    <button id="foobarButton">Get Foobar</button>

</body>
```

A simple button with the id of "foobarButton" has been added. It also displays the label "Get Foobar." Next, we need to make this button do something. Open the renderer.js file and add the following code:

```
const ipcRenderer = require('electron').ipcRenderer

const foobarButton = document.getElementById('foobarButton')

foobarButton.addEventListener('click', () => {
    ipcRenderer.send('foobar', ['hello'])
})

ipcRenderer.on('barfoo', (event, args) => {
    foobarButton.innerText = args
})
```

Let's carefully review this code. First, we are adding Electron's Inter-Process Communication (IPC) module, which allows the Renderer Process and Main Process to communicate with each other. You can find out more about how IPC works in an earlier chapter of this book. Next, we identify the button with the id of "foobarButton" and save it as the variable foobarButton. In the next section, we add a click event listener to our button, which uses the IPC send method to send an event named "foobar" to the Main Process along with the string "hello" inside the argument array. Finally, we create an IPC listener for the "barfoo" event. This event expects an event and an argument to be coming from our Main Process. We use the argument string to change the text of our button.

So, to recap, we've added a button that, when clicked, sends a message "hello" to the Main Process and then waits for the Main Process to send a message back, which we use to change the button's label. Take a moment and run the npm start command just to make sure you do not receive errors and it lays out like Figure 14-7.

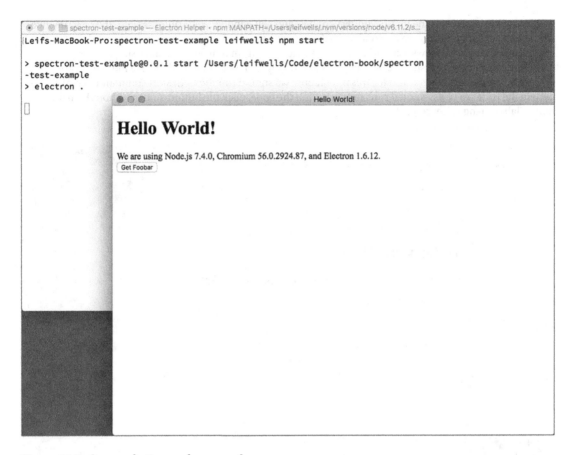

Figure 14-7. *Our new button renders properly*

Now, let's add code to our Main Process to make this actually work. Open the main.js file on your project's root and add the following line near the top of the file, specifically after the electron constant is created:

```
const { ipcMain } = electron
```

Just like the ipcRenderer instance we created in the renderer.js file, the ipcMain gives us access to IPC so that we can send and receive events with the Renderer Process. We use it in the next bit of code we need to place at the bottom of our main.js file:

```
ipcMain.on('foobar', (event, args) => {
  event.sender.send('barfoo', args[0] + '!')
})
```

This piece of code creates an event listener on the ipcMain instance, listening for the "foobar" event coming from the Renderer Process, the event that is sent when the "foobarButton" is clicked. The listener receives an event and arguments. If you remember from the code we placed into the renderer.js file earlier, the arguments are in an array. We use the received event as a reference to send back a message, "barfoo" along with the first item in the argument array. The capturing of the event is important and should not be overlooked. While you could keep a reference to the windows you create (just like the electron-starter code we are using creates the mainWindow variable) and call window.webContents.send, the best practice would be to ensure that you are responding to the proper window. Consider if you want to send the "foobar" event from multiple windows. Capturing and using the event from that window and using that event to communicate back to that specific "sender" will mean only that window would receive the response.

Now, before we build our test for this interaction, we should run the npm start command to make certain the code we've assembled runs properly. Run the code, click the button, and you should see the button label change (Figure 14-8).

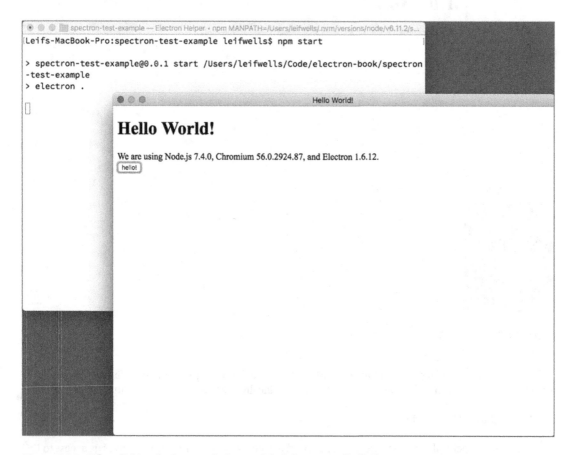

Figure 14-8. *After clicking the button, the button label changes to "hello!"*

Great, now let's build a test for our new feature. Open the test.js file and add the following code to the bottom of our describe, just below the last test:

```
it('should call foobar', () => {
    return app.client.waitUntilWindowLoaded()
                    .then(() => {
                        return app.client.getText('#foobarButton')
                    })
                    .then(text => {
                        expect(text).to.equal('Get Foobar')
                        console.log(text)
```

```
        return app.client.click('#foobarButton')
    })
    .then(() => {
      return app.client.getText('#foobarButton')
    })
    .then(text => {
      console.log(text)
      expect(text).to.equal('hello')
    })
})
```

Now, this code requires careful review because it is a little different that the previous tests. In this test we are chaining together several Promises. Notice that inside each of the then methods, there is a return? That is because we want the code to continue to the next then(). Let's walk through the code and explain what is happening.

We start with the app.client.waitUntilWindowLoaded call that returns a Promise. We capture that Promise and then return the app.client.getText WebDriverIO API call for the id "foobarButton" (the "#" in front of the name means that we are asking for the id). WebDriverIO, the library we are using to control the browser and help get information about what the browser is displaying, can use CSS class names as well as the id attributes as identifiers, so you won't necessarily need to add ids to all the elements with which you are planning to interact. The getText method returns a Promise that we capture and then test that the text returned is "Get Foobar" (which we also log to the console). Next, we return the Promise from the click method. When we pass the id to the click method, WebDriverIO will simulate the clicking action on the element matching that id. We capture the results of the click method, then getText for the "foobarButton" once more, and in the final then we test to see if the message we sent, the string "hello," is returned.

Now that we understand the code for our test, let's run the npm test command and get the results of our test. You'll notice in Figure 14-9 that we are seeing the console logs "Get Foobar" and "hello," so we are capturing the button label, but wait. How did our new test fail? We sent "hello," but we are receiving "hello!"? That's right. We tricked you. We failed to mention that our code alters the string before sending it back.

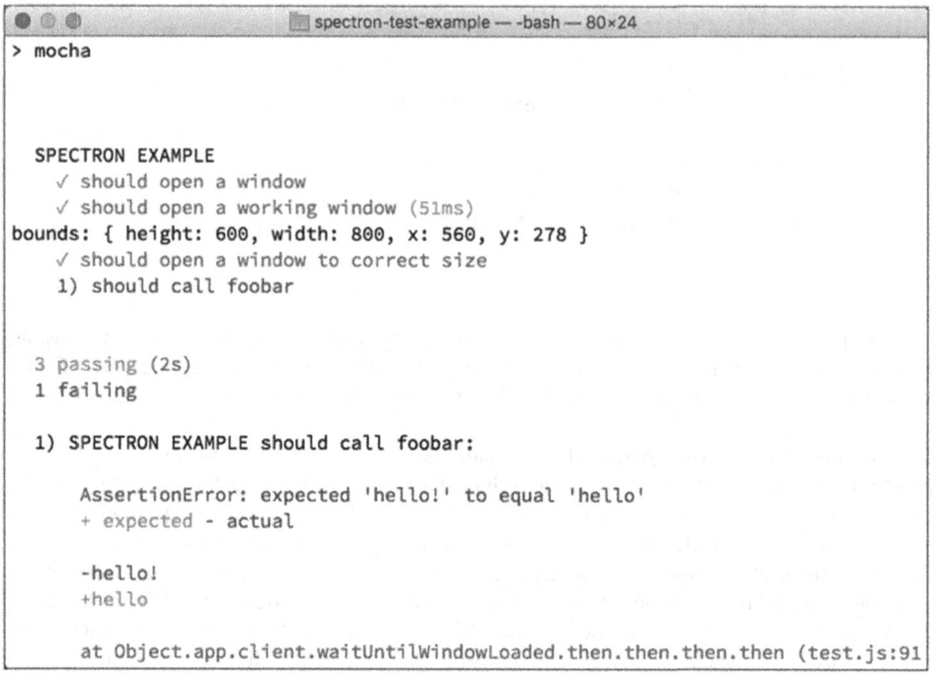

```
● ● ●                      spectron-test-example — -bash — 80×24
> mocha



  SPECTRON EXAMPLE
    ✓ should open a window
    ✓ should open a working window (51ms)
bounds: { height: 600, width: 800, x: 560, y: 278 }
    ✓ should open a window to correct size
    1) should call foobar


  3 passing (2s)
  1 failing

  1) SPECTRON EXAMPLE should call foobar:

     AssertionError: expected 'hello!' to equal 'hello'
     + expected - actual

     -hello!
     +hello

     at Object.app.client.waitUntilWindowLoaded.then.then.then.then (test.js:91
```

Figure 14-9. Our final test fails because "hello!" does not equal "hello."

Take a look at this line of code inside your main.js file:

```
event.sender.send('barfoo', args[0] + '!')
```

See where we added an exclaimation point to the end of the sent string? Let's fix that by adding an exclaimation to this line of the test:

```
expect(text).to.equal('hello!')
```

You should also remove the console.log calls to make our output clean. Now you should see all your tests pass (Figure 14-10).

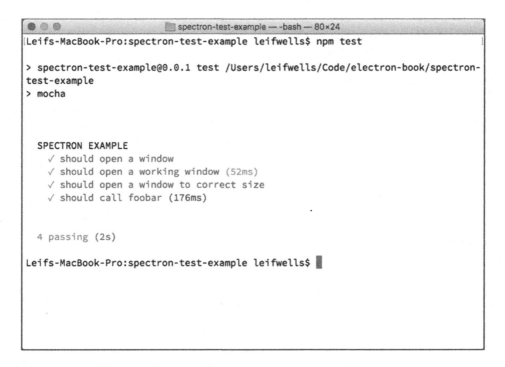

```
●●●                    📁 spectron-test-example — -bash — 80×24
[Leifs-MacBook-Pro:spectron-test-example leifwells$ npm test

> spectron-test-example@0.0.1 test /Users/leifwells/Code/electron-book/spectron-
test-example
> mocha



  SPECTRON EXAMPLE
    ✓ should open a window
    ✓ should open a working window (52ms)
    ✓ should open a window to correct size
    ✓ should call foobar (176ms)


  4 passing (2s)

Leifs-MacBook-Pro:spectron-test-example leifwells$ █
```

Figure 14-10. *All our tests have passed!*

Summary

In this chapter, we installed Spectron, Mocha, and Chai to test our Electron application. We added two new scripts to our package.json so that we can build and test our application. We used the Spectron API in our first test to test if our application created a window, in a second test to check that the window was working as expected, and in a third test to check the window size. We then learned how to access custom functions in the Main Process by setting an environment variable using Spectron and then checking for that variable in our Main Process.

We hope that this chapter is helpful to you in many ways. Do you feel more comfortable with setting up testing for an Electron application? Using the Spectron API for testing an Electron application with Mocha and Chai is reasonably straightforward, right?

Maybe now you will say, "Testing is fun!"

CHAPTER 15

■ ■ ■

Building Your Application

Now is it time to turn our attention to how to transform your Electron application into one that can be easily be distributed. Throughout this book, we have simply been using the stand-alone version of Electron and having it load our collection of HTML and JavaScript files. The de facto solution to take your project's files and create a stand-alone native application is a, npm package aptly called electron-builder. In this chapter, we will look at configuring our application so we can build our stand-alone applications.

We recommend creating a test application to work through setting up the process and exploring the differences that various parameters can have. By exploring with a simple application, you can initially ignore any additional requirements that your actual application might have.

If you are not familiar with Electron Builder, it supports the following:

- Building and Packing your Electron application for macOS, Windows, and Linux.

- Support Code Signing of the application,

- Generates Auto Update ready applications,

Installing Electron Builder

To install Electron Builder simply run

```
npm install electron-builder  --save-dev
```

Once this package is installed, we can begin modifying our package.json file and our directory structure to support using Electron Builder. Let's start with the easy one, the directories.

Adjusting your Build Directories

Electron Builder is going to look for various build assets within a directory named *build*. If you have a directory named this already, you will need to adjust your existing build process. Electron Builder tends to be a bit rigid about directory structure and asset names.

Another directory you will want to create is the *dist* directory. This directory will serve as the location of the outputs from running electron builder.

Finally, create another directory named *app*. Although you don't have to do this, we recommend keeping your actual application within its own directory named app. Move the index.html, main.js and renderer.js files into this new directory, as shown in Figure 15-1.

© Chris Griffith, Leif Wells 2017

C. Griffith, L. Wells, *Electron: From Beginner to Pro*, https://doi.org/10.1007/978-1-4842-2826-5_15

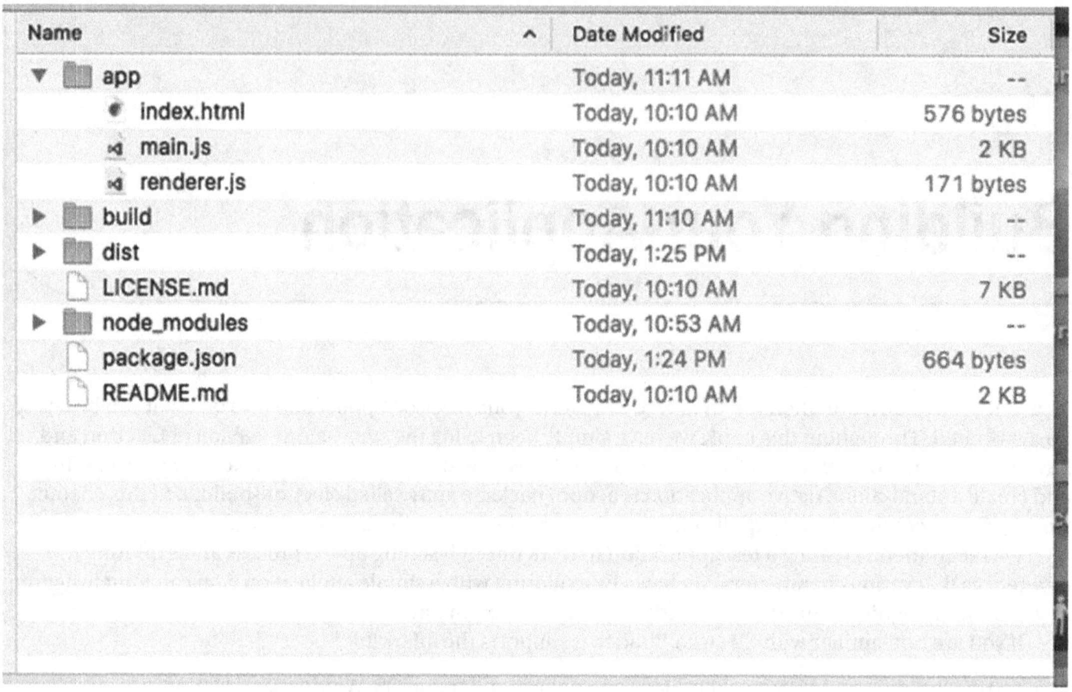

Name	^	Date Modified	Size
▼ 📁 app		Today, 11:11 AM	--
index.html		Today, 10:10 AM	576 bytes
main.js		Today, 10:10 AM	2 KB
renderer.js		Today, 10:10 AM	171 bytes
▶ 📁 build		Today, 11:10 AM	--
▶ 📁 dist		Today, 1:25 PM	--
📄 LICENSE.md		Today, 10:10 AM	7 KB
▶ 📁 node_modules		Today, 10:53 AM	--
📄 package.json		Today, 1:24 PM	664 bytes
📄 README.md		Today, 10:10 AM	2 KB

Figure 15-1. *The revised directory structure*

Updating the package.json file

Electron Builder is controlled through setting properties in the package.json file and executing npm scripts. Let's add in the script that we will call to perform our build. Within the scripts object, we will add our dist script. This script will execute the build command for us. It is here we can define our target platforms and architectures (see tables below)

Build Platforms	Description
--mac, -m, -o, --macos	Build for macOS
--win, -w, --windows	Build for Windows
--linux, -l	Build for Linux

Build Architectures	Description
--x64	Build for x64
--ia32	Build for ia32

So, to build for all three platforms and architectures our script will be:

```
"scripts": {
  "start": "electron .",
  "dist": "build -mwl --x64 --ia32"
}
```

Before we continue defining additional build parameters, we may need to perform some additional installations. If you are developing on a Mac, it is possible to build for both Windows and Linux. Unfortunately, the converse does not apply.

Building for Windows on macOS

To create a Windows executable on a macOS computer, you need to install the following two packages: Wine and Mono. If you are not familiar with these packages, Wine is a free implementation of Windows on Unix, and Mono is an open source implementation of Microsoft's .NET Framework. To install them, we will use Homebrew, another software package manager. Don't worry, it should already be installed on your Mac. From the command line, enter:

```
brew install wine --without-x11
brew install mono
```

Once these two packages have been installed, which can take a few minutes, you can now build Windows-friendly Electron apps.

Building for Linux on macOS

To build an Electron app for Linux on macOS install these two packages:

```
brew install gnu-tar graphicsmagick xz
brew install rpm
```

With those installations in place, we can turn to defining the actual build parameters for each platform.

Configuration Options

Within our package.json file, we will be adding our build configuration options. Here is a bare minimum script:

```
"build": {
  "appId": "com.your-company.electron-app-name",
  "copyright": "Copyright © 2017 YOUR-NAME",
  "productName": "My Electron App",
  "electronVersion": "1.4.1",
  "mac": {
    "category": "public.app-category.developer-tools"
  },
  "win": {
    "target": [
      "nsis"
    ]
```

```
    },
    "linux": {
      "target": [
        "AppImage",
        "deb"
      ]
    }
  }
}
```

Let's look at each parameter in more detail.

appId

This is a reverse domain notation identifier for your application. It is used as CFBundleIdentifier for MacOS and as Application User Model ID for Windows. If none is supplied, electron builder will default to com.electron.${name}. This serves as the unique ID for your application.

copyright

The copyright information that is displayed in the applications information window. If none is provided it will default to Copyright © year author.

productName

Unlike the name property, this value can include spaces and other special characters. This will be the displayed name of the application. If none is provided, the name value is used.

electronVersion

If you want to specify exactly with version of Electron you want to package, set this value. It is recommended that you define this value; otherwise you may package your application with a later version of Electron than the version you may have been developing against.

mac

This is where we will set macOS specific options. We will explore additional options later in this chapter. In this example, we define the category that our application would be sorted by. For the complete list of valid entries, see Apple's documentation at https://developer.apple.com/library/ios/documentation/General/Reference/InfoPlistKeyReference/Articles/LaunchServicesKeys.html#//apple_ref/doc/uid/TP40009250-SW8.

windows

This is where we will set Windows-specific options. We will explore additional options later in this chapter. For this example, we are defining the target build to be the NSIS (Nullsoft Scriptable Install System) format.

linux

This is where we will set Linux specific options. We will explore additional options later in this chapter. For this example, we are we are defining the target build to be the AppImage and Debian formats.

Since we moved our entry point to our app, we need to adjust the value of the main property:

```
"main": "./app/main.js"
```

Testing Our First Build

With our package.json file saved, from the command line run npm run dist. In the terminal you will see the following output, as shown in Figure 15-2:

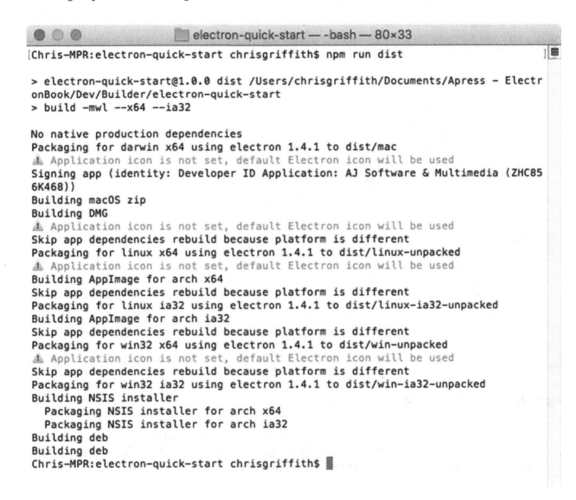

Figure 15-2. *Initial build output*

Go ahead and open the *dist* directory and you will see the various outputs from our build process, as shown in Figure 15-3.

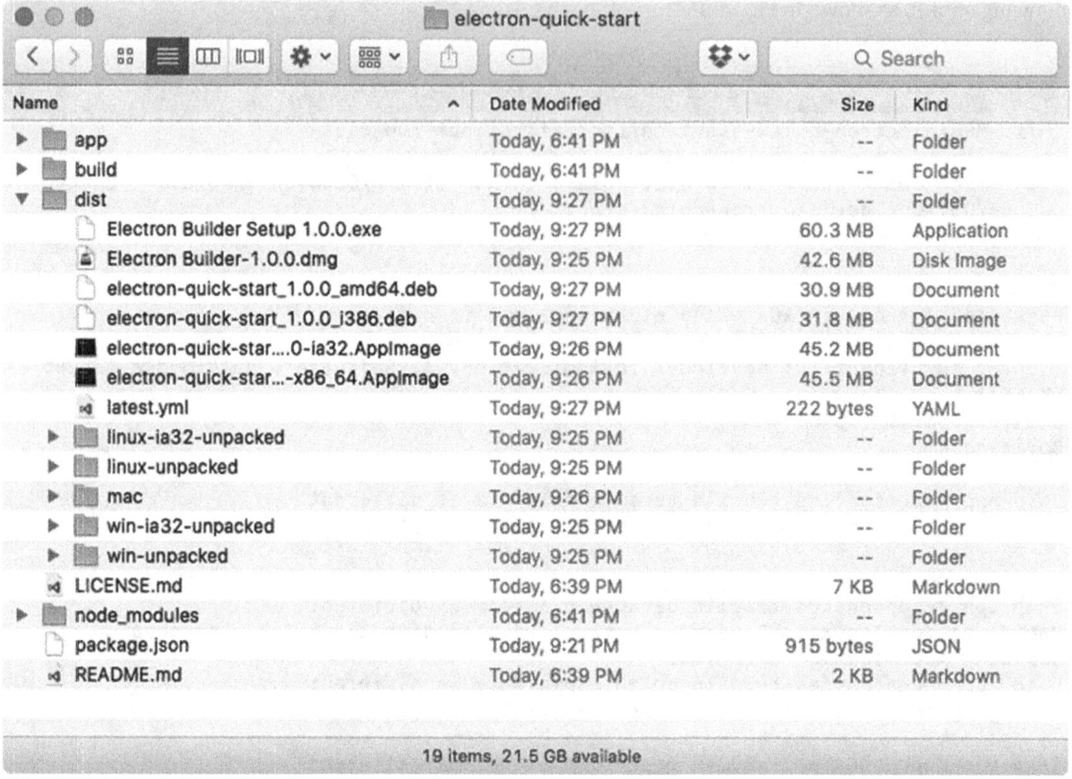

Name	Date Modified	Size	Kind
▶ app	Today, 6:41 PM	--	Folder
▶ build	Today, 6:41 PM	--	Folder
▼ dist	Today, 9:27 PM	--	Folder
Electron Builder Setup 1.0.0.exe	Today, 9:27 PM	60.3 MB	Application
Electron Builder-1.0.0.dmg	Today, 9:25 PM	42.6 MB	Disk Image
electron-quick-start_1.0.0_amd64.deb	Today, 9:27 PM	30.9 MB	Document
electron-quick-start_1.0.0_i386.deb	Today, 9:27 PM	31.8 MB	Document
electron-quick-star....0-ia32.AppImage	Today, 9:26 PM	45.2 MB	Document
electron-quick-star...-x86_64.AppImage	Today, 9:26 PM	45.5 MB	Document
latest.yml	Today, 9:27 PM	222 bytes	YAML
▶ linux-ia32-unpacked	Today, 9:25 PM	--	Folder
▶ linux-unpacked	Today, 9:25 PM	--	Folder
▶ mac	Today, 9:26 PM	--	Folder
▶ win-ia32-unpacked	Today, 9:25 PM	--	Folder
▶ win-unpacked	Today, 9:25 PM	--	Folder
LICENSE.md	Today, 6:39 PM	7 KB	Markdown
▶ node_modules	Today, 6:41 PM	--	Folder
package.json	Today, 9:21 PM	915 bytes	JSON
README.md	Today, 6:39 PM	2 KB	Markdown

19 items, 21.5 GB available

Figure 15-3. *The dist folder contents*

Since the Electron binaries for each platform were not installed, electron builder will automatically download them. Once they are downloaded to the *dist* directory, future builds will not need to perform this task, unless you remove those files. Go ahead and try out the packaged sample app for your platform(s).

For macOS user, double-click on the Electron Builder-1.0.0.dmg. This will display the default app install window for us (see Figure 15-4). Copy our new Electron Builder app into our Applications folder.

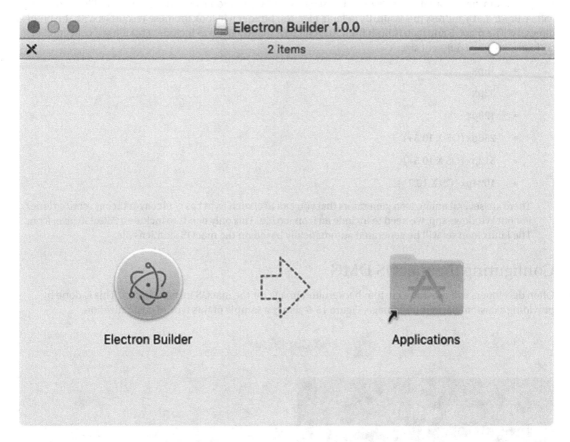

Figure 15-4. *The default OSX installer window*

If you launch it, you will see the same app that you have been playing with throughout this book.
For Windows users, double-click the Electron Builder Setup 1.0.0.exe file to install the Electron Builder app.
For Linux users, use either .deb or .AppImage file for your system.
With our initial test build completed, let's move on to making the actual application a bit more polished.

Configuring the App Icon

As you saw during the build, the process informed us that "Application icon is not set, default Electron icon will be used." Let's address this issue. By default, electron builder will look for these resources with the build directory. The macOS app icon is built from the icon.icns that we need to include. This file is a collection of six icons, each at a different size:

- 16px
- 32px
- 128px
- 256px (OS X 10.5+)
- 512px (OS X 10.5+)
- 1024px (OS X 10.7+)

There are several online icon generators that you can use, such as `https://iconverticons.com/online/`. For our Windows app, we need to include an icon.ico file. This only needs to include a 256x256 pixel icon. The Linux icon set will be generated automatically based on the macOS icon.icns file.

Configuring the macOS DMG

Often developers will provide a custom background image for the macOS install window. This is done by providing a custom background image. Figure 15-5 shows a sample of this type of customization.

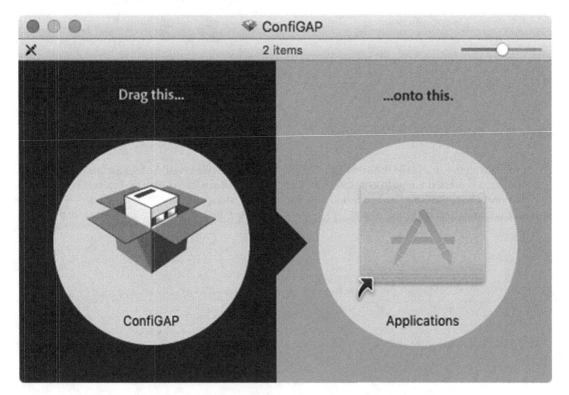

Figure 15-5. *The ConfiGAP install window with the custom background image*

Electron Builder can use either a file named background.png or background.tif. The default size of this image is 540x380. You can change the size of the background to another value; however, you will need to adjust the location of your app's icon and the Applications folder alias icon. To do this you need to use the contents property. This array should contain the x and y locations of each element, the Applications alias, and the app itself.

Another adjustment you can make is the size of the icons that are displayed within the installer window by setting the icon-size. As a reference, the default size is 80 pixels.

We can also change the virtual drive that is created when a user double-clicks the dmg file. Both the name and icon are settable using the title and icon properties, respectively.

Here are the dmg properties for the ConfiGAP dmg:

```
"dmg": {
  "title": "ConfiGAP Installer",
  "background": "./build/background.png",
  "icon": "./build/installer.icns",
  "iconSize": 128,
  "contents": [
    {
      "x": 388,
      "y": 160,
      "type": "link",
      "path": "/Applications"
    },
    {
      "x": 128,
      "y": 160,
      "type": "file",
      "path": ""
    }
  ]
}
```

If you do not want to supply an image, you can set the background color through the backgroundColor property.

Configuring the Windows Installer

The Windows Installer can also be customized for a better user experience. There are two styles of Windows installers, referred to as either one-click (see Figure 15-6) or 'boring' by the Electron Builder documentation. All these options are defined with the nsis properties object. There are several properties that you will want to define for either type of installer:

installerIcon

This is the icon that is shown within the install dialog. The default file is named installerIcon.ico.

installerHeaderIcon

This is the icon that the final installer will use once built. It will default to build/installerHeaderIcon.ico or application icon. This is used by the one-click installer only.

artifactName

This is the name of the installer file itself. By default, it will be the ${productName} Setup ${version}.exe.

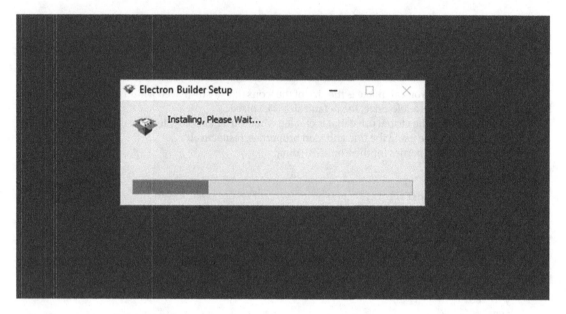

Figure 15-6. *One-Click Installer Dialog*

If you want to use the boring installer, then set the oneClick property to false. When using this style of installer there are several other properties that you will want to configure:

installerHeader

This is the 150 x 57 bmp graphic that is shown in the upper right of the installation screen (see Figure 15-7).

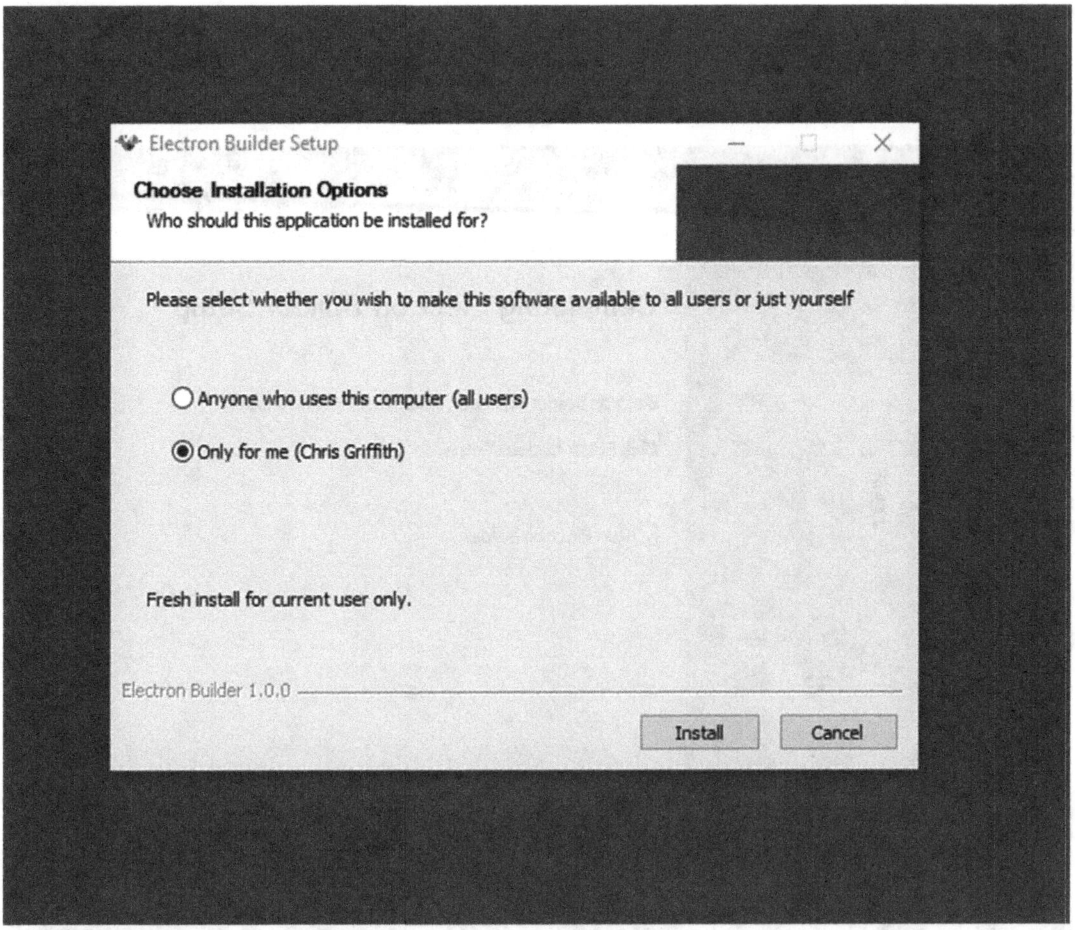

Figure 15-7. *The position of the header graphic in the installer window*

installerSidebar

This is the 164 x 314 bmp graphic that is shown along the left of the installation complete screen (see Figure 15-8).

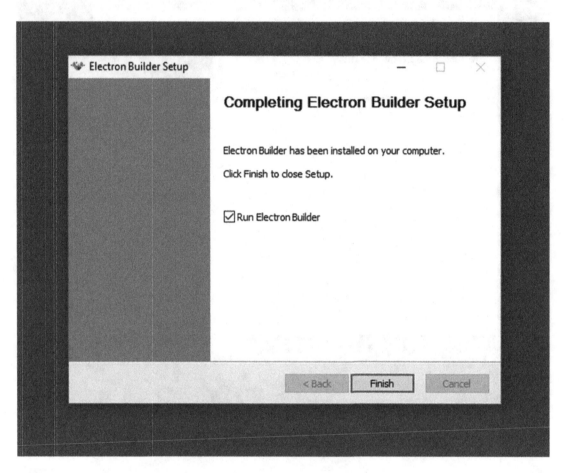

Figure 15-8. *The position of the sidebar graphic in the installer window*

uninstallerSidebar

This is the 164 x 314 bmp graphic that is shown along the left of the uninstallation start screen (see Figure 15-9).

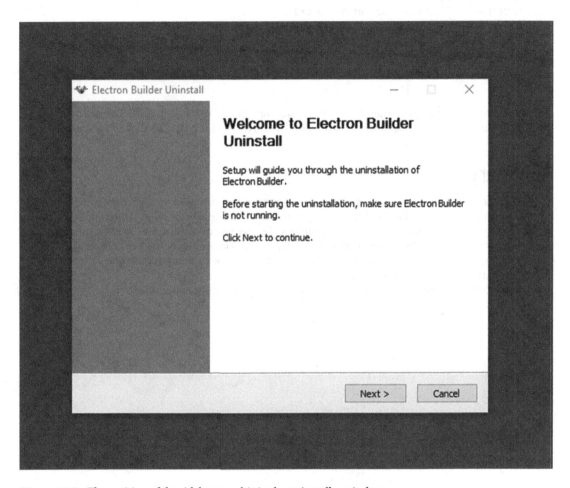

Figure 15-9. *The position of the sidebar graphic in the uninstaller window*

Here is a sample for a one-click installer:

```
"nsis" : {
    "oneClick": true,
    "artifactName": "Electron Builder Setup.exe",
    "installerIcon": "./build/installerIcon.ico",
    "installerHeaderIcon": "./build/installerHeaderIcon.ico"
  }
```

and for a boring installer:

```
"nsis": {
  "oneClick": false,
  "artifactName": "Electron Builder Setup.exe",
  "installerIcon": "./build/installerIcon.ico",
  "installerHeader": "./build/installerHeader.bmp",
  "installerSidebar": "./build/installerSidebar.bmp",
  "uninstallerSidebar": "./build/uninstallerSidebar.bmp"
}
```

There are several other properties that you can define for either NSIS-based installer. To learn more about them, visit https://github.com/electron-userland/electron-builder/wiki/Options#NsisOptions.

Summary

In this chapter we have touched on the major elements you need to include in your package.json file in order to package and build releasable Electron applications. We also looked at some of the supporting assets that are needed to create professional-looking installers. We urge you to take the time and review all the additional options available from this solution. Visit https://github.com/electron-userland/electron-builder/wiki/Options for more information. There are so many other parameters that you can set when building your stand-alone Electron application.

In the next chapter, we will look at how to support auto-updating our applications.

CHAPTER 16

■ ■ ■

Auto Updating Your Application

Now that we have successfully built an app that we can distribute, we need to begin to think long term. How do we inform the user that a new feature has been added to your awesome app (or worse, you had to fix a bug)? Electron includes an auto-update module that we can leverage to assist in the tasks needing to check for an update, and properly install them. This process can be broken down into three primary tasks: the base code we need to include in our Electron application, the modifications needed for the build process, and the proper distribution of the app.

Electron has an auto-updater module that is part of the core framework. This module is just an interface to Squirrel (`https://github.com/Squirrel`). It is this framework that handles the tasks of checking for a new version, downloading, it and performing the actual upgrade. However, both macOS and Windows interact with this module in different ways. Unfortunately, Linux-based Electron apps cannot use this module to auto update themselves.

Before we begin adding this functionality to your Electron app, we strongly recommend that you work through the process with a sample app first, rather than add this to an existing Electron application. This will let you quickly test out the workflow and configurations without the overhead that your full Electron application might have. We will continue to extend the sample app from the previous chapter, as we will need to be using packaged Electron applications in order to test the auto-updating feature.

Auto Updating macOS

The auto updating functionality on macOS is built atop Squirrel.Mac. As such, there is a minimal amount of work we need to do to support this on the client side. First, we need to include the Auto Update module in our main.js file:

```
const autoUpdater =electron.autoUpdater
```

This module broadcasts four events:

- checking-for-update
- update-available
- update-not-available
- error

Using these events, we can manage the life cycle of auto updating. Let's add these to our app:

```
autoUpdater.addListener("update-available", function(event) {
  console.log('Update Available')
})
```

© Chris Griffith, Leif Wells 2017

C. Griffith, L. Wells, *Electron: From Beginner to Pro*, https://doi.org/10.1007/978-1-4842-2826-5_16

```
autoUpdater.addListener("update-downloaded", function(event, releaseNotes, releaseName,
releaseDate, updateURL) {
  console.log("Update Downloaded")
  console.log('releaseNotes', releaseNotes)
  console.log('releaseNotes', releaseName)
  console.log('releaseNotes', releaseDate)
  console.log('releaseNotes', updateURL)

})

autoUpdater.addListener("error", function(error) {
  console.log(Error, error)
})

autoUpdater.addListener("checking-for-update", function(event) {
  console.log('releaseNotes', 'Checking for Update')
})

autoUpdater.addListener("update-not-available", function(event) {
  console.log('releaseNotes', 'Update Not Available')
})
```

We can use these events to provide feedback to the user on the status of the auto-update process. Next, we need to configure our Electron application where to check for a new version.

Squirrel for Mac will ping a remote url and then handle the response. If the server responds with an HTTP status of 204, the Auto Updater will understand that no update is available. If the server responds with an HTTP status of 200, an update is available and a bit of JSON is sent back. Here is a sample response:

```
{
        "url": "http://mycompany.com/myapp/releases/myrelease",
        "name": "My Release Name",
        "notes": "These are some release notes",
        "pub_date": "2017-03-18T12:29:53+01:00"
}
```

This JSON response needs to contain at a minimum the url to the update. The other properties are optional. The Auto Updater will use this url value to automatically download the update for us.

To set the url that the Auto Update will check against, we use the setFeedURL method. Once this is set, we can then call the checkForUpdates method and perform the actual check. Here is some sample code that will get the app's current version, and then call our custom endpoint to perform the auto-update check.

```
let appVersion = app.getVersion()

let updateUrl = 'https://apress-electron-manager.herokuapp.com/updates/latest?v=' +
appVersion

Then within the createWindow function, add this snippet of code:
if (process.platform === 'darwin') {
  autoUpdater.setFeedURL(updateUrl)
  autoUpdater.checkForUpdates()
}
```

User Feedback

Let's update those event handlers to provide some feedback to the user about the auto-update process. These dialogs should be familiar to you from the earlier chapter on dialogs.

```
const dialog = electron.dialog

autoUpdater.addListener("update-available", function (event) {
  console.log('Update Available')
  dialog.showMessageBox({
    type: "info",
    title: "Update Available",
    message: 'There is an update available.' + appVersion,
    buttons: ["Update", "Skip"]
  }, function (index) {
    console.log(index)
  })
})

autoUpdater.addListener("update-downloaded", function (event, releaseNotes, releaseName,
releaseDate, updateURL) {
  console.log('releaseNotes', "Update Downloaded")
  console.log('releaseNotes', releaseNotes)
  console.log('releaseNotes', releaseName)
  console.log('releaseNotes', releaseDate)
  console.log('releaseNotes', updateURL)

  dialog.showMessageBox({
    type: "info",
    title: "Update Downloaded",
    message: "Update has downloaded",
    detail: releaseNotes,
    buttons: ["Install", "Skip"]
  }, function (index) {
    if (index === 0) {
      autoUpdater.quitAndInstall()
    }
    autoUpdater.quitAndInstall()
  })
})

autoUpdater.addListener("error", function (error) {
  console.log('Error')
  console.log(error)
  dialog.showMessageBox({
    type: "warning",
    title: "Update Error",
    message: 'An error occurred. ' + error,
    buttons: ["OK"]
  })
})
```

```
autoUpdater.addListener("checking-for-update", function (event) {
  console.log('releaseNotes', 'Checking for Update')
})

autoUpdater.addListener("update-not-available", function (event) {
  console.log('releaseNotes', 'Update Not Available')
  dialog.showMessageBox({
    type: "warning",
    title: "No Updates",
    message: 'No update available at this time.',
    buttons: ["OK"]
  })
})
```

You will probably want to adjust these for a better user experience.

Auto Update Server Options

There are several prebuilt solutions available for you to use. The Auto Update module's documentation lists these as options:

- **nuts**: A smart release server for your applications, using GitHub as a back end. Auto updates with Squirrel (Mac & Windows). [https://github.com/GitbookIO/nuts]

- **electron-release-server**: A fully featured, self-hosted release server for electron applications, compatible with auto updater. [https://github.com/ArekSredzki/electron-release-server]

- **squirrel-updates-server**: A simple node.js server for Squirrel.Mac and Squirrel. Windows that uses GitHub releases. [https://github.com/Aluxian/squirrel-updates-server]

- **squirrel-release-server**: A simple PHP application for Squirrel.Windows that reads updates from a folder. Supports delta updates. [https://github.com/Arcath/squirrel-release-server]

However, there is not too much to the server-side code, so let's set up our own server using Heroku. Now, this is completely optional; so if you are comfortable working with servers, then please feel free to skip to the next section.

Setting Up Heroku

Heroku is a platform as a service (PaaS) that enables developers to build, run, and operate applications entirely in the cloud. It offers a free development option, so we can test out our Auto Update engine without needing to have to pay for a server.

If you do not have a Heroku account, go to https://signup.heroku.com/login and create one. Select Node.js as the primary development language.

Once, you have completed the signup process, you will be able to create a new Heroku app. Give your app a custom name, and then select the region you wish the app to run from.

Heroku offers several deployment methods: the Heroku CLI, GitHub, or Dropbox. Feel free to use whatever method you are the most comfortable with. Let's get the code together that will power our auto update server.

The Auto-Update Server

What we are doing is running a simple Express server on Heroku that will take the application's version number as a parameter. Our server will check this value, and return the proper response. You certainly could run your own server, but rather than take on the responsibility of being a server admin, using a service like Heroku takes care of that issue. Here is the complete app.js file that will power our server:

```
'use strict'
const fs = require('fs')
const express = require('express')
const path = require('path')
const app = express()

app.get('/updates/latest', function (req, res) {
    const latest = getLatestRelease()
    const clientVersion = req.query.v

    if (clientVersion === latest) {
        res.status(204).end()
    } else {
        let baseURL = getBaseUrl()
        let updateURL = baseURL + '/releases/darwin/' + latest + '/electron.zip'

        res.json({
            url: updateURL,
            name: "My Release Name",
            notes: "These are some release notes",
            pub_date: "2017-04-18T12:29:53+01:00"

        })
    }
})

let getLatestRelease = () => {
    const dir = __dirname + '/releases/darwin'

    const versionsDesc = fs.readdirSync(dir).filter((file) => {
        const filePath = path.join(dir, file)
        return fs.statSync(filePath).isDirectory()
    }).reverse()

    return versionsDesc[0];
}

let getBaseUrl = () => {
  if (process.env.NODE_ENV === 'development') {
    return 'http://localhost:3000'
  } else {
    return 'http://your-company.com'
  }
}
```

```
app.listen(process.env.PORT || 3000, () => {
  console.log(`Express server listening on port ${process.env.PORT || 3000}`)
});
```

There are just a few to note in this code block that you need to be aware of. First, the server resolves the latest version of your app by traversing the /releases/darwin/ directory. Within the darwin directory, you will have addition directories, one for each release. Since this will be our first release, we have a directory named 1.0.0. In order for a git repo to store a directory, it needs to have a file within it. This can be either a .gitkeep file or just a dummy file. Otherwise, our version directory structure will not be captured, and thus not transferred to the Heroku server. As we add new releases of our app, we need to update this directory structure to reflect our new version.

The other note about this code block is the url that is returned in the JSON to where the actual update is stored. This can be on a traditional server, hosted on S3 or GitHub. That choice is up to you to determine. You will need to modify getBaseUrl function to point to the base url, as well as the updateURL's path. This code sample shows a self-hosted solution.

Once you have finished updating your code to point to where you will host your update, deploy this server code to your Heroku account.

Testing Our Auto Update

Once you have deployed your server code to Heroku, let's test it in our browser. Simply go to
`https://<your=app-name>.herokuapp.com/updates/latest?v=1.0.0`
and you should see the following in the window:

```
{"url":"http://your-company.com/releases/darwin/1.0.0/electron.zip","name":"My Release
Name","notes":"These are some release notes","pub_date":"2017-04-18T12:29:53+01:00"}
```

This means our server is running and responding properly. We can now return to our Electron code and complete the changes we need to make.

Signing Your Application

To have auto updating function properly, our Electron applications need to be signed. Otherwise, the auto-updating mechanism will not function. For self-distributed apps and testing, we can generate our own certificate by using the Keychain Access tool, found in the /Applications/Utilities directory.

Create new certificate:

Keychain Access ➤ Certificate Assistant ➤ Create a Certificate...

Give your certificate a name and select Code Signing as the Certificate Type. Next, we need to set the trust level. To do this, locate the newly created certificate in the panel, and double-click to open it. Then change the When using this certificate to Always Trust. This will allow our Electron application to be properly signed.

We need to now set the CSC_NAME environment variable, so the signing can occur when we build our application. In your terminal and in our application's active directory, run

```
export CSC_NAME="Certificate Name"
```

Now, when we build our application it will be signed and auto updating will function.

If you are planning to distribute through the macOS store, you will need a signing certificate from Apple. For more on this process see: `https://github.com/electron/electron/blob/master/docs/tutorial/mac-app-store-submission-guide.md`

Building the Application - macOS

With our update server in place and running, and our signing certificate generated and installed, we are ready to build the first version of our app. In the main.js file, you will need to update the updateURL variable to reflect your Heroku server before proceeding. To reduce our build times, let's only build for macOS. Adjust the dist script in the package.json file to:

```
"dist": "build -m"
```

Now, let's build our application.

```
npm run dist
```

After a few moments, we should have our .dmg file, our .app file, as well as out .zip of our application. Go ahead and run the application. Once it launches, the Auto Update module will ping our server. Since we only have version 1.0.0 of our app, it will report back that there is no update (Figure 16-1).

Figure 16-1. *Our app informing the user that no update is available*

Generating an Update

To generate an update, we need to do three things. First, build a new version of the application with a new version number. To do this, we just need to change the version number in our package.json file:

```
"version": "1.0.1"
```

Then, just rebuild our app. Although we did not make any code changes, the app will still respond as version 1.0.1.

Second, we need to upload our new build to where we store the application.

Third, we need to update our Heroku server to respond correctly based on the proper version number. Just duplicate our 1.0.0 directory and rename it to match our app's new version. Then upload the new structure to Heroku, and have the server restart.

With all three steps complete, go ahead and run the app. After a few moments, the app should inform you that an update is available (Figure 16-2).

Figure 16-2. *The Auto Update module has detected an update*

Click the Update button to update the application (Figure 16-3).

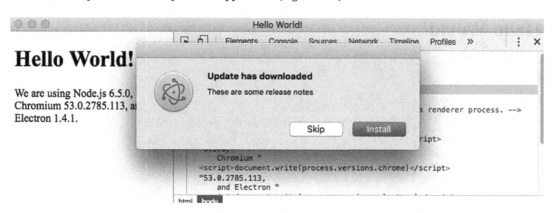

Figure 16-3. *The Auto Update module has downloaded the update and is ready to apply it*

The app will automatically quit and then relaunch. With that, we have a working auto-update system for our macOS Electron applications.

Auto Updating Windows Applications

The auto-update module for Windows is also based on Squirrel; however, it takes a different approach to how it manages the updates. Unlike the Mac, where a custom server response is needed, auto updating on Windows relies on delta packages and a special RELEASES file. We will show how to properly create these files, so auto updating can occur on Windows.

In addition to having Electron Builder installed, we also need to install another node module, Electron Builder Squirrel Windows:

```
npm install electron-builder-squirrel-windows --save-dev
```

This is a plug-in module for use by Electron Builder.

In the previous chapter, we built our Electron application to be built using the NSIS format.

Now, we want to have Electron Builder use Squirrel as our target. In the package.json, change

```
"win": {
    "target": [
      "nsis"
    ],
```

to

```
"win": {
    "target": [
      "squirrel"
    ],
```

You also might want to temporarily change the build flags to only generate Windows builds. This will save some time while you are learning the process. To do this set the dist script to

```
"dist": "build -w --x64"
```

Now, when we execute npm run dist in our terminal, electron builder will generate three files for us:

- Electron Demo Setup 1.0.1.exe

- autoupdatedemo-1.0.1-full.nupkg

- RELEASES

The first file is the installer that you can distribute. It contains both the Squirrel runtime and your application. The second file is your application's source code stored within a special binary. As we generate new versions of our application, Squirrel will reference the .nupkg files to create delta packages. We will touch on this shortly. The final file is a text that contains a listing of all the app versions, along with checksums and the file name of the *.nupkgs.

To build for Squirrel, we need to add a new attribute, squirrelWindows, within our build object in the package.json file:

```
"build": {
    "appId": "com.ajsoftware.electronapp",
    "copyright": "Copyright © 2017 Chris Griffith",
    "productName": "Electron Demo",
    "electronVersion": "1.4.1",
  "win": {
    "target": [
```

```
        "squirrel"
    ]
  },
  "squirrelWindows": {

  }
}
```

Before we generate our first release of our application, there are several attributes we need to define. The first is the app icon. Just like in the previous chapter, we can set the icon attribute to an .ico file.

```
"win": {
    "target": [
      "squirrel"
    ],
    "icon": "./build/icon.ico"
}
```

Signing Your Windows Application

Like building auto-updating apps for macOS, Windows apps must also be signed. Otherwise, anti-virus/malware scanners might flag your application, or Windows SmartScreen may require special actions to enable to run it. We doubt this is the user experience you want. There are a variety of third-party certificate vendors that can issue you a certificate that will allow you to formally sign your application. Unfortunately, these options are not free. Thankfully, there is a method to generate your own certificate for development and testing purposes. If you plan to release your application to the public, you will need to formally sign your application.

To generate your own .pfx file, which Electron Builder uses to sign your application, you will need to use OpenSSL. What is OpenSSL, from their website:

> OpenSSL is an open source project that provides a robust, commercial-grade, and full-featured toolkit for the Transport Layer Security (TLS) and Secure Sockets Layer (SSL) protocols.

If you are building your application on a macOS computer, OpenSSL is already installed. If you are building your Electron application on a Windows computer, you will need to download an installer from https://wiki.openssl.org/index.php/Binaries.

To generate our *.pfx file, we need to first generate a private key and certificate. OpenSSL will allow us to do all three steps. With OpenSSL installed, and then launch your terminal to first generate our private key:

```
openssl genrsa -aes128 -out privateKey.key 2048
```

You will be prompted to enter a passphrase for the key. Enter something that you will remember, and store it in a safe place. This information cannot be recovered.

Next, we can use that key to generate our certificate:

```
openssl req -new -x509 -days 365 -key privateKey.key -out certificate.crt
```

It will prompt you to enter the passphrase you just created for the key file. It will then ask you a series of questions that it will use to identify the certificate. Here is a sample of those questions.

You are about to be asked to enter information that will be incorporated into your certificate request.

```
What you are about to enter is what is called a Distinguished Name or a DN.
There are quite a few fields but you can leave some blank
For some fields there will be a default value,
If you enter '.', the field will be left blank.
-----
Country Name (2 letter code) [AU]:YORU COUNTRY
State or Province Name (full name) [Some-State]:YOUR STATE
Locality Name (eg, city) []:YOUR CITY
Organization Name (eg, company) [Internet Widgits Pty Ltd]:YOUR COMPANY
Organizational Unit Name (eg, section) []:YOUR UNIT
Common Name (e.g. server FQDN or YOUR name) []:YOUR NAME
Email Address []:your-name@somewhere.com
```

Now, with our private key and certificate generated, we can combine them into a .pfx file by using this command:

```
openssl pkcs12 -export -out certificate.pfx -inkey privateKey.key -in certificate.crt
```

You will once again be prompted for the passphrase for your privateKey. Then you will be asked for the password that will be used to unlock the pfx file. Safely store all three files, as they are uniquely generated. With our pfx file created, we can modify the package.json to enable signing of our Windows application. We place our *.pfx file in a cert directory within our general development directory. Set the certificateFile to the location of the *.pfx file, and the certificatePassword to the export password.

```
"win": {
    "target": [
      "squirrel"
    ],
    "certificateFile": "./certificate.pfx",
    "certificatePassword": "your-password",
    "icon": "./build/icon.ico"
},
```

Customizing the Squirrel Installer

Unlike the NSIS installer, using the Squirrel installer actually has very few configurations. The first item we can set is the icon for the generated setup.exe file. Typically, this will be the same as your application's icon. But unlike, the application icon, the location of this file must be remotely hosted. We typically place it in the same directory that we stored the Windows updates.

```
"squirrelWindows": {
    "iconUrl": "http://your-company.com/releases/win/icon.ico",
}
```

Next, we can modify the loading animation that is displayed by Squirrel as it silently installs your application. The default image looks like Figure 16-4, albeit animated.

Figure 16-4. *Default Squirrel Loading GIF*

You can easily replace with your own gif file. Simply set the loadingGif to a file. You do not need to have this image be animated.

```
"squirrelWindows": {
    "iconUrl": "http://your-company.com/releases/win/icon.ico",
    "loadingGif": "./build/loader.gif"
}
```

The next item to adjust is a subtle one. When Squirrel installs your application, it places it within the AppData directory. It will create a new directory based either on your app ID or the name attribute. When Squirrel creates the folder to install your application, and by default it will use your app ID. However, since your app ID will probably follow the pattern of com.company-name.app-name, Windows will truncate the directory name to just com. Instead, we recommend using your name attribute instead. To do this, add useAppIdAsId and set it to false.

```
"squirrelWindows": {
    "iconUrl": "http://your-company.com/releases/win/icon.ico",
    "loadingGif": "./build/loader.gif",
    "useAppIdAsId": false
}
```

This will now enable us to build our Windows application, but we need to make some additional changes to the main.js file to support auto updating with Squirrel. First, we need to set a new updateURL to check for any updates. Here is the new code block for this.

```
if (process.platform === 'darwin') {
  autoUpdater.setFeedURL(updateUrl)
  autoUpdater.checkForUpdates()
} else {
  updateUrl = "http://your-company.com/releases/win/"
  autoUpdater.setFeedURL(updateUrl)
  autoUpdater.checkForUpdates()
}
```

Since our app is now dependent on Squirrel to manage itself, we need to properly handle those events before our application creates its window. These events center around the various installation or uninstall steps that might need to occur. Here is a complete code sample that handles each of the Squirrel events that should be added to the main.js file:

```
if (handleSquirrelEvent()) {
  // squirrel event handled and app will exit in 1000ms, so don't do anything else
  return
}

function handleSquirrelEvent() {
  if (process.argv.length === 1) {
    return false
  }

  const ChildProcess = require('child_process')
  const path = require('path')

  const appFolder = path.resolve(process.execPath, '..')
  const rootAtomFolder = path.resolve(appFolder, '..')
  const updateDotExe = path.resolve(path.join(rootAtomFolder, 'Update.exe'))
  const exeName = path.basename(process.execPath)

  const spawn = function (command, args) {
    let spawnedProcess, error

    try {
      spawnedProcess = ChildProcess.spawn(command, args, { detached: true })
    } catch (error) { }

    return spawnedProcess
  }

  const spawnUpdate = function (args) {
    return spawn(updateDotExe, args)
  }

  const squirrelEvent = process.argv[1]
  switch (squirrelEvent) {
    case '--squirrel-install':
    case '--squirrel-updated':
      // Optionally do things such as:
      // - Add your .exe to the PATH
      // - Write to the registry for things like file associations and
      //    explorer context menus

      // Install desktop and start menu shortcuts
      spawnUpdate(['--createShortcut', exeName])

      setTimeout(app.quit, 1000)
      return true
```

```
case '--squirrel-uninstall':
    // Undo anything you did in the --squirrel-install and
    // --squirrel-updated handlers

    // Remove desktop and start menu shortcuts
    spawnUpdate(['--removeShortcut', exeName])

    setTimeout(app.quit, 1000)
    return true

case '--squirrel-obsolete':
    // This is called on the outgoing version of your app before
    // we update to the new version - it's the opposite of
    // --squirrel-updated

    app.quit()
    return true
    }
}
```

You might be wondering about the spawn code that is referenced in this sample. If you recall, Squirrel installs our app with the AppData folder. Unfortunately, it does not auto generate a shortcut for the user and place it on their desktop. That spawn code will do this as part of the install or update process. Our standard auto-update events will still be triggered, so we need to have the code in place to allow Squirrel to perform its tasks.

Generating Our First Build

With our app's code updated to handle the Squirrel events and the url to check for any updates, let's properly generate our application. From the terminal:

```
npm run dist
```

This process will take a few moments to complete. Once it has completed, go ahead and launch the xxx-setup.exe on a Windows machine. You should see your screen loading gif, then a shortcut created on the desktop. The auto-update check should also run (Figure 16-5).

Figure 16-5. *The No Update dialog*

Since we have not provided any update files, you will see a dialog informing you that no updates are available. So, let's make an update!

Generating an Update

To properly generate an update and the associated files, we need to follow some simple steps. First, those three files that we generated for our first release need to be uploaded to the server that our auto update url is pointing to.

■ **Note**   You technically don't need to use a remote server. If you run a local server, say using Express, you can reference that url instead.

Second, we need to update the package.json file to inform Electron Builder where to reference our remote releases.

```
"squirrelWindows": {
    "iconUrl": "http://your-company.com/releases/win/icon.ico",
    "remoteReleases": "http://your-company.com/releases/win/",
    "loadingGif": "./build/loader.gif",
    "useAppIdAsId": false
}
```

This url should be the same as our auto-update URL in our application code. Now when we build our new application, electron builder will use the files hosted there to generate our *-delta.nupkg file, as well as update the RELEASES file with the new data.

Finally, you need to update the version number in the package.json. If you want to make a simple change to the index.html, you can do that as well.

With those changes in place, execute the npm run dist command again. The process will take a bit longer as the remote files are accessed. When it is complete, we will have several new files alongside of the files from the first build:

autoupdatedemo-1.0.0-full.nupkg

autoupdatedemo-1.0.1-delta.nupkg

autoupdatedemo-1.0.1-full.nupkg

Electron Demo Setup 1.0.0.exe

Electron Demo Setup 1.0.1.exe

RELEASES

Upload these new files, along with the RELEASES file to the server. Once they have transferred, launch the application again on your Window machine. This time, there will be an update available (Figure 16-6).

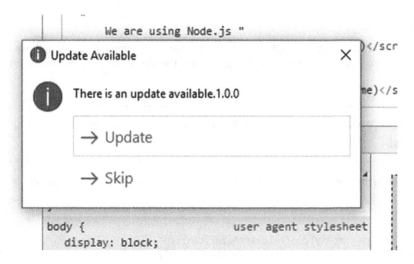

Figure 16-6. *The AutoUpdate dialog*

Click the Update button, and the update will be downloaded for us (Figure 16-7).

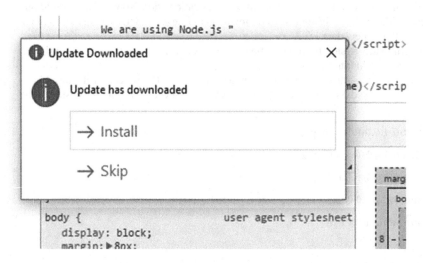

Figure 16-7. *The AutoUpdate Downloaded dialog*

Once that is done, we can install it and relaunch our application. Our application is now up to date! You now have the framework in place to auto update your Electron application on Windows.

Alternative Solutions

Now, using Electron Builder is not the only option to create packaged Electron application. The Electron team also has a Windows installer module. The package can be found at https://github.com/electron/windows-installer. This module does expose more settings for your Squirrel instance. You might want to consider looking at this solution if your application needs additional parameters configured, like a custom-loading Gif.

Another option you might also explore is Electron Forge (`https://beta.electronforge.io/`). Developed by the same team as Electron Builder, this project aims to be a single command-line interface for Electron. It supports packaging to a wide range of platforms. What is interesting is, it uses Electron's Windows Installer for any Squirrel packages. This effort is very intriguing, and it could be a nice solution to for your Electron development workflow.

Finally, we want to touch on Electron Builder itself. If you spend some time reading the documentation, you might notice it has a section on auto updating. Instead of using Electron's built-in Auto Update module, it instead relies on their own electron-updater module. There may be advantages to using this solution instead of the built-in solution, but you will need to make that call yourself.

Summary

You should have the framework in place to enable auto updating for both macOS and Windows. Both platforms require unique solutions to enable this functionality. Now that you have built these exploration apps, you can fold the code into your actual application.

You can also improve the dialog messaging and user interaction of the update process. A common improvement would be to allow the user to check for an update via a menu item. You may also wish to provide some feedback that the update is being downloaded.

■ ■ ■

CHAPTER 17

Additional Resources

Hopefully by now you have a solid starting point to build and code your Electron application. We have touched on many of the core features that most desktop applications require: native menus and dialogs, platform-specific installers, integration with the local file system, and more. The challenge is taking these features and integrating them in your actual application.

Understanding that Electron is built atop two separate systems, you should be able to isolate much of the Electron-specific code from the main process, leaving your renderer process free to your core application. As we come to the end of this book, we want to cover some of the various loose ends that we need to touch upon before you begin writing the next awesome Electron app!

Additional Electron APIs

While we introduced you to a lot of the core APIs that Electron offers, we did not cover every one. But, we would be remiss if we did not touch briefly on some of the other APIs that you should be aware of:

desktopCapturer

This API allows you to capture audio and video from the user desktop. This API is built atop the webkitGetUserMedia API. It should be noted that whenever you access media recording functions, you need to be transparent with the user about performing the recording action.

crashReporter

Electron has this built-in API that will submit crash reports to a remote server. It does require some additional server configurations in order to accept the crash reports from your application.

ClientRequest

This powerful API is used to make HTTP/HTTPS requests via the main process. The actual method implements Node's Writable Stream interface. Some examples of supported streams are the following:

- HTTP request
- HTTP responses
- fs write streams
- zlib streams
- crypto streams
- TCP sockets

© Chris Griffith, Leif Wells 2017

C. Griffith, L. Wells, *Electron: From Beginner to Pro*, https://doi.org/10.1007/978-1-4842-2826-5_17

net

Although like the HTTP and HTTPs modules in Node.js, this API uses Chromium's native networking library instead. Better support for web proxies is one reason you might consider this solution instead of the Node.js modules.

DownloadItem

You can use this API to control file downloads from remote sources. This works well if you need to interact with remote files.

Electron Forge

Billed as the command-line interface for Electron applications, this project is being developed by Electron Userland. You might recognize that name, as they are the developers of the npm modules electron-packager and electron-builder.

The main idea of this project is to provide a CLI for many of the common Electron tasks, including scaffolding a new Electron app, installing new Node modules, packaging and publishing. This is certainly an effort that we are closely following for use in our next Electron application. To learn more about this tool, visit `https://beta.electronforge.io/`.

Community Resources

The success of any open source project is, in part, due to the strength of the community around it. Electron is fortunate to have an active community that new and experienced developers can turn to when dealing with an issue or looking for a solution. Here is a list of some of the more popular channels that you can become a part of:

- Discuss (`https://discuss.atom.io/c/electron`)
- Reddit (`https://www.reddit.com/r/electronjs`)
- Stack Overflow (`http://stackoverflow.com/questions/tagged/electron`)
- @electronjs on Twitter (`https://twitter.com/electronjs`)
- #atom-shell on Freenode (`http://webchat.freenode.net/?channels=atom-shell`)
- #electron on Atom Slack (`http://atom-slack.herokuapp.com/`)
- electron-jp (Japanese) (`https://electron-jp-slackin.herokuapp.com/`)
- electron-br (Brazilian Portuguese) (`https://electron-br.slack.com/`)
- electron-kr (Korean) (`http://www.meetup.com/electronkr`)
- @electron_ru on Telegram (Russian) (`https://telegram.me/electron_ru`)
- electronjs on Facebook (`https://www.facebook.com/groups/electronjs/`)

We should not forget that Electron is an open source project living and breathing on GitHub. Take the time to look over the issues for the project, or you can even contribute to the project.

Summary

This concludes our journey together through this book. We tried to cover many of the various parts of Electron and its supporting technologies at a reasonable depth and in an order that made sense. There is nowhere near enough space or time for this book to cover each and every part of Electron, but this should give you a very strong base on which to rapidly build amazing, sleek, and performant desktop applications. Keep trying new things, and join us in the journey of making Electron a great framework!

Index

Get the eBook for only $5!

Why limit yourself?

With most of our titles available in both PDF and ePUB format, you can access your content wherever and however you wish—on your PC, phone, tablet, or reader.

Since you've purchased this print book, we are happy to offer you the eBook for just $5.

To learn more, go to http://www.apress.com/companion or contact support@apress.com.

Apress®